TEACHER PREP

MERRILL
PRENTICE HALL

Teacher Pr

MW00526555

YOUR CLASS. THEIR CAREERS. OUR FUTURE. WILL YOUR STUDENTS BE PREPARED?

We invite you to explore our new, innovative and engaging website and all that it has to offer you, your course, and tomorrow's educators! Preview this site today at www.prenhall.com/teacherprep/demo. Just click on "go" on the login page to begin your exploration.

Organized around the major courses pre-service teachers take, the Teacher Preparation site provides media, student/teacher artifacts, strategies, research articles, and other resources to equip your students with the quality tools needed to excel in their courses and prepare them for their first classroom.

This ultimate on-line education resource will provide you and your students access to:

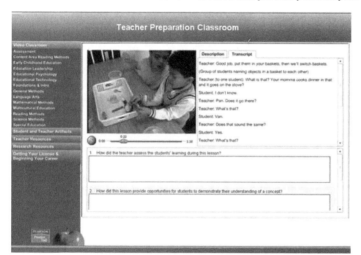

Online Video Library. More than 250 video clips—each tied to a course topic and framed by learning goals and Praxis-type questions—capture real teachers and students working in real classrooms.

Student and Teacher Artifacts. More than 200 student and teacher classroom artifacts—each tied to a course topic and framed by learning goals and application questions—provide a wealth of materials and experiences to help your students observe children's developmental learning.

Lesson Plan Builder. Step-by-step guidelines and lesson plan examples to support students as they learn to build high-quality lesson plans.

Articles and Readings. Over 500 articles from ASCD's renowned journal *Educational Leadership* are available. The site also includes Research Navigator, a searchable database of additional educational journals.

Strategies and Lessons. Over 500 research-supported instructional strategies appropriate for a wide range of grade levels and content areas.

Licensure and Career Tools. Resources devoted to helping your students pass their licensure exam; learn standards, law, and public policies; plan a teaching portfolio; and succeed in their first year of teaching.

HOW TO ORDER *TEACHER PREP* FOR YOU AND YOUR STUDENTS:

For students to receive a *Teacher Prep* Access Code with this text, instructors must provide a special value pack ISBN number on their textbook order form. To receive this special ISBN, please email Merrill.marketing@personed.com and provide the following information:

- Name and Affiliation
- Author/Title/Edition of Merrill text

Upon ordering *Teacher Prep* for their students, instructors will be given a lifetime *Teacher Prep* Access Code.

Assessing Students with Special Needs to Produce Quality Outcomes

CAROL A. LAYTON
Texas Tech University

ROBIN H. LOCK
Texas Tech University

PEARSON
Merrill
Prentice Hall

Upper Saddle River, New Jersey
Columbus, Ohio

Library of Congress Cataloging-in-Publication Data
Layton, Carol A.
 Assessing students with special needs to produce quality outcomes / Carol A. Layton, Robin
H. Lock.
      p. cm.
 Includes bibliographical references and index.
 ISBN–13: 978-0-13-513159-6
 ISBN–10: 0-13-513159-6
 1. Educational tests and measurements—United States. 2. Students with disabilities—Rating
of—United States. I. Lock, Robin H. (Robin Hartman) II. Title.
 LB3051.L387 2008
 371.26—dc22   2007022677

Vice President and Executive Publisher: Jeffery W. Johnston
Executive Editor: Ann Castel Davis
Editorial Assistant: Penny Burleson
Production Editor: Sheryl Glicker Langer
Production Coordination: Shelley Creager, Aptara, Inc.
Design Coordinator: Diane C. Lorenzo
Cover Design: Janna Thompson-Chordas
Cover Image: Jupiter Images
Production Manager: Laura Messerly
Director of Marketing: David Gesell
Marketing Manager: Autumn Purdy
Marketing Coordinator: Brian Mounts

This book was set in Clearface Regular by Aptara, Inc. It was printed and bound by R. R.
Donnelley & Sons Company. The cover was printed by R. R. Donnelley & Sons Company.

Pearson Prentice Hall™ is a trademark of Pearson Education, Inc.
Pearson® is a registered trademark of Pearson plc
Prentice Hall® is a registered trademark of Pearson Education, Inc.
Merrill® is a registered trademark of Pearson Eduation, Inc.

Pearson Education Ltd.   Pearson Education Australia Pty. Limited
Pearson Education Singapore, Pte. Ltd.   Pearson Education North Asia Ltd.
Pearson Education, Canada, Ltd.   Pearson Educación de Mexico, S.A. de C.V.
Pearson Education–Japan   Pearson Education Malaysia, Pte. Ltd

10 9 8 7 6 5 4 3 2 1
ISBN-13: 978-0-13-513159-6
ISBN-10: 0-13-513159-6

This book is dedicated to the individuals, families, and professionals served by the Burkhart Center for Autism Education and Research.

Carol A. Layton and Robin H. Lock

PREFACE

*I*ndividualized student assessment represents one of the most powerful, positive processes of special education. IDEIA 2004 mandates the components of nondiscriminatory evaluation as a key element of the law. These standards create a foundation of specific requirements that establish the most comprehensive assessment system in public schools. IDEIA 2004 assessment requirements incorporate and surpass No Child Left Behind mandates for determining student progress and needs. Used in combination with standardized norm-referenced tools and criterion-referenced measures, authentic assessment methods complete a comprehensive picture of student academic, developmental, and functional needs. Quality authentic assessment reflects an ongoing, continuous tie to the instructional cycle, indicating what a student can do in multiple environments rather than simply denoting weaknesses or deficiencies.

Assessing Students with Special Needs to Produce Quality Outcomes promotes outcome-based evaluation to guide the multidisciplinary team (MDT) in selecting appropriate Individualized Education Program (IEP) goals, classroom modifications and accommodations, and optimal instructional strategies.

Assessing Students with Special Needs to Produce Quality Outcomes advances the development of assessment-based IEPs to enable the MDT to pinpoint and address specific needs to improve student outcomes. Obtaining data from a variety of perspectives and settings improves the opportunity for identifying overall competencies and needs in preparation for higher functioning in all settings.

Accurate assessment leads to increased performance and specific results by improving the teacher's understanding of a student's daily functioning. Various assessment methods produce valid results useful for understanding a student's achievement and higher potential. Just as IDEIA mandates that no one test should be used in isolation, *Assessing Students with Special Needs to Produce Quality Outcomes* endorses the use of multiple assessment techniques to form a complete representation of student achievement.

Formal, informal, and authentic assessment partnerships produce valid special education evaluation results. Formal or standardized assessment allows the MDT to understand a student's performance in relationship to same-age peers. Informal assessment determines the student's functioning on a specific set of competencies or criteria. Authentic assessment appraises individual strengths and needs using specific, realistic classroom-based experiences in natural settings and gathers information across time, different settings, and a variety of perspectives.

The 2004 revisions of the IDEIA call on special educators to increase their understanding of the role and scope of assessment and how they influence all aspects of education. Gone are the days when assessment results depicted weaknesses in isolation separate from instructional decision making. No one can afford to simply teach standardized assessment; federal law mandates that the link between assessment and instruction in special education be forged. *Assessing Students with Special Needs to Produce Quality Outcomes* provides you, the instructor, with the tools to address all three components of effective assessment. The book focuses the following aspects:

- Recommends student-centered, strength-based assessment techniques by providing reality-based figures and examples to aid the reader in understanding how the tools of formal, informal, and authentic assessment merge to provide a more complete understanding of the student.
- Provides specific examples for linking IEP development and daily instruction to highlight the fundamental relationship between assessment and the IEP.
- Emphasizes the growing role of technology in the assessment process as identified by IDEIA 2004 to utilize assistive technology in evaluation and instruction.
- Includes innovative, research-based techniques not extensively explored in other assessment textbooks.
- Explains the impact of cultural diversity on assessment issues and provides specific recommendations for addressing nondiscriminatory, culturally sensitive evaluation to prepare the reader to meet the needs of a diverse society.
- Proposes authentic strategies to increase parent, teacher, and student participation in the IEP process as mandated by IDEIA 2004.

Assessing Students with Special Needs to Produce Quality Outcomes presents an integrated look at a variety of assessment methods in an easy-to-read textbook. End-of-the-chapter activities encourage reader interest in the text. The text layout improves comprehension and mastery of assessment concepts and techniques.

Part I examines Cumulative Measures of Assessment for Educational Interventions that use authentic assessment data from student performance to guide IEP team decision making. Part II, Contextual Measures of Assessment for Educational Intervention, investigates the rationale and techniques for including different individuals' perspectives in the authentic assessment process. Part III provides a description of the process for reporting the results of authentic assessments and decision making within the IEP team process.

Assessing Students with Special Needs to Produce Quality Outcomes offers a distinctive approach to the instruction of evaluation. This approach maximizes the reader's understanding and skill development in formal, informal, and authentic assessment. *Assessing Students with Special Needs to Produce Quality Outcomes* promises to integrate traditional and innovative assessment practices to prepare today's educators to provide quality instructional programming for students with disabilities.

ACKNOWLEDGMENTS

Many people provided valuable assistance in gathering content and assembling this text. We would like to acknowledge particularly the following individuals: Jeffrey P. Bakken, Illinois State University; Larry Beard, Jacksonville State University; Gerlinde G. Beckers,

Louisiana State University; Dawn J. Behan, Upper Iowa University; Sherrie Bettenhaussen, College of Charleston; Dorota Celinska, Roosevelt University; Lynne Chalmers, University of North Dakota; Bert Chiang, University of Wisconsin, Oshkosh; Greg Conderman, Northern Illinois University; Sara C. Davis, College of Charleston; Preston D. Feden, La Salle University; Dan Fennerty, Central Washington University; Barbara M. Fulk, Illinois State University; Jo Holtz, Edinboro University of Pennsylvania; Barbara Hong-Foster, Texas A & M International University; Kim Knesting, University of Northern Iowa; Christine A. Macfarlane, Pacific University; Carol Moore, Troy State University; Stephanie M. Peterson, Idaho State University; Ellen H. Ratcliff, Southeastern Louisiana University; and Jane Williams, Towson University.

Discover the Merrill Resources for Special Education Website

Technology is a constantly growing and changing aspect of our field that is creating a need for new content and resources. To address this emerging need, Merrill Education has developed an online learning environment for students, teachers, and professors alike to complement our products—the *Merrill Resources for Special Education* Website. This content-rich website provides additional resources specific to this book's topic and will help you—professors, classroom teachers, and students—augment your teaching, learning, and professional development.

Our goal is to build on and enhance what our products already offer. For this reason, the content for our user-friendly website is organized by topic and provides teachers, professors, and students with a variety of meaningful resources all in one location. With this website, we bring together the best of what Merrill has to offer: text resources, video clips, web links, tutorials, and a wide variety of information on topics of interest to general and special educators alike. Rich content, applications, and competencies further enhance the learning process.

The *Merrill Resources for Special Education* Website includes:

- Video clips specific to each topic, with questions to help you evaluate the content and make crucial theory-to-practice connections.
- Thought-provoking critical analysis questions that students can answer and turn in for evaluation or that can serve as basis for class discussions and lectures.
- Access to a wide variety of resources related to classroom strategies and methods, including lesson planning and classroom management.
- Information on all the most current relevant topics related to special and general education, including CEC and Praxis™ standards, IEPs, portfolios, and professional development.
- Extensive web resources and overviews on each topic addressed on the website.
- A search feature to help access specific information quickly.

To take advantage of these and other resources, please visit the *Merrill Resources for Special Education* Website at

http://www.prenhall.com/layton

BRIEF CONTENTS

CONTENTS

Note: Every effort has been made to provide accurate and current Internet information in this book. However, the Internet and information posted on it are constantly changing, and it is inevitable that some of the Internet addresses listed in this textbook will change.

CUMULATIVE MEASURES OF ASSESSMENT FOR EDUCATIONAL INTERVENTION

I

Authentic Assessment and Individual Education Programs

Chapter Focus

Authentic assessment reflects a strength-based method for evaluating student achievement in naturalistic settings by collecting data over time and from a variety of perspectives. Informal assessment is a broad term that constitutes any assessment that is not standardized. While informal and authentic assessment share some common tools, the two methods differ in the manner used to collect data, as well as in the settings for evaluation. Authentic assessment includes information concerning the application of strength-based assessment, naturalistic data, multiple intelligences, and preferred modalities. This method allows for the consideration of cultural and linguistically diverse student needs in assessment/classroom settings to provide realistic information about performance. In addition, technology plays a dual role in authentic assessment. It serves as an aid to the examiner in data collection and organization and as an accommodation for students engaged in the assessment process. Authentic assessment strengthens the IEP team's decision-making process by including all members in a student-centered, collaborative endeavor.

Learner Objectives

- Define authentic assessment.
- Explain the differences between informal and authentic assessment.
- Identify the common features of authentic assessment.
- Describe the relationship between authentic assessment and No Child Left Behind.
- Discuss the impact of authentic assessment on the special education evaluation process.
- Depict the results from authentic assessment.
- Recognize the information gained from authentic assessment.
- Explain authentic assessment and its impact on issues of cultural and linguistic diversity.
- Portray the benefits of and concerns regarding authentic assessment.
- Explain the role of technology in authentic assessment.

WHAT IS AUTHENTIC ASSESSMENT?

Authentic assessment reflects **real-world functioning**. This type of assessment involves the development of a contextual picture of a student's abilities rather than comparison of student test scores with same-age peers. Authentic assessment provides realistic and practical information about student performance. Venn (2004) identifies three significant contributions of the authentic assessment process. First, it measures progress based on what students do in the classroom rather than how they perform on a standardized measure. Second, authentic assessment creates a realistic framework for assessment by relating evaluation results to classroom instruction. Third, authentic assessment validates classroom work and the observations of those involved in that environment.

Authentic assessment portrays children's development and learning in daily activities and routines to guide and support children's learning. Using the results of authentic assessment creates an educational environment that concentrates on student strengths rather than on deficits. Authentic assessment relies on a straightforward examination of student products related directly to the curriculum (Salvia & Ysseldyke, 2004).

Spinelli (2006) defines authentic assessment as a process based on student performance using relevant, real-world tasks. Naturalistic environments such as the classroom or playground allow for examination of routine activities to gather information about the student's daily life at school. Furthermore, information gathered from a variety of sources allows for multiple perspectives.

DISTINGUISHING INFORMAL AND AUTHENTIC ASSESSMENT

According to Goh (2004), authentic assessment reflects the real-world input obtained in the evaluation process. Informal assessment measures student skills in isolation without reference to daily tasks. For example, using a criterion-referenced instrument to measure money skills prior to instruction in that area would be considered informal and diagnostic

Figure 1.1   Questions for Verifying Authentic Assessment Techniques

1. Is assessment tied to daily activities?
2. Is assessment tied to material already mastered and currently being studied?
3. Is assessment performed on an ongoing basis?
4. Does assessment occur in naturalistic settings?
5. Is the assessment continuous (noting progress over time rather than comparing students to others)?
6. Does the assessment include a variety of techniques and a variety of sources?
7. Does the assessment require students to synthesize and analyze knowledge in pragmatic applications?
8. Are the assessment tasks meaningful to students in a real-life context?

but not authentic. **Curriculum-based assessment** used to isolate student progress on a set of objectives without obtaining additional classroom evidence represents informal assessment. Adding evidence of the ability to generalize those skills into other settings changes the informal technique to authentic assessment. Authentic assessment takes place in the naturalistic environment. The technique provides a holistic view of student progress while using a variety of informal assessment techniques. Figure 1.1 presents the elements needed to ensure that the assessment remains authentic.

FOUNDATIONS OF AUTHENTIC ASSESSMENT

Authentic assessment features five relevant facets. These include strength-based evaluations, the use of naturalistic data, considerations concerning multiple intelligences, respect for preferred modalities, and reflection about strengths available from outside sources. These foundations permeate the planning and implementation process for any authentic assessment.

Strength-Based Evaluations

Strength-based evaluations represent an underlying construct of authentic assessment intended to direct the evaluation toward identifying the student's competencies. Creating a plan based on strengths rather than weaknesses highlights a positive direction for student development. It steers the assessment toward the student's accomplishments rather than failures. A strength-based assessment plan focuses the next goals on progress rather than dwelling on the student's deficiencies (Oosterhof, 2003).

Strength-based assessment emphasizes a student's capacity for learning, aptitudes, and personal interests. It concentrates on the accomplishments and best avenues for learning. In contrast, a deficit-based model highlights weaknesses in the learning process, cognitive deficits, and a student's lack of motivation. Choosing a strength-based model over a **deficit-based model** influences not only the content of the report but clarifies a holistic picture of the student.

According to Alper, Ryndak, and Schloss (2001), a simple method for determining whether an assessment report relies on strengths or deficits involves the use of highlighter pens. Underline strengths in one color and deficits in another. The highlighting demonstrates the focus of the report and paints a picture for all who read the report. The report characterizes the student as competent or inadequate, which ultimately impacts the thought and planning process of the Individualized Education Program (IEP) team. Understanding the impact of strength-based decision making from authentic assessment data proves priceless.

A strength-based assessment provides a balanced and more complete view of the student. It earns the trust of families and students by involving them in data collection rather than simply gathering scores without input. Concentrating on a student's strengths creates an atmosphere of improved self-esteem and self-advocacy. It also enables IEP team members to utilize a student's strengths in the learning environment and provides an impetus for planning for the achievement of success.

Figure 1.2   Outline of a Student's Strength-Based Assessment

1. Identifying information
   a. Background
   b. Life goals
   c. Referral information
   d. Personal interests
2. Historical records
3. Current IEP goals
   a. Academic competencies
   b. Preferred avenues for learning
      i. Multiple intelligence areas
      ii. Dominant learning modalities
      iii. Learning aptitude
   c. Family strengths
   d. School strengths
   e. Community partner strengths
   f. Transition plan strengths
4. Summary of strengths
5. Tools used for assessment
6. Synopsis of the data collected
7. Identification of strengths and priority needs
8. Creating a cumulative report
9. Ensuring reliability and validity

The authentic process in strength-based evaluations sets the tone for the student's educational environment. Building from strengths rather than dwelling on deficits produces a learning climate that encourages student progress by capitalizing on positives. From the parental perspective, strength-based plans highlight the student's value. Authentic assessment techniques encourage the teacher to gather a variety of naturalistic data to make classroom evaluation decisions reflecting this positive attitude. Figure 1.2 provides an example of an outline for a strength-based assessment plan.

Naturalistic Data

Naturalistic data form the basis for a focus on strength-based assessment. Such data include information gained in the student's daily environment. Naturalistic data collected from several different perspectives in multiple settings enhance the evaluator's ability to see the student more clearly. Naturalistic data include classroom, community, and home-based experiences. To gather this type of data, the evaluator must involve various individuals familiar with the student.

Figure 1.3 Strength-Based Component Questions Obtained from Naturalistic Data

1. What areas of home life are advantageous to the student?
2. What activities in the home setting help this student achieve personal goals?
3. What activities in the community help this student achieve personal goals?
4. What people in this student's life are positive influences in achieving personal goals?
5. What other supports could be put in place in the community to help this student achieve his or her goals?
6. What areas of school life are positive aspects of the student's day?
7. What other supports at school are needed to help this student achieve?
8. What other environments are potentially positive places where this student's goals can be achieved?
9. What persons can be added to this child's support team to help facilitate success?

Naturalistic data collection occurs over time and provides more in-depth information than does traditional assessment. It allows the IEP team to examine how the student functions using a variety of particular skills in the environment. This generalization influences student success in various settings. Figure 1.3 presents questions to be used to determine strengths obtained from naturalistic data.

Multiple Intelligences

Student learning comes from a multitude of intellectual sources such as those described by Gardner (1993) in his Multiple Intelligences Theory (MI). Gardner described the theory of MI as a method for viewing cognitive strengths by recognizing eight different types of cognitive styles. These specific strengths and styles describe the student's ability to think and solve problems. Gardner suggests that using a person's area of MI strength reinforces learning to enhance performance.

Gardner's MI areas consist of the following:

1. Verbal/linguistic
2. Mathematical/logical
3. Musical
4. Visual/spatial
5. Kinesthetic/tactile
6. Interpersonal
7. Intrapersonal or reflective
8. Naturalistic (Gardner, 1993)

Identification of cognitive preferences regarding these eight areas illuminates the learning process. For example, if a student really loves music and incorporates it into

Figure 1.4   Multiple Intelligence and Strength Areas

Linguistic—good with words, likes to write and read a lot

Mathematical/logical—good with numbers and prefers sequential, logical explanations

Visual/spatial—good at art, visualizing, and navigating

Musical—good at music and has natural rhythm

Bodily/physical—good at sport and dance

Interpersonal—good at persuading, selling, or teaching others and can detect other people's moods well

Intrapersonal or reflective—good at reflection, drawing conclusions from personal experience

Naturalistic—good at activities involving nature and interested in subjects like ecology and agriculture

---

every aspect of daily living, then music should be part of that student's academic and functional skills. The use of Gardner's theories encourages teaching competencies through strong areas of multiple intelligence. Figure 1.4 presents a description of the components of multiple intelligence and strength areas.

Preferred Modalities

Sensory modality preferences include auditory, tactile/kinesthetic, and visual (Wallace, 1995). Most students utilize these modalities in fairly evenly distributed ways. While people may be able to identify one modality preference, they concede that all three prove useful in their learning process. Most people have a predominant style with secondary strengths that complement their abilities (Vail, 1992). For students with learning disabilities, however, the absence or faulty operation of one modality may cause the student to depend on one or both of the others more heavily (Vaughn, Bos, & Schumm, 2000).

Students with auditory modality deficits experience difficulty when presented with isolated auditory learning tasks (e.g., lecture courses without visual aids). Likewise, teachers who insist on using visual examples for students with visual modality deficits may be wasting valuable time. The identification of the student's modality strengths and weaknesses clarifies the most appropriate methods for facilitating the student's learning. However, while pinpointing these preferences through standardized methods remains difficult, authentic assessment techniques capture this information through a variety of techniques. Table 1.1 presents strength-based factors based on a student's learning modalities.

Strengths Available from Outside Sources

Authentic assessment yields results that identify strengths in the community, school, and family. This type of support becomes a critical component of student development

Table 1.1   Strength-Based Factors Regarding Learning Modalities

Type of Modality	Learner Preference
Visual: Learning by seeing	• Demonstrations • Copying notes • Highlighting textbooks • Flash cards • Color coding • Diagrams, photographs, charts, graphs, maps • Maps • Movies
Auditory: Learning by hearing	• Auditory tapes • Reading aloud • Oral instructions • Lectures • Using rhythmic sounds • Word association • Discussions • Music • TV
Tactile/kinesthetic: Learning by doing	• Experiments • Role-playing • Games • Problem solving • Field trips • Taking notes • Preparing lists • Physical examples • Associating emotions with concepts

and learning. The Individuals with Disabilities Education Improvement Act (IDEIA) 2004 guidelines stress the identification of and focus on academic, developmental, and functional progress for students. These strengths provide support to increase the opportunity to meet annual goals.

RELIABILITY AND VALIDITY IN AUTHENTIC ASSESSMENT

Issues of reliability and validity in authentic assessments remain difficult to ascertain due to the nature of this evaluation technique. Traditional, research-based reliability and validity studies using large numbers of students completing the same standardized assessment obviously do not apply to authentic assessments. Reliability proves difficult to establish through accepted technical needs.

Validity, however, relies on the notion that the assessment complements the desired goals of the evaluation. In this respect, authentic assessment suggests a more consistent match between the actual daily curriculum and the appraisal. Although weaker than other forms of validity, the **face validity** of authentic assessments presents strong evidence. Authentic assessments precisely connected to a set of knowledge and skills, such as state-mandated standards, also offer construct, criterion-related, and content validity that may be verified only through qualitative research techniques.

AUTHENTIC ASSESSMENT AND NO CHILD LEFT BEHIND

No Child Left Behind (NCLB) compels local districts to provide students with disabilities with the appropriate accommodations to take statewide assessments. NCLB defines accommodations in testing material and procedures as those necessary to access student abilities rather than disabilities. These accommodations must be listed on the student's IEP. Since authentic assessment examines real-world functioning, it offers insight into what these modifications and accommodations need to be. Techniques used in authentic assessment monitor how a student works best and under what conditions optimal learning occurs. This information becomes critical to student success on state-mandated tests.

For students with **significant cognitive disabilities** NCLB provides the option for alternate assessments. The IEP team makes the determination if a student needs alternative assessments. Authentic assessment allows for data-driven decision making concerning the need for alternative assessments. The IEP team utilizes information obtained from an authentic assessment to create IEPs based on facts rather than on assumptions concerning student needs.

AUTHENTIC ASSESSMENT AND SPECIAL EDUCATION

Beginning with the reauthorization of the Individuals with Disabilities Education Act (IDEA) of 1997 through the IDEIA of 2004, stronger language linked nondiscriminatory evaluation, informal assessment data, and the general curriculum. According to Turnbull and Cilley (1999), the reauthorization mandated that nondiscriminatory evaluation information must be explicit and well-connected to program and placement. Evaluation serves as the basis for eligibility determination (Salvia & Ysseldyke, 2004). It also guides the IEP team in developing pragmatic IEP goals for use in the general setting and selecting the most appropriate placement (Oosterhof, 2003). Authentic assessment helps provide that linkage by systematically collecting information to enable the student to progress in his or her curriculum (Alper, Ryndak, & Schloss, 2001). IDEIA 2004 continues this emphasis.

Authentic assessment entails a variety of tools and strategies to identify academic, functional, and developmental information. IDEIA 2004 requires that supporting data be collected from parents and other team members to ensure the use of multiple procedures for determining eligibility, programming, and appropriate placement. IDEIA 2004 stipulates the use of technically sound instruments to evaluate cognitive, behavioral, physical, and developmental domains. Standardized instruments usually fulfill this portion of the law. Authentic assessment supports the results of standardized instruments and provides additional information to guide the development of the IEP and appropriate placement (Alper, Ryndak, & Schloss, 2001).

RESULTS OF AUTHENTIC ASSESSMENT

In the past, IEP teams may not have linked assessment information for annual reviews and IEP development to classroom data. Often IEP teams relied on special education teachers to administer a series of standardized or criterion-referenced assessment devices not necessarily tied to the curriculum. This practice provided information about the student's growth only in terms of that particular instrument. In comparison, authentic assessment supplies a strategic method for linking the IEP with evaluation results in a variety of vital areas.

Importance of Matching Plans with Individual Education Program Goals

To ensure that the authentic assessment actually provides the IEP team with information to indicate goal mastery, a written authentic plan must be developed. Without **stakeholder** responsibilities clearly outlined and followed, the assessment depends too heavily on one person's perspective or on results from standardized assessments.

First, goals and objectives are examined to determine which sources of authentic information provide the best, real-life examples of mastery. Second, the IEP team develops a system for obtaining and storing the specific data. Next, IEP team members collect the data. Finally, summaries of the data are prepared for presentation. Developing a written plan guides the authentic assessment process through the year and encourages the collection of quality data.

Authentic assessment enables the IEP team to gather data to answer specific questions concerning student growth. These areas include standards-based IEPs, demonstrating depth of development, planning for the future, annual IEP development, evaluating service delivery, evaluating the success of inclusionary programs, and evaluating potential for transitions. Careful planning of the authentic assessment yields valuable information for the team during IEP meetings.

Standards-Based Individual Education Programs

When using authentic assessment to validate a standards-based IEP, the team incorporates additional sources of authentic products from the classroom to aid in understanding the student's specific level of achievement. NCLB measures student achievement using a state-mandated criterion-referenced test that produces a set of scores indicating the objectives achieved on the assessment. Authentic assessment provides a more detailed understanding of the student's actual abilities by gathering data about progress not measured on the state-mandated assessment.

When combining this information with the results of a systematically planned authentic assessment, IEP teams become aware of the areas in which the student excels compared to those areas in need of continued attention. The teacher instructing a student with a standards-based IEP analyzes the student's performance on the assessment, reviews the IEP goals and objectives, and then plans an authentic assessment to determine how well the student actually generalizes the knowledge.

Demonstrating Depth of Development

To show progress on a standardized instrument, development must be equal or better than the progress demonstrated by same-age or -grade peers. Standardized instruments reflect one grade-level progress per academic year. Measuring students with disabilities according to this standard often diminishes their perceived progress. Although increasing in skills, students with disabilities may not be learning at the same rate as their peers without disabilities.

Authentic assessment provides the IEP team with a vehicle to demonstrate the student's depth of growth. Additionally, authentic assessment includes all members of the team gathering real-life data. It removes the element of error or false indicators of progress obtained through guessing or memorization of test items without comprehension. This type of assessment includes multiple sources of data, gathered in various settings and under realistic conditions, to document progress for the IEP team. Using authentic assessment summaries to validate mastery of IEP goals and objectives helps the IEP team to understand the student's present level of functioning and then to create meaningful, appropriate goals for the next academic year.

Planning for the Future

IEP teams review annual goal attainment and make future service delivery decisions. Incomplete information about the student leads to faulty decision making with inaccurate and inappropriate plans. Authentic assessment provides additional data—such as mastery, generalizability, and readiness to use the skills—and improves decision making.

Annual Individual Education Program Development

By collecting information on a daily basis, the teacher tracks the progression of student learning and decides on the next steps for instruction. By viewing the record of achievement, the IEP team discusses new annual goals needed for further development with increased confidence. Data collected in authentic assessment validate the student's progress on the state-mandated curriculum and provides input as to needed modifications or supports.

Students with significant cognitive deficits participating in alternative curriculum also benefit from authentic assessment techniques. Authentic assessment allows the teacher to collect data on an ongoing basis in multiple settings to validate progress on alternative standards and verify results on alternative assessments.

Evaluating Service Delivery

Determining the effectiveness of a program based solely on high-stakes testing and standardized achievement tests proves difficult. **Goodness of fit**, or the matching of IEP and curricular goals, remains essential when evaluating the adequacy of service delivery. Individually designing the authentic assessment process to correspond to IEP goals enables the teacher to measure annual goals using realistic products and observations in actual classroom settings. Failure to meet goals, ineffective instruction, or inappropriate settings for goal attainment reflect the need for changes in service delivery. Authentic assessment provides a specific plan for gathering the necessary data to support these decisions.

Evaluating the Success of Inclusionary Programs

Authentic assessment focuses on the student and draws together the efforts of the entire IEP team for the benefit of the student. General education teachers become full partners alongside the special educator. Parents have more opportunity to participate fully in the authentic process. Soliciting information from the parent during assessment and the IEP planning process enables the parent to continue to give input into inclusionary placement. Success in inclusionary programs depends upon the skill of general educators in implementing the IEP and, specifically, modifications and additions. Hearing the voice of the general educator and incorporating this knowledge establish a strong collaboration with the entire IEP team.

Evaluating Potential for Transitions

High stakes and standardized instruments typically lack the ability to incorporate personal strengths and likes or dislikes into the results. These instruments fail to provide the IEP team with enough specific authentic data regarding strengths of the student and his or her family. **Transition planning** considers many ways for enriching a student's life. For all students, outcomes should be couched in terms of ability, personality, and future happiness. The **Individual Transition Plan** (ITP) brings the IEP team, the student, parents, and community service providers together to formulate preparations for real-world settings.

The ITP reflects strategies for improving postsecondary outcomes in seven areas:

1. Vocational/Education
2. Community Living
3. Home and Family Issues

4. Recreation/Leisure Activities
5. Financial Planning
6. Health Issues
7. Transportation Skills

Authentic assessment allows for an organized method to collect data on student development in each of these skill areas from a variety of sources. This empowers the ITP team, including the student, to create real-world goals in transition planning based on evaluation in the naturalistic setting.

INFORMATION OBTAINED FROM AUTHENTIC ASSESSMENT

As part of the process in the development of an authentic assessment plan, certain guiding principles dictate the selection of the items or processes to be included during the assessment (Spinelli, 2006). Each of the following items or processes relates to classroom functioning either in the general curriculum or through the IEP:

- **Performance**—creating examples, solving problems, generalizing a concept to another situation
- **Product**—drawings or illustrations, written or oral classroom work
- **Portfolio**—selection of self-evaluated classroom work over time
- **Personal communication**—interviews from a variety of sources, checklists, communication journals
- **Observations and anecdotal records**—direct observations, narratives, miscue analysis, running records, functional behavioral analysis

Authentic assessment techniques naturally group themselves into two distinct classification measures: cumulative and contextual. By using both categories of tools, a variety of information completes the assessment picture. **Cumulative measures** use tools to examine the student's mastery from an observable perspective. **Contextual measures** delve into perceptions of attitudes or feelings, observations of specific behaviors, and environment or naturalistic concerns.

Cumulative Measures

Cumulative measures in authentic assessment provide real-life documentation of student mastery of IEP annual goals. Common tools include portfolios, work samples, electronic portfolios, curriculum-based measures such as homework and classroom tests, curriculum-based assessment, diagnostic teaching using in-class learning opportunities, task analysis of activities tied to the curriculum, and observation. Figure 1.5 presents a description of each cumulative tool and the products obtained.

To gather indications of mastery over time and in a variety of settings, these activities produce data specifically observable in products or actions. For example, cumulative

Figure 1.5 Authentic Assessment Cumulative Measurement Tools

- **Portfolios:** a collection of student- and teacher-evaluated work indicating student achievement
- **Electronic portfolios:** a collection of student- and teacher-evaluated work indicating student achievement stored on CD format
- **Work samples:** specimens of daily work
- **Curriculum-based measurement:** a set of tasks that document classroom progress by isolating specific skills to indicate progress
- **Diagnostic teaching:** notes obtained by talking through a lesson to determine the level of understanding and reasoning possessed by a student
- **Task analysis:** detailed information about a student's ability to complete a complex task that has been divided into individual steps
- **Curriculum-based assessment:** samples of classroom activities that document specific daily progress
- **Observations:** notes taken to describe a student's behavior

measures produce tangible products to supplement scores on state-mandated assessments and provide the IEP team with evidence of continued progress. This evidence proves extremely useful when the student's achievement on the state-mandated assessment appears negligible. The input results in decisions concerning the level for instruction and evaluation, as well as possible modifications needed for success.

Contextual Measures

Contextual measures evaluate student progress in meeting goals across settings from a secondary perspective while rating student mastery. The student also provides information concerning progress using contextual measures, which describe feelings, naturalistic factors, and attitudes. Contextual measures examine student interactions with others, including peers, parents, teachers, school personnel, and persons directly involved in the student's life.

Contextual measures include checklists, rating scales, interviews, surveys, questionnaires, communication notebooks and journals, and ecological assessment. Figure 1.6 describes contextual measures and the types of information gained.

Contextual measures utilize an authentic process in which members of the IEP team seek knowledge from others who have directly observed the student's learning or dispositions. Often, these data provide feedback about the student's feelings, attitudes, desires, or parental concerns and goals regarding real-life experiences in the classroom, home, and community. Collecting this information from people who have direct contact with the student ensures the creation of a more complete and complex picture.

Figure 1.6 Contextual Authentic Assessment Measures and Tools

- **Interviews:** a group of conversations that aid in the understanding of the student
- **Questionnaires:** a collection of written responses to specific questions concerning the student solicited from a variety of sources
- **Checklists:** ratings on a list of skills sequenced to measure student progress
- **Rating scales:** a set of rankings of student achievement on a specific numerical scale
- **Communication notebooks:** written dialogue between individuals concerning student behaviors or activities
- **Journals:** reflective thoughts recorded daily

Contextual techniques also examine how a student problem solves or uses knowledge in a more generalized manner. Naturalistic measures, such as environmental checklists and sociograms, offer a dimension of assessment critical to the success of students with special needs. The IEP team decides to use contextual measures in authentic assessment to complete its understanding of the student. Contextual measures often provide a glimpse into a student's life that work samples and standardized scores cannot accomplish. For example, a student arrives continuously late to school and misses much of math class. His teacher assumes that the behavior indicates avoidance and defiance. After interviewing the student and his mother, the teacher discovers that the student walks a long distance to school after dropping younger siblings at another school, due to his mother's work schedule. This simple contextual measure provides the impetus for the IEP team to explore transportation options to address this issue.

The IEP team determines which assessment techniques to select to develop a clearer picture of a student's day-to-day development. Certain techniques provide information about the student's progress toward annual goals based on the student's learning characteristics. A technique may be selected as appropriate for one student but not for another. For example, task analysis proves to be appropriate for a student with low-functioning skills as she learns small segments of a task incrementally. A high-functioning student, who learns larger and more complex amounts of information in each lesson, might be assessed through a work sample from class.

Cumulative and contextual measures work in tandem in authentic assessment to provide information for decision making. Authentic assessment based on annual goals results in an ongoing process to obtain a clear picture of progress from a variety of perspectives. Both methods supply valuable insights and create a more in-depth picture of student achievement and functioning. Figure 1.7 portrays the cyclical nature of authentic assessment with respect to the development and evaluation of IEP annual goals.

Figure 1.7 Annual Goals and the Tools of Authentic Assessment

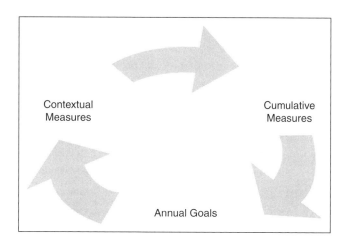

Contextual
Measures

Cumulative
Measures

Annual Goals

CULTURAL DIVERSITY AS A DEFINING COMPONENT

The holistic view obtained through authentic assessment provides insight into many aspects of student functioning. However, without cultural understanding the picture remains incomplete. Bauer and Shea (2003) list several guidelines for integrating cultural competence into the authentic assessment process.

- Use parent and family strengths to lessen the deficit model approach.
- Draw on family involvement to improve student success.
- Provide the family with many different options for involvement.
- Highlight the unique individuality of the student by viewing the student through the family's perspective.

The process of authentic assessment encourages the IEP team to learn as much as possible about the student, including his or her culture, so that learning environments remain compatible with the student's daily life outside the classroom. The process underscores the importance of involving all team members, with particular emphasis on the parent. Incorporating the student's history, family, and community traditions, as well as other aspects of the home environment, strengthens the IEP team's ability to plan effectively (Baca & Cervantes, 2004).

The IEP team improves communication among members and improves understanding of a student's strengths and needs when cultural differences remain in focus. Figure 1.8 presents cultural responsibilities in the authentic assessment process as described by Bondurant-Utz (2002).

The authentic assessment process allows the IEP team to create a data collection system specific to the student. First, communication in the language most likely to yield

Figure 1.8   Cultural Responsibilities of the IEP Team in the IEP Process

- Include at least one person on the IEP team who speaks the student's or parent's language.
- Emphasize the importance of background information.
- Value language dominance.
- Highlight cultural differences as an important feature of the student rather than as a deficit.
- Provide options for the location of interviews and meetings.
- Accept the hospitality of the family; spend time building rapport.
- Be patient in developing an understanding of the family's values and differences.
- Adjust communication style and body language to the family.
- Keep parents up to date on the learning/assessment cycle.

information forms the basis for authentic assessment. Second, respect for cultural mores, such as the method for asking questions in an interview, fits within the model of authentic assessment. Third, the avoidance of inappropriate questions based on the student's culture reflects the flexibility of authentic assessment. Finally, authentic assessment encourages the IEP team to discover the family's perceptions about the student's ability, disability, or progress in a more informal setting.

ADVANTAGES OF AUTHENTIC ASSESSMENT

Several advantages warrant the use of authentic assessment:

1. Authentic assessment encourages the use of multiple sources from a variety of perspectives to gain a more in-depth understanding of student performance.
2. Authentic assessment allows for student evaluation over a longer period of time, thus enabling the evaluator to pinpoint small increments of progress.
3. This process creates a record of achievement rather than a simple indication of student function on one specific occasion.
4. Authentic assessment engages many individuals in the process of evaluation to encourage their participation in determining educational programming for students.
5. Authentic assessment involves students in self-examination to allow for the development of knowledge about strengths and needs to increase self-determination skills.

For special educators, authentic information provides valid data for program planning and goal setting that affect the student's ability to participate in the general curriculum. When instruction reflects appropriate goals, assessment becomes an impetus for the continual cycle of assessment, planning, and instruction. Daily lessons should be planned, taught, and evaluated by the teacher, and changes should be made if necessary regarding the effect of instruction.

DISADVANTAGES OF AUTHENTIC ASSESSMENT

One concern about using authentic assessment focuses on the reliability of the techniques. The lack of technical adequacy forces examiners to carefully consider additional methods for ensuring result consistency. This process also requires a considerable amount of time and organization. Due to these constraints, untrained teachers may question the viability of authentic assessment. An additional concern revolves around the construction of the authentic assessment. Poorly constructed or unmatched processes lead to inaccurate results impacting instructional decisions.

THE INDIVIDUAL EDUCATION PROGRAM TEAM PERSPECTIVE

The IEP team includes a variety of individuals providing critical information for the development of the authentic assessment plan. By involving the individuals throughout the school year, the IEP team strengthens assessment and instructional results. Each team member, as well as others involved with the student, supplies critical information in the authentic assessment process. Planning for these various contributions enriches the evaluation and ensures a broad base for decision making.

What Does Authentic Assessment Contribute to IEP Development?

- It offers student data based on real-world performance.
- It presents results that have already been generalized into pragmatic use.
- It gives information that provides a holistic view of student performance.
- It uses strength-based assessment to meet clearly defined priority needs.
- It produces positive outcomes for students with disabilities.
- It provides information that verifies results from informal testing and formal standardized testing.

THE DUAL ROLE OF TECHNOLOGY

According to Golden (2000), the efficiency of assistive technology devices becomes apparent while viewing a person make use of the equipment or software program. Knowledge about how well the person manipulates the technology and its impact on skill development form the basis for understanding user efficiency. Authentic assessment provides the opportunity to examine technology use in a natural setting and ascertain the level of efficiency. Beigel (1996) suggests the following questions to be answered regarding a student's **assistive technology** usage:

- What does the learner need to make academic progress?
- What is the learner willing to use?
- How can assistive technology be used to support the student?
- How will the teacher react to a student using assistive technology?
- Is the device/program easy to use? Is the device portable?
- Is the device durable?

These questions can be best answered using cumulative and contextual measures of authentic assessment. Viewing the student working with the assistive technology in a variety of settings can provide several perspectives on its validity. Additionally, authentic assessment allows the IEP team to gather information regarding the competence of using the technology, as well as the student's attitude toward that particular accommodation. As a part of authentic assessment, already existing technological assistance needs to be integrated in the evaluation of academic skills. Careful planning, flexible implementation, and ongoing naturalistic assessment are the keys to integration of assistive technology into the lives of students with special needs (Male, 2003).

Technology plays a dual role in authentic assessment. The proliferation of computers and software for teaching and assessing students promises to create new and exciting ways for evaluating student progress (Venn, 2004). Technology systems store data from curriculum-based assessments and curriculum-based measurement sessions, computer-based journals, and electronic communication notebooks. Scanning provides the opportunity for students to develop and house their work on the computer. Additionally, software to encourage written language proficiency aids students in developing quality products while writing in journals and communication notebooks. Teachers indicate substantial results in portfolios from students who produced otherwise substandard daily written work (Male, 2003). Finally, the IEP team uses technology to create a summary specifically designed for each student using word processing or spreadsheet software.

SUMMARY

- Authentic assessment obtains data from naturalistic settings and a variety of perspectives to create a strength-based description of a student's performance.
- Informal and authentic assessments differ in their practical application.
- Authentic assessment features a strength-based focus using naturalistic data, relies on the tenets of multiple intelligences, and utilizes a student's preferred modalities.
- Verifying NCLB results through authentic assessment improves IEP team decision making.
- Special education evaluation gains validity from authentic assessment.
- The tools of authentic assessment allow for issues of cultural and linguistic diversity.
- Technology used in authentic assessment improves the evaluation process for all concerned.

COMPREHENSION CHECK

1. What is authentic assessment?
2. Describe the difference between formal, informal, and authentic assessment.
3. Why is strength-based assessment critical to the authentic assessment process?
4. List five methods for ensuring that a student's culture has been considered and honored in an authentic assessment.

ACTIVITIES

1. Make a list and role-play the different individuals involved in an authentic assessment.
2. Demonstrate each of the varying modalities commonly employed by students (visual, auditory, kinesthetic, oral, and olfactory).
3. Based on what you know, create a short, basic outline to assess a student in one area using authentic assessment measures.

REFERENCES

Alper, S., Ryndak, D. L., & Schloss, C. N. (2001). *Alternate assessment of students with disabilities in inclusive settings.* Boston: Allyn & Bacon.

Baca, L. M., & Cervantes, H. T. (2004). *The bilingual special education interface* (4th ed.). Upper Saddle River, NJ: Merrill/Prentice Hall.

Bauer, A. & Shea, T. (2003). *Parents and schools: Creating a special partnership for students with special needs.* Upper Saddle River, NJ: Merrill/Prentice Hall.

Beigel, A. (1996). Developing computer competencies among special needs educators. *Learning and Leading with Technology, 23*(6), 69–71.

Bondurant-Utz, J. (2002). *Practical guide to assessing infants and preschoolers with special needs.* Upper Saddle River, NJ: Merrill/Prentice Hall.

Gardner, H. (1993). *Multiple intelligences: The theory in practice.* New York: Basic Books.

Goh, D. S. (2004). Assessment accommodations for diverse learners. Boston: Allyn & Bacon.

Golden, D. C. (2000). Instructional software accessibility: A status report. *Journal of Special Education Technology, 14*(1), 57–60.

Male, M. (2003). *Technology for inclusion: Meeting the special need of all students* (4th ed.). Boston: Allyn & Bacon.

Oosterhof, A. (2003). *Developing and using classroom assessments* (3rd ed.). Upper Saddle River, NJ: Merrill/Prentice Hall.

Salvia, J., & Ysseldyke, J. E. (2004). *Assessment* (9th ed.). Boston: Houghton Mifflin Company.

Spinelli, C. G. (2006). *Classroom assessment for students in special and general education* (2nd ed.). Upper Saddle River, NJ: Merrill/Prentice Hall.

Turnbull, R., & Cilley, M. (1999). *Explanations and implications of the 1997 Amendments to IDEIA.* Upper Saddle River, NJ: Merrill/Prentice Hall.

Vail, P. L. (1992). Learning styles: Food for thought and 130 practical tips for teachers K–4. Rosemont, NJ: Modern Learning Press.

Vaughn, S., Bos, C. S., & Schumm, J. S. (2000). Teaching exceptional, diverse, and at-risk students in the general education classroom (2nd ed.) Boston: Allyn & Bacon.

Venn, J. J. (2004). *Assessing students with special needs* (3rd ed.). Upper Saddle River, NJ: Merrill/Prentice Hall.

Wallace, J. (1995). Accommodating elementary students' learning styles. *Reading Improvement, 32*(1), 31–41.

CURRICULUM-BASED ASSESSMENT

2

Chapter Focus

Curriculum-based assessment (CBA) acquires information about a student's classroom functioning by directly observing performance. Using a variety of assessment procedures, CBA encourages the teacher to plan instruction based on the student's actual performance in the classroom. Described as an alternative to norm-referenced testing, CBA provides a close link between assessment and intervention (Burns, 2002). An informal, teacher-developed method for ascertaining a student's academic levels and subsequent achievement makes CBA a tremendous link between instruction and evaluation (Hargrove, Church, Yssel, & Koch, 2002). CBA provides a useful method for enabling the teacher to evaluate students using materials based on the classroom curriculum (Howell & Nolet, 2000). This chapter explores CBA and its contributions to the IEP process. Advantages and disadvantages, as well as the mechanics for developing quality CBA, enhance understanding of this authentic assessment tool. Methods for summarizing CBA results and reporting those results to the IEP team are used to describe how the tool influences the development of quality IEPs. As in other chapters of this book, information about the impact of CBA techniques on cultural considerations and methods for using technology suggest useful steps for implementing CBA.

LEARNER OBJECTIVES

- Describe curriculum-based assessment (CBA).
- Explain the primary role of CBA.
- Discuss the advantages and disadvantages of CBA.
- Give examples of how CBA reflects individual diversity.
- Identify the reasons for using CBA.
- List the four models of CBA and describe the unique characteristics of each.
- Isolate the steps in the implementation of CBA.
- Provide illustrations for summarizing CBA data.
- Specify ways that technology would benefit the teacher and student in CBA.

WHAT IS CURRICULUM-BASED ASSESSMENT?

CBA focuses on performance and emphasizes more direct examination of student progress in basic school curriculum areas (Fuchs & Fuchs, 1996). CBA relies on the content of the student's curriculum as a foundation for assessment (Taylor, 2003). CBA performs as an "ingredient of instruction" rather than a separate assessment activity that allows the teacher to measure a student's progress during the instructional day (Venn, 2004). A CBA system for examining the instructional needs of a student based on the student's continual performance with existing course curriculum provides specific knowledge about actual day-to-day performance. The design varies from setting to setting and differs with each student's needs (Howell & Nolet, 2000).

Peverly and Kitzen (1998) describe CBA as a collection of assessment techniques that utilize information gained in the instructional setting to evaluate student performance. They indicate that five models of CBA exist and that each of the five looks at a slightly different aspect of the student's performance:

- Curriculum-and-instruction-based assessment (CIBA) documents adequate progress as a measure of appropriate placement.
- Curriculum-based assessment for instructional design (CBA-ID) monitors the level of instructional materials.
- Curriculum-based evaluation (CBE) provides an analysis of student errors and skill deficits.
- Criterion-referenced curriculum-based assessment (CR-CBA) evaluates student progress on specific goals in the curriculum, by state-mandated skills, or standardized instruments.
- Curriculum-based measurement (CBM) uses a standardized method to systematically monitor student progress through a series of short, intermittent samples.

A complete discussion of CBM appears in Chapter 3.

BENEFITS OF USING CURRICULUM-BASED ASSESSMENT

CBA in all its forms provides many benefits in the instructional process. First, CBA supplies a connection between the curriculum and instruction that assists the teacher in determining what to teach based on the progress made. CBA techniques afford the opportunity for frequent use when included as part of the instructional cycle (Cohen & Spenciner, 2003, p. 148). Additionally, CBA offers a **noncompetitive approach to instruction.** Measurement of the student's progress occurs against the curriculum and not among classmates and also gives the teacher the ability to offer explicit feedback concerning the student's **level of mastery** (Nitko, 2004). This feature improves the IEP team's ability to communicate through the detailed information obtained in the CBA (Taylor, 2003).

Additional benefits of CBA include the following:

- Alignment of the student's instructional IEP goals or state-mandated knowledge and skills
- Determination of baseline information to facilitate understanding of the student's progress, especially when progress remains limited or slow

DISADVANTAGES OF CURRICULUM-BASED ASSESSMENT

Criticism of CBA revolves around the concern that the testing process becomes the curriculum. Actual student development depends upon the validity of the curriculum measured by the CBA (Taylor, 2003). Taylor also indicates that CBA emphasizes outcomes but not process so that the IEP team may have little information about a student's ability to generalize or use the skill to produce a realistic product. CBA used in isolation to simply grade or determine mastery produces a diminished effect on student progress. CBA tied to actual instructional decisions and modification of instruction produces greater academic achievement (Overton, 2006). Howell and Nolet (2000) caution that a thorough understanding of the curriculum prior to determining the standards for mastery is necessary to create a quality CBA.

CULTURAL AND LINGUISTICALLY DIVERSE CONSIDERATIONS

Typical CBA evaluates the student's mastery of the academic curriculum. In addition to the academic curriculum, a **hidden curriculum** exists within the school setting (Losardo & Notari-Syverson, 2001). This hidden curriculum includes the student's awareness of the rules of the dominant culture, accepted norms for communication and behavior, and expertise concerning peers and friendships. To respect cultural differences, CBA must include evaluation in both the academic and hidden curricula. Losardo & Notari-Syverson indicate the following methods for respecting cultural and linguistic diversity while using CBA.

- Assess in culturally emphasized areas such as oral language versus more formal written language development.
- Consider issues such as the amount of eye contact, amount of personal space, and voice level and tone.
- Use probes and questions to facilitate a more culturally sensitive approach.
- Incorporate both home-based language and the language of the school to provide a more complete picture of the student.
- Include social interactions as another source of data to validate the results obtained during the CBA.

Bondurant-Utz (2002) stresses the importance of diagnostic teaching when evaluating students with CBA. Diagnostic teaching gives students the opportunity to show their ability to learn from instruction in the diagnostic teaching cycle. It encourages students to internalize instruction based on their own cultural experiences. Bondurant-Utz also promotes the use of CBA and CR-CBA as naturalistic, comprehensive, and practical approaches that inform and include parents in the evaluation process.

Other methods for ensuring that the CBA uses culturally sound techniques include the following:

- Design CBAs that reflect the community's cultural values (Baca & Cervantes, 2004)
- Select CBAs that diminish bias by allowing for varied responses
- Include the family in determining what activities are important or particularly valued (Baca & Cervantes, 2001)

DECIDING TO IMPLEMENT CURRICULUM-BASED ASSESSMENT

The IEP team chooses to include CBA as an element within the student's authentic assessment because it produces data impacted by the direct relationship between testing, teaching, and evaluation of progress (Losardo & Notari-Syverson, 2001). CBA provides the IEP team with explicit evidence of the student's learning performance on a daily basis. The CBA model matches the IEP team's goal for inclusion in the general education program with accessible accountability (Taylor, 2003). Through CBA, teachers focus on the development of skills embedded in the curriculum rather than on the student's disability. Additionally, CBA promotes increased decision making about instruction and the instructional cycle in the classroom (Taylor).

IEP teams select CBA as a part of the IEP process when they do any or all of the following:

- Identify gaps in the student's mastery levels
- Note that a student has trouble with a state mandated assessment but does well in class
- Require documentation of progress in incremental steps
- Need more structure in the student's instructional processes
- Determine that the learner is not making consistent and timely progress
- Call for validation of learning through testing and decide to use a criterion-referenced test
- Want to use authentic information gathered in a more traditional or systematic manner

TYPES OF CURRICULUM-BASED ASSESSMENTS

CBA recognizes several different approaches that are dependent upon the procedures followed during instruction. As previously noted, the approaches include curriculum-and-instruction-based assessment (CIBA), curriculum-based assessment for instructional design (CBA-ID), curriculum-based evaluation (CBE), curriculum-based measurement (CBM), and criterion-referenced curriculum-based assessment (CR-CBA). In the following section, each of these approaches is described and illustrated.

Curriculum-and-Instruction-Based Assessment

CIBA provides for **direct daily measurement** to ascertain the student's current skills and determine the next skills needed for mastery of curricular goals (Overton, 2006). CIBA uses the following steps to link instruction and daily assessment (Cohen & Spenciner, 2003):

- Identify the purpose for using CIBA, including deciding entry levels, establishing instructional **benchmarks,** or evaluating rate of progress.
- Break down the **curricular goals** into the specific tasks needed to accomplish mastery.
- Isolate the behaviors that demonstrate mastery of the goals.

CIBA ensures that the instructional process is tied to the curriculum at an appropriate level for the student's existing mastery level. Using CIBA in the classroom enables the teacher to pinpoint exact deficits, provide for remediation, and move the student forward.

One CIBA process used effectively to assess and instruct includes diagnostic teaching. Diagnostic teaching utilizes a decision-making cycle to inform the teacher regarding the effectiveness of instruction for each child. Diagnostic teaching remains an internal process that occurs between the student and teacher. As the student performs the task, the teacher problem solves, evaluates the success or mastery of the student, and makes choices regarding the next step in instruction. Typical instructional/assessment questions include these:

- Does the student demonstrate mastery?
- Are problem-solving techniques used by the student?
- Can the student inform the teacher about what is not understood?
- What techniques have worked in the past?
- What modifications impact the student's success?

The decision-making cycle of diagnostic teaching contains an initial phase of assessment and instruction (Walker, 2004). The teacher then formulates a **diagnostic picture** of the student's weaknesses. The teacher selects appropriate instructional techniques used for the lesson. After the lesson, evaluation of progress and effectiveness of the instructional process occurs. Adjustments take place. If performance levels fail to reach the independent level, then the diagnostic decision-making cycle begins again. When mastery occurs, the student moves to the next goal.

In diagnostic teaching, assessment transpires as an ongoing activity just as in other CIBAs. As the student learns, the teacher documents diagnostic information and uses it to formulate changes in instruction. Diagnostic teaching, as well as other CIBA, allows the teacher to make continuous changes in the instructional process while monitoring the effectiveness for use by the IEP team. The evidence provided by diagnostic teaching reflects not only the student's response to instruction but also the teacher's attempts to make changes in the instruction to match the learner's needs. Figure 2.1 provides a sample based on a CIBA of an activity done with a student.

Curriculum-Based Assessment for Instructional Design

CBA-ID carefully controls learning on a task-by-task basis by monitoring the instructional sequence to lower the **frustration level** of students (Alper, Ryndak, & Schloss, 2001). In one technique described by Glicking and Thompson (1985), teachers manage the amount of unfamiliar and challenging materials presented in a given lesson. The practice of **folding-in** recommends that the teacher establish a ratio of 70:30 between known and unknown new concepts in a lesson. Several other schedules also exist. One schedule for oral reading suggests a ratio of 93% known words versus 7% unknown words. Another for reading comprehension uses a 75:25 ratio. In other words, the student deals with more known than unknown content in each lesson.

Figure 2.1   A CIBA for Carley, a Student

Money-Related Mathematics Skills

Instruction

After completing a unit on nickels, dimes, and quarters, Carley will learn to use the vending machine in the school cafeteria to purchase a drink or snack.

1. Carley orally reviews coins by naming nickels, dimes, and quarters.
2. Carley walks down the hall to the vending machines.
3. Carley selects the correct beverage machine.
4. Carley looks at the drinks and decides to purchase one that costs 60 cents.
5. Carley tells the teacher how many nickels, dimes, and quarters she needs to make 60 cents.
6. Carley places the correct amount of change in her left hand.
7. Carley puts the correct amount of change in the coin slot with her right hand.
8. Carley pushes the correct button to get her drink.

Assessment

1. Carley names each piece of money.
2. Carley names the coins to use to make 60 cents.
3. Carley determines the correct button to select to obtain her snack.

Instructional Direction

1. Activities for selecting items from various vending machines will be developed.
2. Carley will work on using a variety of machines to choose different snacks.
3. Carley will complete the exercise using different types of vending machines.
4. Carley will also practice selecting correct change for a variety of differently priced snacks.

CBA-ID evaluation focuses on establishment of beginning skill levels with the provision of high levels of success within any given lesson. Pretests and posttests happen every day to establish high success. More challenging skills must be added slowly to the instructional design as mastery of lower skills becomes evident. Figure 2.2 presents a CBA-ID for a student named Keith.

Curriculum-Based Evaluation

CBE involves monitoring student difficulties during instruction to establish component subskills that the student must learn prior to mastering curricular goals (Alper, Ryndak, & Schloss, 2001). The emphasis of this type of assessment rests on the determination of

Figure 2.2   Curriculum-Based Assessment for Instructional Design for Keith, a Student

Increasing Sight Words for Reading

Keith has been learning new sight words each week. However, the number of new sight words needs to be controlled so that he will become less frustrated and exhibit increased motivation. Known materials consist of the following words from the pre-primer and primer list of sight words. Keith is starting on the first-grade list of sight words. The teacher will use the folding-in method of teaching new words at a ratio of 9:1. For every nine mastered words listed in his word bank, one new word will be added each day. New words will remain in the unknown (new) words section until they have been continually mastered for 2 weeks. If this method proves successful, as Keith increases his knowledge and ability, the ratio of 9:1 may be increased sequentially. For example, 8 known sight words will be drilled 5 times daily and 2 new words may be added. (Keith's performance chart is shown here.)

Date	Known words + mastered new word(s)	New word(s)	% correct after 5 drills
9-1	Primer List (PL)	of	100
9-2	PL + of	his	100
9-3	PL + of, his	had	100
9-4	PL + of, his, had	him	100
9-5	PL + of, his, had, him	her	100

CBA-ID will continue, and changes in the number of new words presented will be made as needed. The student must retain this high average of success, or the ratio must be changed to increase the ability of the student to be highly successful.

student **error and error patterns** within the instructional sequence. According to Alper, Ryndak, and Schloss, errors indicate a lack of conceptual knowledge, confusion about the rules or procedures, or both. By understanding the reason for the student's error, appropriate **remediation** or **reteach** can be focused for successful learning.

Error analysis involves the (a) identification of patterns of errors, (b) understanding of why a student makes the errors, and (c) determination of specific instruction to help the student correct the error (Cohen & Spenciner, 2003). Many people recognize error analysis in reading as miscue analysis. Common **miscues** include substitutions, omissions, reversals, repetitions, and insertions. This type of assessment determines specific errors in oral reading. The steps for developing an error analysis in reading include the following:

- Selection of a passage for oral reading from three different levels, including the student's independent, instructional and frustration levels (each with approximately the same number of words)

- Recording of the student's oral reading of each passage
- Marking of substitutions, omissions, reversals, repetitions, and insertions on a printed copy of each passage
- Summarization of the numbers of substitutions, omissions, reversals, repetitions, and insertions for each passage
- Analysis of the types of miscues that frequently occur

All this information pinpoints how the instruction should be modified or changed to better instruct the student.

Task analysis represents another technique used in CBE and other classroom assessment situations. Task analysis involves breaking down the steps in a given task into their smallest units, providing specific instruction on these steps, and subsequent assessment of the mastery of the component parts (Bigge, Best, & Heller, 2001). Task analysis describes both a process and a product and results in a detailed analysis of the student's mastery of each individual step in a complex skill. Task analysis provides a method for instruction and assessment when a student seems unable to accomplish a complex task. By breaking down the task into smaller parts and evaluating the student's mastery of each of these pieces, the teacher pinpoints the problematic areas and begins the reteach process. Task analysis reflects two perspectives: student deficits in skill development and student mastery in that same skill development.

Bigge, Best, and Heller (2001) describe two types of CBE that occur using task analysis. Formative assessment provides information about how the student achieves and how the instruction must be modified to continue achievement. Summative assessment portrays what the student learned at the end of the instructional cycle. Task analysis uses the following steps (Snell & Brown, 2000):

- Identify a skill or desired goal.
- Define the observable skill in precise terms.
- Watch others and take notes about the exact steps involved.
- Perform the task noting the specific steps.
- Adapt the actions to match the student's abilities.
- Validate the task analysis by having the student attempt each step while keeping notes.
- Explore adding simple adaptations to revise the task for the student while keeping notes.
- Write the task analysis based on observable behavior, logical sequence, and verbal prompts.
- Teach the components of the task analysis while noting progress and continue the cycle of modifying instruction until the student is successful.

Figure 2.3 presents an example of a task analysis CBE for a student named Beth.

Criterion-Referenced Curriculum-Based Assessment

In CR-CBA, the student's performance is compared to a set of predetermined criteria rather than to another student's functioning. The predetermined characteristics include state-mandated knowledge and skills standards or other forms of published skill lists. CR-CBA pinpoints the gaps in the student's understanding and mastery. The teacher then attends to these gaps prior to the second administration of the assessment.

Figure 2.3   A Curriculum-Based Evaluation Using Task Analysis for Beth, a Student

Increase the Use of Picture Vocabulary Cards

Task Analysis

1. Pick up a card.
2. Move to the actual object.
3. Match the card and appropriate object.
4. Place the picture vocabulary card on the object.
5. Indicate completion by using the sign for "finished."

Assessment

1. Beth is successful with the following signs: chair, table, block, doll.
2. Beth is unsuccessful with these signs: door, book, easel, puzzle, beads.

Criterion referenced approaches fall into three categories: developmental, spiraling, and unestablished CR-CBAs (Alper, Ryndak, & Schloss, 2001).

Developmental CR-CBA.   In developmental curricula, the learning tasks are listed by level of difficulty. The curriculum divides concepts into sequential steps related to typical development. Students progress through the curriculum in a stepwise fashion according to developmental scope and sequence. Often a scope and sequence chart provides the basis for this type of assessment. The developmental CR-CBA utilizes the sequential listing of skills as the goals for the assessment.

Spiraling CR-CBA.   Spiraling curricula represent repeated topics that examine student growth in relationship to their ability to perform more complex tasks. Most examples of spiraling curricula are found within a textbook series. In sequential textbooks, the same topics appear multiple times throughout the series. These topics represent increasingly intricate skills to be mastered. As the student progresses through the sequential textbooks, he or she acquires more multifaceted and difficult skills. The same topics repeat yearly; the topics grow in difficulty within a fixed scope. Science and social studies commonly utilize spiraling curricula. A spiraling CR-CBA looks across time to document student progress through this expanding learning process.

Unestablished Curriculum CR-CBA.   In unestablished curricula, the teacher defines the developmental scope and learning sequence based on research-based practices uniquely fitting the student's learning profile and educational program. CR-CBA isolates baseline information to create data for instructional decision making to take the student from baseline to generalization. This type of curriculum presents opportunities for students to progress without keeping pace with same-age peers in an individualized approach to the curriculum. The curriculum depends on the use of data-driven choices regarding goals and strategies to complete those instructional objectives.

Figure 2.4   Criterion-Referenced Curriculum-Based Assessment with Taylor, a Student

Example of Self-Help Skills (Brigance, 1991) for Taylor		
Getting Dressed		
Self-Help Skills Subtest		
1. Puts on socks	Accomplished	September
2. Puts feet in correct shoes	Accomplished	October
3. Closes Velcro fastener	Accomplished	November
According to the results obtained by the CR-CBA, Taylor demonstrates readiness for putting on his shoes correctly. The next step in this sequence will be to select a more complex dressing skill for Taylor and subsequently to teach it to him.		

The unestablished curriculum allows the IEP team to select a curriculum uniquely designed for each individual student's learning profile and goals.

Many CR-CBAs utilize formal, standardized, published criterion-referenced tests that include both a scope and sequence or developmental view of the skills necessary for mastery of a certain academic subject area and grade-level scores. Criterion-referenced tests allow for multiple testing of a student's development in the particular skill areas, and they detect small steps of progress. Additionally, standardized CR-CBAs allow the IEP team to compare the student's progress on the criterion-referenced test over time. The Brigance Inventories are an example of a criterion-referenced test. Several different versions of the Brigance exist, including early development, basic skill development, and essential skills for various levels. The IEP team selects the inventory that best suits the type of information needed for instructional decision making. A record book, available for each inventory, records responses for several administrations and documents the student's progress over time. One major disadvantage of published CR-CBAs, as well as the Brigance, includes the misuse of the instrument as a curriculum rather than a complete listing of requisite skills. Figure 2.4 presents a sample of a CR-CBA for a student named Taylor, using the Brigance Inventory of Basic Skills (Brigance, 1981).

CREATING A CURRICULUM-BASED ASSESSMENT

When the IEP team decides to use a CBA, several steps for development of the evaluation occur, including the following:

1. Specify the purpose for the CBA. This will aid the IEP team in determining which of the five models of CBA should be used: curriculum-and-instruction-based assessment (CIBA), curriculum-based assessment for instructional design (CBA-ID), curriculum-based evaluation (CBE), criterion-referenced curriculum-based assessment (CR-CBA), and curriculum-based measurement (CBM).
2. Analyze the curriculum to pinpoint learner goals.
3. Isolate performance criteria from the IEP goals.

4. Choose appropriate assessment procedures, including evaluation activities such as test items, observations of performance, and demonstrations of behaviors (Cohen & Spenciner, 2003).
5. Apply the assessment procedures.
6. Compile the information into a usable format.
7. Use the data to make **informed decisions** about the instructional cycle. Continue the cycle for further instruction or practice. In mastery situations, document the achievement and move to the next goal or objective.
8. Readminister any criterion-referenced test periodically to document retention of the skill (Alper, Ryndak, & Schloss, 2001).

Bondurant-Utz (2002) encourages the assessor to consider the importance of tracking the reasons why a student does not succeed during the lesson. She indicates that knowledge about why the student failed allows the examiner to target the exact changes needed in the instructional cycle. Other useful information from a CBA includes the following:

- Knowledge of the setting in which instruction occurs
- The materials used during instruction
- The tasks required of the student during the instructional phase
- The level of comprehension needed for the student to complete the task
- The pace of response required to demonstrate mastery
- The quality or efficiency of the student's achievement to complete the picture of a quality CBA

Figure 2.5 presents an example that demonstrates how the IEP team created a CBA for a student named Connor, including the rationale for selecting certain procedures.

Figure 2.5   Creating a CBA for Connor, a Student

---

1. *Purpose:* To evaluate Connor's ability to understand receptive language.
2. *Isolate performance criteria:* 90% of the time.
3. *Select appropriate assessment activities:*
   - Administer Brigance Diagnostic Inventory of Early Development, Knowledge and Comprehension Subtest (Brigance, 1991) as a pretest.
   - Create a matching game and keep records on performance.
   - Establish centers for general classroom activities and use checklist for maintaining play-based records.
   - Read stories and point to the objects and name them, while using a tape recorder to record performance.
   - Readminister the Brigance to document possible growth.
4. *Apply the assessment activities* in the classroom.
5. *Compile information* into a usable format.
6. *Use data to make decisions* both in the instructional cycle and for the annual review.

SUMMARIZING CURRICULUM-BASED ASSESSMENT DATA

CBA data summaries allow the IEP team to easily follow the results of the evaluation and see how the information fits with other authentic assessment information. Bondurant-Utz (2002) suggests several qualities of an effective CBA summary. The first section of a CBA summary reports identifying information, such as the student's name, the names of the evaluator(s), the dates of the assessments, and where the assessment was administered, and provides valuable data. Any published criterion-referenced tests used in the past should also be documented. The second section of the summary highlights background information about the student, including a brief summary of the student's developmental, medical, and educational history. A narrative of the methods used during the CBA completes the summary. This narrative section includes the following (Bondurant-Utz):

- A description of the student's independent performance on the specific skills measured
- A depiction of the types of support and the level of success when the supports are in place
- An explanation of the instructional strategies used and their efficiency
- An account of any intervening variables in the intervention plan, including issues such as information about why a student was unsuccessful or the factors that interfered with the instruction
- A report of the student's behavior during the lessons
- A description of the strategies that enhanced the student's attention or on-task behaviors during the lesson
- An explanation of the student's strengths and weaknesses as discovered in the CBA

Summaries for CBA reflect a variety of formats, including rubrics, rating scales, checklists, semantic webs, growth charts, and graphs. Each type of summary displays information describing the student's areas of improvement, as well as deficits. It is important to provide the facts to the team in the most readable and understandable structure.

Rubrics for summarizing CBA provide scoring criteria with which the evaluator rates the student's progress on a prescribed system developed to indicate different levels of mastery of the goals being assessed. A rubric usually includes both a numerical scale (often 1 to 5) and a written description of each level on the scale to help the evaluator isolate the highest level of mastery (Kubiszyn & Borich, 2003). Summarizing CBAs using a rubric involves gathering of data collected over time, sorting of the data into piles that represent each of the categories identified on the rubric, and determining which category best represents the student's mastery level. Figure 2.6 presents a sample summary rubric.

Rating scales also aid in summarizing CBA information and prove particularly useful when the IEP team desires information about a student's particular level of performance on a task (Kubiszyn & Borich, 2003). Kubiszyn and Borich identify two key issues for determining the scoring system for the rating scales: (a) first, pinpoint the most important features of the task that really identify mastery and (b) second,

Figure 2.6   Summary Rubric for the IEP Team for Whitney, a Student

Increasing the Use of Picture Vocabulary Cards						
How often does Whitney select the correct communication card to express herself?						
1 Never 2 Seldom 3 Sometimes 4 Frequently 5 Always						
Vocabulary	First Time	Second Time	Third Time	Fourth Time	Fifth Time	Sixth Time
drink	3	3	4	5	5	5
doll	2	2	2	2	3	3
play	1	2	3	3	3	4
book	2	2	2	3	3	3
sit	1	2	3	3	4	5
restroom	1	2	3	4	5	5
eat	3	3	3	4	5	5
angry	3	3	4	4	5	5
happy	3	3	5	5	5	5
go	1	2	2	3	4	4
finished	1	2	2	2	3	4
help	1	3	3	3	4	4
teacher	2	3	3	4	5	5
blocks	1	2	2	2	3	4
out	1	2	3	4	5	5

describe which errors in performance indicate lower performance. These two questions help the IEP team to focus on the most important components for mastery without scoring successive approximations too highly. A rating scale includes five or six indicators that are necessary performance characteristics. Figure 2.7 presents a rating scale sample showing a summary of a student's performance on a CBA measuring writing skills.

Checklist formats often summarize instructional results through CBA. Checklist systems effectively and efficiently summarize data on very complex behaviors, such as tying a shoelace (Kubiszyn & Borich, 2003). In the initial stage of development, the

Figure 2.7   An IEP Team Summary Rating Scale for Claire, a Student

Composing a Topical Essay

Performance Indicators for the Month of October

Claire will correctly use the following:

	Week 1	Week 2	Week 3	Week 4
1. Periods	20/25	22/25	23/25	24/25
2. Sentences	16/25	17/25	20/25	21/25
3. Capitals	15/25	16/25	18/25	20/25
4. 5 sentences	3/5	4/5	4/5	5/5
5. 4 to 5 paragraphs	2/5	2/5	3/5	4/5

Summary: Continue to work to achieve these indicators of mastery.

IEP team describes the list of behaviors necessary for mastery of a specific task and asks the evaluator to gather information about the student's performance on the task and then to collapse the findings into a single checklist. Scoring consists of a "yes/no", "0/1", or "observed/not observed" basis (Kubiszyn & Borich). The IEP team uses this type of summary to identify the gaps in skills development needed for progress. These skills then appear on subsequent IEPs. Figure 2.8 provides a sample of a checklist form for a CBA for math.

Semantic webbing provides another method for an IEP team to summarize information about a student's CBA. A semantic web utilizes a visual display of a specific objective listed on the IEP that is connected to explicit examples of the student's growth in several different, generalized areas. The IEP team determines the precise areas for collection of the web data. The evaluator engages in the CBA to evaluate the student's abilities in a variety of generalized settings. The evaluator then creates the semantic web to provide the IEP team with a picture of the student's mastery over time. Figure 2.9 presents an example of a summary semantic web in the area of algebra.

A growth chart supplies another method for visually presenting a student's skill development as obtained through a CBA. Developmental milestones form the basis for the indicators of progress on a growth chart. Growth charts present particularly interesting information for parents and provide the IEP team with a look at progress without emphasizing deficit abilities. The IEP team initially selects an appropriate scale with identified developmental milestones. The IEP team looks at the developmental milestones in conjunction with the defined goals from the IEP. The IEP team decides which milestones to pinpoint. The evaluator collects records through

Figure 2.8 A Summary Checklist of Charle's Math-Related Daily Living Skills for the IEP Team of Charles, a Student

Generalizing Functional Money-Related Skills						
Activity	**1st 6 weeks**	**2nd 6 weeks**	**3rd 6 weeks**	**4th 6 weeks**	**5th 6 weeks**	**6th 6 weeks**
Vending machines	10/20	13/20	14/20	17/20	18/20	20/20
Lunch line	8/20	12/20	16/20	19/20	20/20	20/20
School store (various)	3/20	7/20	8/20	14/20	13/20	14/20
Receipts from office	0/4	1/4	2/4	3/4	4/4	4/4
Count money from wrapping paper sales	3/20	5/20	8/20	9/20	14/20	15/20

Mastery: Vending machines, lunch line, receipts from office.
Summary: Continue to work on buying various items from school store and counting money from wrapping paper sales.

Figure 2.9 A Summary Semantic Web in Algebra for a Student and Her IEP Team

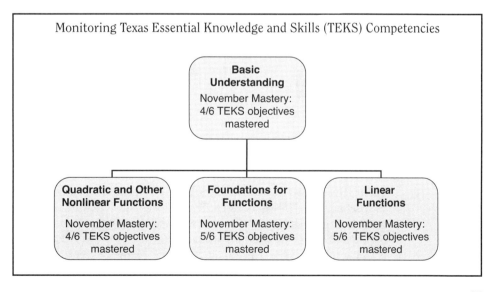

Figure 2.10 A Growth Chart Illustrating Proficiency with Describing Personal
Information for Marshall, a Student

	Class Expectation	Entry	Exit
First name	✓	✓	✓
Full name	✓	✓	✓
Address	✓		✓
Phone number	✓		✓
Birthday	✓	✓	
Teacher's name	✓		✓
Room number	✓		✓
School name	✓		✓

CBA that provide evidence of student growth on the developmental milestones. The summarized data appear on a growth chart for the IEP team. Figure 2.10 provides a sample of
a growth chart illustrating a student's proficiency with describing personal information.

Graphing involves the representation of levels of achievement measured by the extent of mastery of the curriculum. Graphing takes several forms, including bar graphs or
scatterplots. Bar graphs depict the level of student mastery in a certain area of the curriculum, as well as in other subject areas. IEP teams view the extent of growth across the
curriculum by comparing mastery among subjects. The bar graph also allows for problem solving to identify areas for continued intervention. Scatterplots pinpoint beginning
knowledge and sequential progress. Scatterplots provide motivation for students and
permit self-monitoring opportunities. Seeing success on a scatterplot often provides the
motivation to work harder and longer to achieve the mark of progress. Figure 2.11 presents a summary growth chart as a bar graph depicting a student's need for assistance
when using headphones.

USING CURRICULUM-BASED ASSESSMENT DATA IN THE INDIVIDUALIZED EDUCATION PROGRAM

The IEP team uses the results of the CBA to determine the level of success experienced in
the particular skill areas assessed. The first step involves the determination of the number
of skills or goals mastered outright. Second, the IEP team examines the CBA summaries
to pinpoint the goals still unmastered. These goals become discussion points for the development of the new IEP. Finally, the team examines the summary data to identify the
factors that must be addressed for instruction to become more successful, including

Figure 2.11   A Growth Chart Bar Graph for Phillip, a Student

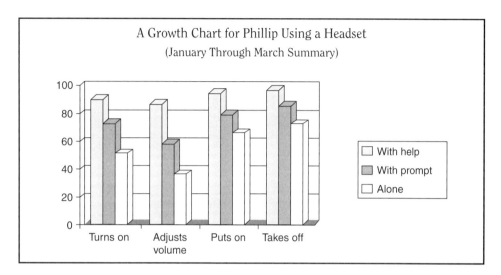

issues such as (a) placement for instruction, (b) specific materials to aid the student's comprehension, (c) lowering the difficulty level of each lesson to increase the student's success rate, and (d) determining if oral, written, or some other response mode changes the student's outcomes or the student's ability to generalize across settings. Once the IEP team considers these three steps, it begins to formulate new IEP goals and essential modifications in the classroom or it determines the need for additional assessment.

What Does Curriculum-Based Assessment Contribute to IEP Development?

- It produces information linked to curriculum used in the classroom.
- It offers information easily understood by parents.
- It supports classroom grades appearing in report cards.
- It reflects daily functioning in the classroom.
- It occurs during the course of daily activities.

CURRICULUM-BASED ASSESSMENT AND TECHNOLOGY

Technology plays a part in CBA through the use of daily instructional software programs that automatically assess skills. This type of software creates lessons to represent specific skill development. The teacher obtains a daily log of the student's success on that particular lesson. Knowing the outcome of each day's lesson allows for immediate intervention in the instructional cycle. The teacher reteaches the lesson to avoid gaps in the student's development. This type of system also provides continual feedback for students and their parents as to the amount of progress being made.

Male (2003) identifies several different software programs that provide for this type of instruction. Online Reader (EBSCO), Reading Counts (Scholastic), and Accelerated Reader with Advantage Learning System provide three examples of reading programs that provide for CBA. Quick Flash supplies a mathematics program that utilizes the CBA format.

SUMMARY

- Curriculum-based assessment (CBA) links the curriculum to the cycle of learning through effective intervention.
- The primary role of CBA revolves around the creation of opportunities to connect IEP teams, teachers, parents, and students by providing feedback through daily assessment of skill mastery and successful growth related to IEP goals.
- CBA addresses necessary changes in instruction to impact student outcomes.
- CBA monitors the learning cycle by documenting student mastery. If the student remains unsuccessful, the teacher changes the intervention or instructional delivery to ensure student learning and mastery.
- CBA honors cultural diversity by incorporating the student's values into instructional lessons.
- The models of CBA include curriculum-and-instruction-based assessment (CIBA), curriculum-based assessment for instructional design (CBA-ID), curriculum-based evaluation (CBE), criterion-referenced curriculum-based assessment (CR-CBA), and curriculum-based measurement (CBM) (discussed in the Chapter 3).
- The creative use of technology in CBA offers teachers the ability to infuse daily record keeping into the curriculum, thereby aiding their own understanding of student mastery and daily performance.

COMPREHENSION CHECK

1. List three benefits and three disadvantages of CBA. Describe how the teacher compensates for the concerns.
2. Explain how CBA addresses issues of cultural and linguistic diversity.
3. Name the steps in developing a CBA.

ACTIVITIES

1. Interview several teachers in your district about the incorporation of CBA into their curricula. Prepare a list of the ways that CBA is used in their classrooms.
2. In a small group, prepare true–false questions, multiple choice questions, and essay questions that cover this chapter. Next, design a performance assessment covering the content of this chapter. Which assessment approach captured your understanding of the chapter more completely? Why?
3. The purpose of CBA is to inform instruction. It encourages the teacher to base instructional plans and interventions on student learning. Explain how the use of CBA provides the teacher with the needed information to make instructional plans and intervention decisions.

REFERENCES

Alper, S., Ryndak, D. L., & Schloss, C. N. (2001). *Alternate assessment of students with disabilities in inclusive settings.* Boston: Allyn & Bacon.

Baca, L. M., & Cervantes, H. T. (2004). *The bilingual special education interface* (4th ed.). Upper Saddle River, NJ: Merrill/Prentice Hall.

Bigge, J. L., Best, S. J., & Heller, K. W. (2001). *Teaching individuals with physical, health, or multiple disabilities* (4th ed.). Upper Saddle River, NJ: Merrill/Prentice Hall.

Bondurant-Utz, J. (2002). *Practical guide to assessing infants and preschoolers with special needs.* Upper Saddle River, NJ: Merrill/Prentice Hall.

Brigance, A. H. (1981). *Brigance Diagnostic Inventory of Basic Skills.* North Billerica, MA: Curriculum Associates.

Brigance, A. H. (1991). *Brigance Diagnostic Inventory of Early Development.* North Billerica, MA: Curriculum Associates.

Burns, M. K. (2002). Comprehensive system of assessment to intervention using curriculum-based assessments. *Intervention in School and Clinic, 38*(1), 8–13.

Cohen, L. G., & Spenciner, L. J. (2003). *Assessment of children and youth with special needs.* Boston: Pearson, p. 148.

Fuchs, L. S., & Fuchs, D. (1996). Combining performance assessment and curriculum-based measurement to strengthen instructional planning. *Learning Disabilities Research and Practice, 11*(3), 183–192.

Glicking, E., & Thompson, V. (1985). A personal view of curriculum-based assessment. *Exceptional Children, 52*, 205–218.

Hargrove, L. J., Church, K. L., Yssel, N., & Koch, K. (2002). Curriculum-based assessment: Reading and state academic standards. *Preventing School Failure, 46*(4), 148–151.

Howell, K. W., & Nolet, V. (2000). *Curriculum-based evaluation* (3rd ed.). Belmont, CA: Wadsworth/Thompson Learning.

Kubiszyn, T., & Borich, G. (2003). *Educational testing and measurement: Classroom application and practice* (7th ed.). New York: John Wiley & Sons, Inc.

Losardo, A., & Notari-Syverson, A. (2001). *Alternative approaches to assessing young children.* Baltimore, MD: Brookes.

Male, M. (2003). *Technology for inclusion: Meeting the special need of all students* (4th ed.). Boston: Allyn & Bacon.

Nitko, A. J. (2004). *Educational assessment of students* (4th ed.). Upper Saddle River, NJ: Merrill/Prentice Hall.

Overton, T. (2006). *Assessing learners with special needs: An applied approach* (5th ed.). Upper Saddle River, NJ: Merrill/Prentice Hall.

Peverly, S., & Kitzen, K. (1998). Curriculum-based assessment of reading skills: Considerations and caveats for school psychologists. *Psychology in the Schools, 35,* 29–48.

Snell, M. E., & Brown, F. (2000). *Instruction of students with severe disabilities* (5th ed.). Upper Saddle River, NJ: Merrill/Prentice Hall.

Taylor, R. L. (2003). *Assessment of exceptional students: Educational and psychological procedures* (6th ed.). Boston: Pearson.

Venn, J. J. (2004). *Assessing students with special needs* (3rd ed.). Upper Saddle River, NJ: Merrill/Prentice Hall.

Walker, B. J. (2004). *Diagnostic teaching of reading: Techniques for instruction and assessment* (5th ed.). Upper Saddle River, NJ: Merrill/Prentice Hall.

CURRICULUM-BASED MEASUREMENT

LEARNER OBJECTIVES

- Understand the importance of curriculum-based measurement (CBM) and how it guides instruction.
- Describe the advantages and disadvantages of CBM.
- Explain how cultural considerations integrate easily into CBM.
- Clarify the reasons for using CBM.
- Name the types of CBM.
- Discuss the steps for creating a CBM.
- Identify methods for summarizing CBM results.
- Reveal the ways in which CBM results aid the IEP team in decision making.
- Describe the use of technology in CBM.

Chapter Focus

Curriculum-based measurement (CBM) represents a well-developed method of authentic assessment, grounded in research, and considered both valid and reliable (Allinder, Fuchs, & Fuchs, 2004). CBM creates a measurement system to document a student's academic progress in learning basic academic skills (Fuchs & Fuchs, 2002). Fuchs and Fuchs aptly describe CBM as a method for discerning what to assess, how to quantify it, and how to use the results of the measurement. CBM includes a set of standardized procedures that allow the IEP team to access the student's database of daily performance (Hosp, 2003). CBM yields rate-based information useful in planning day-to-day instruction (Stoner, Scarpati, Phaneuf, & Hintze, 2002). Simple, low-cost and repeated measures characterize CBM as a time-efficient, easy-to-implement enhancement for instructional planning.

In the past decade, CBM gained recognition for predicting the success of student performance in high-stakes assessment (Deno, 1992). This chapter provides information concerning the definition of CBM, a discussion of the difference between CBM and curriculum-based assessment (CBA), the steps to completing CBM, and a description of summarization procedures. This valuable, motivational tool creates an opportunity for teachers and students to view firsthand graphs of progress.

WHAT IS CURRICULUM-BASED MEASUREMENT?

CBM comprises a systematic way for determining student progress in the scope and sequence of classroom expectations. CBM involves four segments: (a) the creation of measurement materials called **probes**, (b) the administration and scoring of the probes, (c) the graphing of the probes and estimations of how much the student can learn and achieve during the academic year, and (d) the comparison of actual growth with the expected rate of growth (Allinder et al., 2004). Allinder et al. also describe some of the basic features integrated into CBM. These include reliability and validity, simple and repeated administrations, and cost and time effectiveness.

DIFFERENCES BETWEEN CURRICULUM-BASED MEASUREMENT AND CURRICULUM-BASED ASSESSMENT

The link between CBM and CBA lies in the mastery and automaticity of basic skill development. The two procedures differ, however, in several distinct aspects. Most CBA techniques focus on mastered knowledge and skills, including teacher-made chapter tests and items derived from classroom lessons. CBM evaluates **general outcome measures** (GOM). Repeated small assessment trials evaluate progress on basic skills (Hosp, 2003). GOMs allow teachers to make decisions about student progress in reading, spelling, written expression, and math computation. CBM improves instruction by measuring performance on basic tasks of equal difficulty linked to the curriculum over time.

CBM demonstrates reliability and validity through its standardized guidelines and procedures using repeated measures or probes to establish a baseline and subsequent achievement. The probes or small, standardized assessments represent the overall goals learned in a general curriculum rather than specific lessons. CBM requires procedures for selecting the testing material and recording the student's progress.

Although tied to the classroom curriculum, CBA often includes teacher-created instruments that lack this measure of standardization. Furthermore, CBA data include data collection specific to or formed from actual classroom activities. Also, CBA consists of more casually grouped items that allow the teacher to include a variety of sources of information for decision making. Figure 3.1 presents a list of typical testing materials used in CBA and CBM.

BENEFITS OF USING CURRICULUM-BASED MEASUREMENT

CBM presents many advantages for assessment. First, it provides a technically strong evaluation method effective in determining academic progress (Deno, Fuchs, Marston, & Shin, 2001). Second, it entails well-researched methods confirmed over the past two decades. CBM enjoys established validity beginning with the work of Deno, Mirkin, and Chiang in 1982 through the research conducted by Fuchs and Fuchs in 2002. CBM

Figure 3.1   Comparison of Testing Materials Used in CBA and CBM

Curriculum-Based Assessment

- Teacher-made tests used during daily instruction or present unit
- Chapter tests available from the curriculum
- Work samples of paragraphs written by the student during class
- Classroom activities tied to state-mandated standards
- Mathematics worksheets covering a specific objective, such as addition from the day's instruction
- Sight word lists used during reading instruction
- Running records consisting of notes made by the teacher during oral reading
- Use of teacher intuition to modify instruction
- Emphasis on accuracy

Curriculum-Based Measurement

- Short tests of 1- to 3-minute duration taken from words and skills taught for the entire year
- Tests or probes measuring a specific skill in reading, spelling, math, or written language
- Probes representing the curriculum but not taken directly from daily instruction
- Student performance graphed
- Computer-based software that provides both the probes and graphing functions sometimes available
- Standardized procedures for administration and scoring
- Constructed by teams following CBM guidelines
- Emphasis on rate

combines the principles of standardized assessment with established reliability and validity and the usefulness of observational data and qualitative descriptions of student behavior in the classroom on a daily basis, which proves more sensitive to student growth than commercial standardized instruments (Fuchs & Fuchs). CBM assesses not only the student's progress but also the curricular match between the learner and instruction, as well as the learning environment. Finally, research reports that CBM provides an effective measure for informing teachers regarding the impact of instruction on student development (Allinder et al., 2004).

Other beneficial uses of CBM include using the technique to document the need for a student to be reintegrated into the general education classroom. Powell-Smith and Stewart (1998) describe a model for reintegration that includes a systematic, **data-based decision making** method, in which the IEP team used the information collected in this system featuring CBM to determine the appropriate placement for the student. Fuchs

Figure 3.2   Reasons to Use CBM

- To provide obvious, visual representation of specific growth in fluency with math or reading
- To highlight small increments of change
- To increase ability to perform basic skills in reading, spelling, written language, and mathematics quickly and accurately
- To demonstrate any patterns of growth that emerge

and Fuchs (2002) identify four reasons for making data-based decisions using CBM. The four include (a) shaping academic growth, (b) differentiating between unproductive instruction and undesirable student learning, (c) enlightening instructional planning, and (d) continually updating instructional effectiveness of student programs.

Other positive outcomes have been noted for using CBM (Taylor, 2003):

- Increased academic improvement
- Correlation of the ratio of planning time to increases in student achievement
- Increased efficient uses of academic programs

Taylor (2003) also suggests that CBM can be used effectively in conjunction with CBA to create a planning, monitoring, and decision-making process. Figure 3.2 reflects the reasons a teacher should use CBM.

DISADVANTAGES TO CURRICULUM-BASED MEASUREMENT

Although many advantages exist with CBM, several valid criticisms appear in the literature. Taylor (2003) enumerates several disadvantages. First, CBM accentuates skills in isolation rather than the learning process. Second, although CBM proves useful in determining when a change in instruction appears, it does not indicate what type of change in instruction may be the most valuable. Third, studies report bias in CBM as it overestimates reading ability in girls and underestimates the ability in boys (Kranzler, Miller, & Jordan, 1999). Fourth, the implementation of CBM requires considerable training.

CULTURAL AND LINGUISTICALLY DIVERSE CONSIDERATIONS

VanDerHeyden, Witt, Naquin, and Noell (2001) discuss how CBMs can be used to directly measure student progress on basic skills. They point to CBM as a method that more accurately identifies students with special needs and problems. Using a more objective method, such as CBM, may provide information that remains freer from cultural bias and concentrates on student achievement rather than on cultural differences.

Kranzler, Miller, & Jordan (1999) report that CBM reading scores overestimated reading comprehension in African American fourth- and fifth-grade students and that the exact reason for the bias remained unidentified. Evans-Hampton, Skinner, Henington, Sims, and McDaniel (2002) describe CBM in relation to two possible sources of bias in mathematical evaluation. First, the reduction of content bias occurs when using CBM. CBM provides a closer correspondence between the curriculum and the actual assessment, and this relationship impacts the teacher's ability to eliminate cultural bias by maintaining the proper focus on the curriculum. Second, in situational bias, CBM may increase the influence of cultural differences.

Several factors associated with CBM affect students from different cultural backgrounds, grades, or gender. First, CBM includes a timed procedure that may alter the ability of certain ethic groups to perform at their maximum capacity (Evans-Hampton et al., 2002). Students from particular ethnic backgrounds may have better outcomes through CBM than will others. Younger students produce more valid CBM scores than do older students (Malecki & Jewell, 2003). This information must be considered by the IEP team when determining the rationale for using CBM for assessment purposes.

DECIDING TO IMPLEMENT CURRICULUM-BASED MEASUREMENT

The IEP team decides to utilize CBM as a data collection method for the following reasons (Scott & Weishaar, 2003):

- To monitor progress on an ongoing basis
- To quickly determine if what is being done in instruction is effective so that necessary interventions can be implemented
- To improve motivation by using progress graphs

RESPONSE-TO-INTERVENTION MODEL

With the reauthorization of the IDEIA (2004), the **response-to-intervention model** (RTI) based on CBM principles increased in acceptance as a systematic, ongoing measurement of progress (Haager & Klinger, 2005). RTI based on CBM reflects the growing need to track student progress more closely than with yearly state-mandated assessments. The model uses an ongoing CBM approach to carefully evaluate student progress to determine those who respond well to intensive instruction and evaluation. Particularly useful in the prereferral state, RTI established through CBM encourages the teacher to determine the strategies and interventions having meaningful impact on performance and to avoid referral for special education. RTI using CBM promotes the evaluation of instructional progress based on current functioning leading to intense intervention rather than waiting for a discrepancy between ability and achievement to surface.

RTI models display three tiers of instructional design. Tier 1 includes the use of research-based strategies for instruction that cover a comprehensive core of academic requirements. Tier 2 provides for supplemental instruction to students demonstrating difficulties with the curriculum after several weeks of instruction. Tier 2 requires concentrated, supplemental instruction in the general education classroom for a period of 20 to 30 minutes per day in addition to continued core instruction. Techniques such as CBM may prove helpful in documenting and tracking student progress in this tier. In Tier 3 students displaying continued deficits in progress will be considered for additional, more extreme intervention or referral to special education. Once again, CBM techniques help to support this decision.

Assessing Progress

The curricular areas most often assessed with CBM include reading, spelling, written language, and mathematics (Gansle, Noell, VanDerHayden, Naquin, & Slider, 2002). CBM consists of a series of informal, brief tests directly tied to basic skills. Frequent administration and inexpensive development of multiple forms provide the teacher with many samples of the performance to indicate slight growth as student achievement increases (Gansle et al.).

The IEP team selects CBM as an evaluation method if it wants to obtain general assessment of global skills using repeated measures (Hosp, 2003). In addition, the use of CBM increases a student's academic gains through the individualized instructional planning and monitoring of progress (Scott & Weishaar, 2003). CBM involves students in monitoring their advancement, thereby providing an excellent motivational tool. CBM identifies slight changes in achievement, creating a more in-depth understanding of the student's improvement (Hosp).

In the behaviorist tradition, CBM's direct link to fluency in reading, written language, spelling, and mathematics expands development of basic skills more rapidly than a more global approach (Stoner, Scarpati, Phaneuf, & Hintze, 2002). Additionally, CBM increases the IEP team's knowledge of the student's progress through the visual representations of weekly growth evident through the charting procedures (Taylor, 2003). Research indicates that monitoring procedures for CBM progress correlate with other standardized measures and often produce a more sensitive short-term measurement (Dunn & Eckert, 2002). The increase in time that teachers spend planning prior to instruction appears to have a positive impact on the student's achievement levels (Taylor, 2003).

The **database** created for each student assessed through CBM continually documents for the IEP team the progress made by individual students. This database also documents long-term progress of general skills over time. CBM also provides input for teacher-designed modifications. CBM graphs indicate progress and supply good communication tools for teachers to convey to parents the student's achievement at school. Research suggests that parents who receive CBM reports become more involved in their child's education and instructional programs. Easy to administer, score, and feature in corresponding graphs, CBMs provide the IEP team with usable data. These graphs offer comparisons made across students, classrooms, and entire districts (Hosp, 2003).

TYPES OF CURRICULUM-BASED MEASUREMENT

CBM represents a classroom-based procedure used to measure academic progress in basic skills in the areas of reading, writing, spelling, and mathematics. CBM procedures collect data, report progress, and provide the teacher with the necessary information to change and modify instruction (Pemberton, 2003). Administration and scoring directions should be easy to follow, straightforward, and reliable.

Reading Curriculum-Based Measurement

Several different types of CBM rate reading skills. Taylor (2003) suggests that CBM effectively measures oral reading fluency. **Oral reading rate** can be calculated by dividing the number of words in a passage by the number of seconds required to read it and multiplying the quotient by 60 (Carver, 1990). Using this method, the teacher establishes a written record of student accuracy and speed in reading words. Figure 3.3 provides an example of an oral reading rate calculated with a CBM.

Establishing **oral reading fluency** includes using a prepared passage at the student's instructional reading level and having the student read the segment aloud. Issues such as slow pace, choppy reading, poor phrasing or intonation, numerous pauses, or repetitions appear during the assessment (Walker, 2004). **Rates of reading speed** and miscues can be recorded in chart form to better represent the student's progress. Figure 3.4 presents an oral reading fluency example.

CBM measures reading comprehension through the **maze procedure** to ascertain level of understanding. Omit every nth word (as in every 10th word) from the assessment passage. The student selects the word that best completes the sentence from three choices. The maze procedure provides an indication of the student's level of

Figure 3.3   Calculating an Oral Reading Rate

1. Count the *total number* of words read in the passage and multiply by 60.
2. That number becomes the *dividend*.
3. The *divisor* is the number of seconds it takes to read the passage.
4. The *quotient* is the number of words read per minute.

Total number of words in passage   100

$$\frac{\times\,60}{6000} \div 70 \text{ seconds} = 85.7 \text{ words per minute}$$

Figure 3.4   A CBM Graph of a Student's Oral Reading Fluency

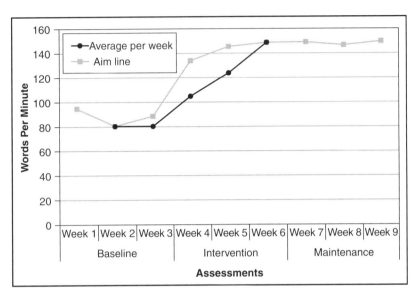

understanding. Research on reliability, validity, and sensitivity of the maze procedure points to excellent and consistent results using CBM (Shin, Deno, & Espin, 2000). Figure 3.5 illustrates a maze procedure.

Written Language Curriculum-Based Measurement

CBM often includes both writing samples and spelling assessments. Allinder, Fuchs, and Fuchs (1998) describe a procedure for using CBM to assess spelling progress. The teacher selects 20 spelling words at random from the entire list of words for the year. The student spells a list of words read aloud at approximately 10-second intervals. The entire procedure requires 2 minutes. The number of **correct letter sequences** (CLS) provides the score for the procedure rather than the number of correctly spelled words. These letter sequences chart growth. For example, Emily's teacher wants to document

Figure 3.5   Example of a Maze Procedure

Directions: Read each word silently, then circle the one word that makes the sentence correct.

1. The little green frog _____ at the pond.

    lived   walked   read

2. The little frog liked to _____ on the lily pads.

    sick   sit   sip

3. He _____ to eat flies and bugs.

    danced   sang   liked

her progress on the fourth-grade spelling words. She selects 20 words from the list at random and gives them orally to Emily at 10-second intervals. The following list features the correct word, Emily's spelling, and the graded word. The evaluator must remember to place a space holder or phantom letter at the beginning and end of each word.

Correct Word (Number of Correct Letter Sequences)	Emily's Spelling	Graded Word
simple (7)	simple	^ ^ ^ ^ ^ ^ _simple_
guide (6)	giude	^XXX^^ _giude_
fence (6)	fence	^ ^ ^ ^ ^ _fence_
study (6)	study	^ ^ ^ ^ ^ _study_
order (6)	order	^ ^ ^ ^ ^ _order_
pound (6)	pound	^ ^ ^ ^ ^ _pound_
package (8)	package	^ ^ ^ ^ ^ ^ ^ _package_
paint (6)	paint	^ ^ ^ ^ ^ _paint_
noise (6)	noise	^ ^ ^ ^ ^ _noise_
clothes (6)	cloes	^ ^ ^XXX _cloes_
information (12)	information	^ ^ ^ ^ ^ ^ ^ ^ ^ _information_
find (5)	find	^ ^ ^ ^ _find_
sorry (6)	sorry	^ ^ ^ ^ ^ _sorry_
noise (6)	noise	^ ^ ^ ^ ^ _noise_
carry (5)	cary	^ ^X^ _cary_
save (5)	save	^ ^ ^ ^ _save_
guide (6)	guide	^ ^ ^ ^ ^ _guide_
many (5)	many	^ ^ ^ ^ _many_
hope (5)	hope	^ ^ ^ ^ _hope_

Figure 3.6   A Spelling CBM Graph for Candace

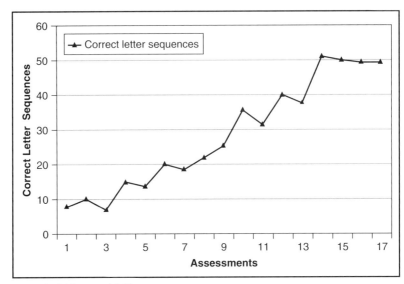

Emily's score is 111 out of 118.

Twice-weekly repetitions occur for a spelling CBM. These test results can be put to-gether over a period of time to demonstrate progress on the list of words. Figure 3.6 shows Candace's spelling CBM graph that features CLS growth over an 8-week period.

Writing evaluated with CBM determines the **correct word sequences** (CWS) written in a passage minus the incorrect sequences (Espin, Shin, Deno, Skare, Robinson, & Benner, 2000). Certain descriptors form the basis for the evaluation process in a writing CBM. First, "words written" include the number of words in the student's written sample. Sec-ond, a "word" refers to any series of letters separated by a space. Third, "words spelled cor-rectly" include any English word without respect to grammar or context. Fourth, "words spelled incorrectly" represents words not correctly spelled in the English language. Fifth, "characters" refer to all letters, spaces, and punctuation marks. Sixth, a "sentence" con-sists of any series of words separated from any other series of words with a period, ques-tion mark, or exclamation point. Seventh, "characters per word" means the number of characters written divided by the number of words written. Eighth, "words per sentence" stands for the number of words written divided by the number of sentences written. Word processing programs aid in the calculation of these eight measures. Using this procedure produces growth indicators of written language development.

Gansle et al. (2002) describes a method for evaluating writing through CBM that ex-amines **predictor variables** to go beyond simply looking at the total number of words. First, the examiner calculates the total number of words by counting what was written in a 3-minute period. The examiner disregards correct spelling and grammatical usage in the total word count. The next step includes the recording of the total number of nouns, verbs, and adjectives. Then the examiner denotes the number of words spelled correctly. Other categories evaluated include total punctuation marks, correct use of punctuation marks, correct capitalization, use of complete sentences, the number of words in complete sentences, words in correct sequence, sentence fragments, and simple sentences. This procedure also uses computer scoring. Gansle et al. (2002) report that this method provides a more detailed and reliable measure of student progress than just looking at total word count analysis.

Mathematics

Evans-Hampton et al. (2002) describe a CBM procedure for documenting student growth in the area of mathematics. The student completes a mathematics worksheet with 35 problems constructed to represent the current curriculum using a timed administration. The examiner calculates the "number of digits correct per minute," as well as the "number of digits incorrect per minute," while documenting the effects of covert versus obvious timing procedures. Once again the examiner must include placeholder digits; 0's as well as spaces are counted as correct digits; digits carried are not counted. A teacher could use a similar procedure to document growth on each state-mandated skill or every IEP goal.

THE MECHANICS OF CURRICULUM-BASED MEASUREMENT

After the IEP team determines that CBM will yield appropriate assessment and instructional information, certain steps must be followed. CBM involves some aspects that are similar across the subject areas. These include repeated administration of particular probes or sample items taken from the year's curriculum, graphing the results to examine trends, and changes to the instructional cycle based on the trends.

Probes

A probe represents a sample from the student's overall curriculum used in a diagnostic manner to determine the effectiveness of instructional strategies by taking small samples of daily performance. Figure 3.7 presents Roberto's completed math probe.

Figure 3.7   Roberto's Completed Math Probe

Roberto completed the following math probe.

4	5	7	3	6	8
+5	+5	+4	+5	+7	+3
9	10	**12**	**7**	**14**	11

The problems were scored correct or incorrect (bolded). Roberto received a score of 3 out of 6 or 50%. It is also possible to score this probe using all digits computed. For instance, Roberto answered correctly with one digit on the problem 7 + 4 = 12; the one is correct and the two is incorrect. When scoring probes, CBM can be very sensitive to the student's individual progress.

Figure 3.8 Brandon's Writing Graph for a 6-Week Period

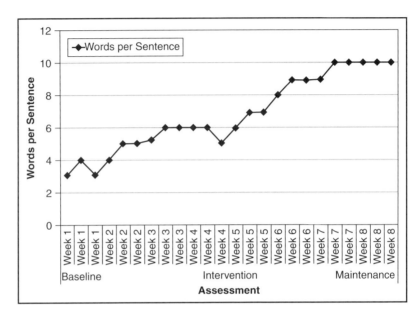

Graphing

Graphing is another component of CBM that is consistent across subject areas. CBM graphing uses two separate axes. The horizontal axis represents the number of sessions during the CBM. The vertical axis indicates the number of correct responses per time unit obtained through the probes. The initial graph represents the **baseline**, which reports the student's correct and incorrect words or number of words per minute read by averaging the performance. Once the baseline has been established, the teacher then determines the aim line. Figure 3.8 presents Brandon's initial graph of average words per sentence over the course of a week.

Aim Lines

The **aim line** represents the number of correct responses expected as a result of student learning, which is also the goal of instruction. Plotting the aim line on the graph allows the teacher to monitor the student's progress toward the goal. For example, if a student reads at a rate of 67 words per minute during the three baseline data collections, then the baseline would be 67. By examining a chart of *expected weekly growth rates* (Deno, Fuchs, Marston, & Shin, 2001), the teacher then determines that a realistic growth rate would be one word per week for an average third-grade student without disabilities. The teacher would then determine the number of weeks of instruction left in the school year (in the following case, 33) and calculate the following:

Baseline: 67
Weekly increase in number of words expected for third-grade student = 1

Number of weeks of instruction following the baseline period = 33
$$1 \times 33 = 33 + 67 = 100$$

This aim line of 100 would be plotted on the graph by drawing a line between the baseline score of 67 and the goal of 100 words. This allows the instruction to be monitored by plotting student performance twice a week to determine if the student progresses satisfactorily. The aim line also permits the teacher to adjust instruction. Students failing to meet the aim line projections on three consecutive attempts receive additional instruction with less difficult material. Those excelling during the trials engage in more demanding instruction.

Trend Lines

Trend lines represent connected plots on the graph with a solid line. This line creates a visual representation of change. Trend lines connect the baseline or the performance prior to the instruction to the achieved level of performance at the end of the intervention. In each subject area, however, specific procedures exist for reading, written language, spelling, and mathematics. The mechanics for the individual subject areas are explained in the following sections.

Reading Curriculum-Based Measurement Mechanics

According to Scott and Weishaar (2003) general steps for developing a CBM for reading consist of the following:

*   Choose textbook excerpts from the student's curriculum.
*   Avoid poetry or plays.
*   Select materials on the student's instructional reading level. (This is why an informal reading inventory is essential.)
*   Compute the readability for each passage.
*   Type, organize, and copy the selections.
*   Create two copies; the teacher's copy will contain a cumulative word count.
*   Use the sample to test the student once or twice a week for every week of instruction.
*   Use a new excerpt for each testing session.
*   Mark miscues on the teacher's copy to calculate the reading rate.
*   Draw graphs to monitor student progress.

Written Language Mechanics

Hosp (2003) describes a method to conduct a CBM of written language focused on spelling skills. The teacher begins by gathering the appropriate materials, including a list of spelling words equivalent to the student's typical spelling words, a stopwatch or timer, and an answer sheet with lines for the student to record responses. The examiner needs a recording copy of each spelling probe marked with the correct number of letter sequences for each word. Hosp defines a CLS as the correct letters written in order in the student's response. The teacher notes these CLSs on the recording copy. Initially, three equivalent tests are administered to establish a baseline. After the initial assessment, the probes are administered 30 different times throughout the school year. The probes are administered to an individual or to a group and consist of 12 to 13 words for Grades 1 through 3. For students in Grades 4 through 8, 17 to 18 words are used.

Mathematics Mechanics

To develop a mathematics CBM, the teacher follows the procedures described by Calhoun and Fuchs (2003) for a math CBM based on *The Math Operations Test–Revised* (MOT–R; Fuchs, Fuchs, Hamlett, & Stecker, 1991). Using the MOT–R, the teacher selects 50 problems that match the goals to be accomplished. Using a standardized instrument, such as the MOT–R, provides the teacher with information about the reliability and validity of the procedure, thereby strengthening the results. The student completes the problems in a 2- to 3-minute period. The number of correct answers forms the basis for the results. Similar CBM probes administered on a regular basis demonstrate student growth over the academic year. The chart of fluency in addition problems demonstrates Keith's growth over an 8-week period.

Published Curriculum-Based Materials for All Subject Areas

As mentioned, published CBM materials that include preselected probes, answer and scoring sheets, and summary sheets prove very helpful to the teacher. Using this type of system frees the teacher from having to constantly construct individualized probes.

Figure 3.9   Keith's Chart of Fluency Addition Problems

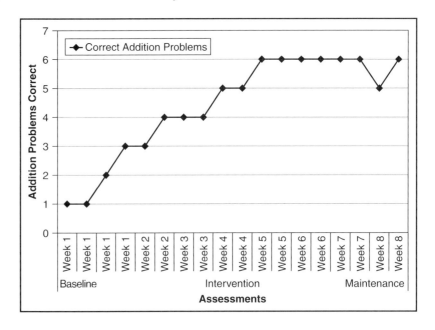

For reading, something as simple as the features built into word processing software—such as Microsoft Word, which uses the Flesch-Kinkaid readability system—provides tremendous help (Gunning, 2002). The steps for accessing this feature appear in the Curriculum-Based Measurement and Technology section of this chapter.

The *Monitoring Basic Skills Progress* (MBSP) systems include four software programs that allow students to complete a series of short probes with automatic computer scoring (Taylor, 2003). This type of system provides an excellent way to cut the time the teacher must devote to preparing, scoring, and charting probes. Immediate feedback to the student is also part of the MBSP. The four tests include the basic reading tests (Fuchs, Hamlettt, & Fuchs, 1997), the basic spelling tests (Fuchs, Hamlett, & Fuchs, 1990), the basic math computation tests (Fuchs, Hamlett, & Fuchs, 1998), and the basic math concepts and applications tests (Fuchs, Hamlett, & Fuchs, 1999).

The basic reading tests (Fuchs, Hamlettt, & Fuchs, 1997) include a maze procedure omitting every seventh word in a 400-word reading probe. The student supplies the correct word for three choices. Students take this test as often as twice a week on a computer. The software analyzes the student's responses and automatically provides a graph and saves it for the teacher.

The basic spelling tests (Fuchs, Hamlett, & Fuchs, 1990) require the teacher to dictate to the student one of the 30 spelling lists that include 20 words. The student completes responses on the computer. Once again, the software analyzes the results and produces a computer-generated graph to demonstrate the student's improvement over the course of the year.

The basic math computation tests (Fuchs, Hamlett, & Fuchs, 1998) and the basic math concepts and applications tests (Fuchs, Hamlett, & Fuchs, 1999) evaluate student progress in two different aspects of mathematics. The basic math computation tests examine computation skills with 180 different probes (20 at each grade level). Each probe includes 25 computation problems that are completed using paper and pencil and are scored by a computer. The program provides graphs to display changes in performance. The basic math concepts and applications tests include 30 three-page probes per year from Grades 2 through 6 concerning the student's ability to apply math rather than merely complete a simple computation. This program also scores and graphs the results of each administration over time.

The Academic Competence Evaluation Scales (ACES; Psychological Corporation, 2001) uses a technology-based rating scale to identify students with academic difficulties and provide links to specific interventions. ACES offers a prereferral problem-solving process to identify three to five descriptions of possible research-based instructional strategies. The technology isolates academic strengths and classroom attitudes in the areas of motivation, engagement, study skills, and interpersonal skills. ACES reports have consistently demonstrated reliability and validity.

Dynamic Indicators of Early Literacy Skills

Reading First was authorized as a part of the No Child Left Behind Act. It is historically the largest reading initiative ever undertaken in the country. Reading First focuses on the implementation of proven methods of reading. The goal of Reading First is to have all children reading at grade level or above by the end of third grade. One of the most important initiatives that has emerged from the Reading First research focuses on the Dynamic Indicators of Early Literacy Skills (DIBELS) assessment tool. Researchers at the University of Oregon developed DIBELS as a scientifically based framework. It is a powerful evaluation tool for beginning literacy and assists teachers in pinpointing student progress on the reading targets needed to pass high-stakes tests. DIBELS enables teachers to know the type of instruction needed and the intensity level required to ensure that all students will be reading on grade level, or above grade level, by the end of third grade.

DIBELS takes about 15 minutes to administer for each child. Schools can download all of the DIBELS materials from the University of Oregon Web site. Currently, the university charges a fee per child to score the instrument. Some states have established their own database for scoring. DIBELS measures consist of the following: initial sound fluency, letter naming fluency, phoneme segmentation fluency, nonsense word fluency, oral reading fluency, **oral retelling fluency**, and **word use fluency**.

Use of this research-based assessment helps teachers to make informed decisions about instruction. DIBELS appears to be quick, valid, and effective. Its inclusion as a CBM tool enables states to provide the mandated screening, progress monitoring, diagnostic data gathering, and outcome measures required by NCLB.

SUMMARIZING CURRICULUM-BASED MEASUREMENT

Summarizing the information obtained from CBM involves specific steps that are easy to follow. First, the teacher gathers baseline or everyday functioning information prior to the intervention or instruction. The probes occur daily. In reading, the probes involve reading words aloud. The teacher counts the number of correct words and calculates the average. This average signifies the student's starting point or baseline (Scott & Weishaar, 2003).

Next, a graph is developed, featuring the student's baseline, progress during the **intervention phase**, and the goal for the student. The goal represents the amount of expected progress occurring within a designated period of time. In the reading example described, the **expected rate of growth** could be one to two new words per week. This results in an average of two new words learned a week. For example, if a student reads 48 words in his baseline, he would be reading approximately 66 words at the end of the 9-week intervention. This would be indicated on the graph with a straight line connecting the baseline of 48 to the expected growth point of 66 words.

Expected growth rates for spelling, as described by Hosp (2003), are determined by obtaining a baseline average of correct letter sequences (CLS) and then projecting one additional correct letter sequence per week times the number of weeks divided by 100. For example, improvement of one CLS per week might be appropriate for a third-grade student. Teacher judgment also serves as a valuable predictor of rate of growth.

In mathematics, a baseline average occurs by administering three probes within a short time. The number of correct digits (CD) per minute is counted for each probe.

CBM instruction seeks to achieve an average improvement of one CD per minute per week until the student reaches the next or appropriate grade level. Graphs are used to monitor changes and note success.

Third, the student's performance during intervention on each probe is plotted on a graph. The results of each instructional session appear on the graph with a trend line connecting these plots. The trend line shows whether the student's performance demonstrates improvement, remains stagnant, or decreases. Hopefully, the trend line corresponds to or surpasses the aim line. Graphing should be done at the end of each instructional session so that instruction can be wisely modified to improve progress.

To analyze this data, the probes must be collected at least weekly, and perhaps twice a week, to increase the amount of information obtained (Scott & Weishaar, 2003). Scott and Weishaar also report the following rules for making instructional modifications when using CBM:

- Three consecutive data points falling below the aim line warrant instructional changes. These changes might take the form of environmental support, time of the intervention, or instructional design of the intervention.
- Performance above the aim line on three consecutive data points to the need for changes in the rate.
- Performance consistently above or right below the aim line requires assessment of the instructional level.
- Performance consistently below the aim line for more than three consecutive data entries necessitates changes in the instruction.
- Intervention warrants continual monitoring.

USING THE CURRICULUM-BASED MEASUREMENT DATA IN THE INDIVIDUAL EDUCATION PROGRAM

What Does Curriculum-Based Measurement Contribute to IEP Development?

- It monitors student academic growth regularly using specified probes to determine progress.
- It provides formative and summative information useful in redirecting instruction for individual students.
- It offers opportunities for students to visually graph their progress on academic mastery.
- It gives results that are easy to explain and interpret to IEP members.
- It lends documentation to strategies and methods that meet research-based criteria.

Benefits to Parents

CBM data benefit parents by helping them to see and to understand students' growth in both general and special education. The graphs provide visual displays of improvement over time and allow parents to see both the speed with which students demonstrate mastery and the level of their performance. When presented with CBM data, parents and the IEP team can develop a shared understanding of the ways in which the instruction has taken place, and they can identify areas of progress and slower development. Deno (1992) indicates that performance graphs that display CBM data in bar graph form allow parents to do the following:

- Have a reference between current and former achievement
- See the performance in relationship to the actual goals of instruction
- Understand the relevance of the program by viewing the actual areas of emphasis
- Visualize how changes to the instructional program impact their students
- Recognize the difference in their students' performance with regard to peers using classroom norms

The Individualized Education Program Team as a Whole

The IEP team applies the results of CBM in several ways. First, the team uses the information to determine student readiness for the general education classroom. Second, the information also determines future instructional strategies, such as appropriate modifications that can be used. Third, the IEP team employs the results of the CBM in discussions aimed at exploring small increments of progress and making necessary changes in the direction of the student's school career. Fourth, the IEP team finds decision making easier as the choices are based on graph results rather than on emotion (Pemberton, 2003). This type of system may improve communication with parents by providing reliable data showing daily progress rather than a single standardized assessment score.

CURRICULUM-BASED MEASUREMENT AND TECHNOLOGY

AIMSweb (http://aimsweb.com) provides users with an online formative assessment system that continuously evaluates student performance data, allowing for evidence-based, data-driven, instructional decision making. The Web site supplies assessment materials in the areas of reading, early literacy, early numeracy, mathematics, spelling, and written expression through the use of CBM techniques. AIMSweb delivers universal screening and progress monitoring of student progress in a three-tier problem-solving model using response-to-intervention in a Web-based data management and reporting system. The Web site includes information concerning products, including data capture tools and CBM sets, assessments for a variety of academic subjects, research articles and links, training and support for teachers.

Intervention Central (http://www.interventioncentral.org/index.php) provides free tools and resources for schools and parents to identify and encourage positive behaviors and effective learning activities. The Web site provides a variety of online tools, including the CBM List Builder IKAPI! Reading Probe Generator, the Chart Dog tool to create CBM charts, and Test Score Analyzer 2.0. The Web site also includes special downloads, including the CBM Warehouse and other related items.

SUMMARY

- CBM provides a research-based method for linking instruction and assessment in such basic academic skills as reading, written language, and mathematics.
- CBM bases decision making on classroom performance, thereby diminishing the impact of cultural considerations.
- CBM monitors progress and determines the effectiveness of specific instructional processes.
- CBM clarifies decision making through the use of graphs to chart both the student's expected progress and actual achievement over a period of time.
- Summarizing CBM results provides visual displays of growth in charts and graphs.
- CBM functions as an excellent source of information about a specific student to aid in the development of quality IEP goals.
- Technology in CBM includes the development of records, charts, and graphs and the use of several computer-based CBM programs.

COMPREHENSION CHECK

1. Explain the reasons that CBM provides more reliable and valid results than CBA does.
2. Why would an IEP team use the information provided by CBM to make instructional planning decisions? Why would the teacher use CBM to make adjustments in classroom instruction? How would a student benefit from CBM?
3. What problems can you foresee in using the CBM method in a classroom?

ACTIVITIES

1. Select a CBM program for a student who needs help with fluency in reading. Be sure to include the goal, probes, and measurement/graphing plan.
2. Use the Internet to make a list of five CBM programs for use with reading, spelling, written language, and math.
3. Motivation is a by-product of CBM. Demonstrate scenarios that highlight the ways in which CBM motivates teachers and students.

REFERENCES

Allinder, R., Fuchs, L., & Fuchs, D. (1998). Curriculum-based assessment. In H. B. Vance (Ed.), *Psychological assessment of children* (2nd ed., pp. 104–127). New York: John Wiley & Sons.

Allinder, R. M., Fuchs, L. S., & Fuchs, D. (2004). Issues in curriculum-based assessment. In A. M. Sorrells, H. Rieth, & P. Sindelar (Eds.), *Critical issues in special education: Access, diversity, and accountability* (pp. 106–124). Boston: Allyn & Bacon.

Calhoun, M. B., & Fuchs, L. S. (2003). The effects of peer-assisted learning strategies and curriculum-based measurement on mathematics performance of secondary students with disabilities. *Remedial and Special Education, 24*(4), 235–245.

Carver, R. P. (1990). *Reading rate: A review of research and theory.* San Diego, CA: Academic Press.

Deno, S. (1992). The nature and development of curriculum-based measurement. *Preventing School Failure, 36*, 5–10.

Deno, S. L., Fuchs, L. S., Marston, D., & Shin, J. (2001). Using curriculum-based measurement to establish growth standards for students with learning disabilities. *School Psychology Review, 30*(4), 507–524.

Deno., S. L., Mirkin, P., & Chiang, B. (1982). Identifying valid measures of reading. *Exceptional Children, 49,* 36–45.

Dunn, E. K., & Eckert, T. L. (2002). Curriculum-based measurement in reading: A comparison of similar versus challenging material. *School Psychology Quarterly, 17*(1), 24–36.

Espin, C., Shin, J., Deno, S. L., Skare, S., Robinson, S., & Benner, B. (2000). Identifying indicators of written expression proficiency for middle school students. *The Journal of Special Education 34*(3), 140–153.

Evans-Hampton, T. N., Skinner, C. H., Henington, C., Sims, S., and McDaniel, C. E. (2002). An investigation of situational bias: Conspicuous and covert timing during curriculum-based measurement of mathematics across African American and Caucasian students. *School Psychology Review, 31*(4), 529–539.

Fuchs, L. S., & Fuchs, D. (2002). Curriculum-based measurement: Describing competence, enhancing outcomes, evaluating treatment, effects, and identifying treatment nonresponders. *Peabody Journal of Education, 77*(2), 64–84.

Fuchs, L. S., Fuchs, D., Hamlett, C. L., & Stecker, P. M. (1991). Effects of curriculum-based measurement and consultation on teacher planning and student achievement in mathematics operations. *American Educational Research Journal, 28,* 617–641.

Fuchs, L., Hamlett, C., & Fuchs, D. (1990). *Monitoring basic skills progress—spelling.* Austin, TX: Pro-Ed.

Fuchs, L., Hamlett, C., & Fuchs, D. (1997). *Monitoring basic skills progress—reading.* Austin, TX: Pro-Ed.

Fuchs, L., Hamlett, C., & Fuchs, D. (1998). *Monitoring basic skills progress—mathematics.* Austin, TX: Pro-Ed.

Fuchs, L., Hamlett, C., & Fuchs, D. (1999). *Monitoring basic skills progress—math concepts and applications.* Austin, TX: Pro-Ed.

Gansle, K. A., Noell, G. H., VanDerHayden, A. M., Naquin, G. M., & Slider, N. J. (2002). Moving beyond total words written: The reliability, criterion validity, and time cost of alternative measures for curriculum-based measurement in writing. *School Psychology Review, 31*(4), 477–497.

Gunning, T. B. (2002). *Assessing and correcting reading and writing difficulties*. Boston: Allyn & Bacon.

Haager, D., & Klinger, J. K. (2005). Differentiating instruction in inclusive classrooms. The special educator's guide. Boston: Pearson/Allyn & Bacon.

Hosp, M. K. (2003). Curriculum-based measurement for reading, spelling, and math: How to do it and why. *Preventing School Failure, 48*(1), 10–17.

Kranzler, J. H., Miller, M. D., & Jordan, L. (1999). An examination of racial/ethnic and gender bias on curriculum-based measurement of reading. *School Psychology Quarterly, 14*(3), 327–342.

Malecki, C. K., & Jewell, J. (2003). Developmental, gender, and practical considerations in scoring curriculum-based measurement writing probes. *Psychology in the Schools 40*(4), 379–390.

Pemberton, J. B. (2003). Communicating academic progress as an integral part of assessment. *Teaching Exceptional Children, 25*(4), 16–20.

Psychological Corporation. (2001). The *Academic Competence Evaluation Scales* (ACES). San Antonio, TX: Author.

Powell-Smith, K., & Stewart, L. (1998). The use of curriculum-based measurement in the reintegration of students with mild disabilities. In M. Shinn (Ed.), *Advanced applications of curriculum-based measurement* (pp. 254–307). New York: Guilford Press.

Scott, V. G., & Weishaar, M. K. (2003). Curriculum-based measurement for reading progress. *Intervention in School and Clinic, 38*(3), 153–159.

Shin, J., Deno, S., & Espin, C. (2000). Technical adequacy of the maze test for curriculum-based measurement of reading growth. *Journal of Special Education, 34*, 164–172.

Stoner, G., Scarpati, S. F., Phaneuf, R. I., & Hintze, J. M. (2002). Using curriculum-based measurement to evaluate intervention efficacy; *Child and Family Behavior Therapy, 24*(1), 101–112.

Taylor, R. L. (2003). *Assessment of exceptional students: Educational and psychological procedures* (6th ed.). Boston: Pearson.

VanDerHeyden, A. M., Witt, J. C., Naquin, G., & Noell, G. (2001). The reliability and validity of curriculum-based measurement probes for kindergarten students. *School Psychology Review, 30*(3), 363–382.

Walker, B. J. (2004). *Diagnostic teaching of reading: Techniques for instruction and assessment* (5th ed.). Upper Saddle River, NJ: Merrill/Prentice Hall.

BEHAVIORAL OBSERVATIONS AND ASSESSMENT

Chapter Focus

Behavioral observation provides the IEP team with specific information about a student's performance in the classroom from both academic and social perspectives. Qualitative observations involve the recording of a detailed account of all the behaviors demonstrated in a classroom setting. Quantitative observations focus on a specific behavior to determine how often it occurs, how long it lasts, or the amount of time it takes a student to respond to a particular request. Quantitative observation forms the basis for functional behavioral assessment required by IDEIA for all students with disabilities facing removal from the current placement due to inappropriate behaviors. The IEP team uses behavioral observations to make decisions about placements, instructional arrangements, modifications, or IEP goals.

LEARNER OBJECTIVES

- Define behavioral observation and functional behavioral assessment.
- Explain the benefits and disadvantages of behavioral observation and functional behavioral assessment.
- Describe how behavioral observation and functional behavioral assessment address issues of cultural and linguistic diversity.
- Determine when to use behavioral observation or functional behavioral assessment.
- Depict the different types of behavioral observations.
- Identify the steps for developing behavioral observations or functional behavioral assessments.
- Explain how to summarize information from behavioral observations or functional behavioral assessments.
- Clarify the use of data from behavioral observations or functional behavioral assessments for use with IEPs.
- Characterize the role of technology in behavioral observation and functional behavioral assessment.

WHAT ARE BEHAVIORAL OBSERVATIONS?

Observation entails the most objective and widely used method of assessment (Taylor, 2003). Behavioral observation consists of watching and recording the actions of an individual student (Maag, 2004). Observation provides a systematic method for gathering information by examining a student in his or her environment (Cohen & Spenciner, 2003). Observation, the most direct method of assessment, yields a wide variety of information that can be gathered during a school day (Taylor, 2003). It directly mirrors how students approach problems in the context of their learning needs (Albert, Mayotte, & Sohn, 2002). Using well-defined behavioral observations clarifies academic performance and academic-related behaviors (Salend, 2000).

Salvia and Ysseldyke (2004) describe two principal methods of behavioral observation: **qualitative** and **quantitative**. Qualitative observations provide a broad, descriptive base of a student's daily functioning (Bondurant-Utz, 2002). Data collected from qualitative observations can be analyzed in isolation or in a group of observations collected on a specific student. Quantitative observations measure specific behaviors. These behaviors, defined in detail, require specific procedures for gathering the observable behavior (Salvia & Ysseldyke).

Behavioral observations can also be delineated as **unstructured** and **structured** (Kubiszyn & Borich, 2002). Unstructured observations collect essentially qualitative data using open-ended information. Such observations involve recording as much data as possible about a student's behavior during a given period of time. The teacher does not have a preconceived idea about the exact behaviors to be detailed and must make sense out of the information after completion of the observation.

Structured observations consist of specifically defined behaviors that the observer prepares to monitor. This preparation may take more time and planning than an unstructured observation, but the results yield specific indicators of the student's actual performance on those behavioral tasks. Three key components comprise structured observations: (a) isolation of the behavior observed, (b) anticipation of expected behavior, and (c) recording of the behavior using a measurable tally system (Kubiszyn & Borich, 2002).

BENEFITS OF USING OBSERVATION

Quality instruction requires the teacher to constantly monitor the progress and behavior of both the students and self in the learning environment. Observations ensure that classroom instruction proves conducive to achievement. They provide information about student behavior in a general sense or by looking at specific behaviors. Environmental events that instigate and maintain inappropriate behaviors reveal themselves best during direct examination. These valued glimpses of student behavior help IEP teams to deliver effective prescribed interventions (Strain & Joseph, 2004).

Salvia and Ysseldyke (2004) identified three important points regarding observations: (a) information gathered about significant behaviors requiring intervention serves as a focus point for action, (b) observation plays a critical role in the identification of acceptable social behaviors, and (c) **on-task behavior** and skill performance in a variety of settings prove invaluable to the teacher and IEP team for instructional decision making.

Cohen and Spenciner (2003) consider observation to be a key component in the initial evaluation and reevaluation of students. Classroom observations form a basis for understanding individual functioning on standardized measures and aid the IEP team in constructing a more complete picture of the student's educational activity. Often, observations identify disabling conditions or pinpoint harmful and **inappropriate behaviors** (Salvia & Ysseldyke, 2004). Venn (2004) identified four reasons to observe behaviors of students with special needs: (a) uncover specific signs of disabilities, (b) consider the realm of possible disabling conditions, (c) create management programs for the classroom, and (d) monitor the effectiveness of interventions and classroom instruction.

Early deficits in student performance are often detected during observation (Taylor, 2003). An observation can provide information about readiness for instruction and can guide the teacher in determining where instruction should begin. The use of systematic observation to document incremental growth directs the teacher in determining small successes that have been achieved.

In addition to observing the student's behavior, teacher actions and classroom information can also be collected. Details about the arrangement of the classroom, grouping for instruction, teacher response rates and expectations, and other daily routines prove easily obtained through direct observations (Cohen & Spenciner, 2003).

Another benefit of observation involves the inclusion of parents or others familiar with the student's functioning in various settings (Bondurant-Utz, 2002). By including the observations of these individuals, the IEP team begins to understand the student's generalization outside the classroom. Multiple sources of information provided by the IEP team members serve to reinforce the findings of other data, whether collected from standardized or authentic sources. Through the collaboration of the IEP team, support extends to the student, parents, peers, and all stakeholders in the student's environment (Hunt, Soto, Maier, & Doering, 2003).

DISADVANTAGES OF USING OBSERVATION

Bondurant-Utz (2002) identifies several disadvantages to using observations. First, she cautions that students may be sensitive to the observer's presence and that, therefore, observations must be undertaken in a variety of environments before the results can be generalized. Second, observers must be acutely aware of their influence in the outcome of an observation. Positive or negative observer responses color the results of the process. In addition, both **systematic** and random errors contribute to unreliable observations (Salvia & Ysseldyke, 2004). **Systematic errors** include inaccurate recording equipment, a departure from standardized procedure, or other unintended changes in the observation. **Random errors** include such factors as unfamiliarity with the recording system, inadequate time spent during the observation, or lack of concentration by the observer.

The expertise of the observer includes knowledge of a variety of observation techniques, accuracy in recording, and the ability to integrate the obtained material into useable components of intervention (Cohen & Spenciner, 2003). Awareness of observer bias is instrumental in good observational training. The development of observer self-awareness to obtain reliable observations increases observation validity (Sattler, 2001). Recognizing personal attitudes and values minimizes preconceptions and helps observers to create a neutral perspective toward students being observed. Sattler encourages observers to be attentive, cautious, and impartial, yet always concerned and sensitive.

The effect on the student being observed represents one of the most typical problems with observation. Many students react negatively to changes in the environment and additional people in the classroom. This practice tends to result in an impetus for the student or classroom to change normal behavioral patterns. This type of sensitivity alters the results and leads to faulty decision making. Bondurant-Utz (2002) strongly suggests that observations be performed across familiar settings to gain more accurate information. Overall, observations remain subjective and, especially for young students, change dramatically over a short period of time.

CULTURAL AND LINGUISTIC DIVERSITY

To ensure objectivity, reliable observers engage in self-examination concerning their understanding of cultural, ethnic, and socioeconomic groups. Sattler (2001) encourages observers to be aware of their own attitudes, values, and feelings. A conscious and alert attitude toward distractions caused by personal appearance, deformities, tattoos or body piercings, stereotypic behavior, or body odors limits or diminishes personal bias. This internal personal bias greatly reduces the effectiveness of the observer's ability to obtain accurate information.

Awareness of internal feelings guards against bias. Care must be taken to create precise, realistic findings (Sattler, 2001). When the observer's self-awareness increases, so can the ability to eliminate bias and increase respect for cultural and linguistic diversity. Inferences that color factual observations negatively impact objectivity, but understanding the influences of culture and language can have a positive impact on accurate observations. For example, an Asian American may avoid looking his teacher in the eye (the fact) as a symbol of respect (the cultural influence).

Observers should understand and correctly utilize information about cultural nuances. Sattler (2001) cautions observers to be specific and accurate, without making judgments that may be biased by lack of knowledge of the culture. Baca and Cervantes (2004) stress the need for observer competence in identifying second-language acquisition. The characteristics of second-language acquisition sometimes mirror language deficits resulting from a disability. Observers need to be able to ascertain the difference between language acquisition and disability.

Baca and Cervantes (2004) also offer several guidelines to help teachers and evaluators provide a culturally relevant, appropriate education that includes children with diversity and linguistic differences. First, interpreting observations of students requires help from families and communities. These individuals offer culturally sound interpretation of certain behaviors. Second, forming a strong relationship with parents can assist the observer in learning about traditions and practices related to language and culture: parents help teachers, and observers avoid inaccurate assumptions. Third, observers should keep an open mind and remember not to impose their own cultural values on students. Fourth, observers must examine themselves to determine biases and opinions. Asking questions regarding underlying assumptions about language, culture, and the necessity of English can help eliminate biases unknown to observers without training. Fifth, encouraging use in school of the child's home language and cultural values signifies that all languages and cultures have value.

DECIDING TO IMPLEMENT OBSERVATIONS

The IEP team decides to use observations as part of the assessment package when data collection must come directly from the student's performance. Unlike other authentic assessment techniques, which may look at a student's output in terms of work samples or self-analysis, behavioral observations record events as they occur. To determine the observation procedures to be used, the IEP team must carefully consider the type of information needed to make decisions about instruction.

For example, the team selects a more formal observational system when attempting to diagnose a particular inappropriate behavior in order to increase the understanding of a student's functioning in the classroom. In this case, the team chooses a formal instrument that includes behavioral observation as its data collection method. The Direct Observation Form (Achenbach, 1986) enables the observer to identify specific observed behaviors and to rate the severity of these behaviors to determine the difference in the student's performance from other same-age and grade-level peers (Overton, 2006). The observation of the student's specific behaviors occurs in several different settings.

On the other hand, if the IEP team desires less structured types of observations related directly to behaviors noted by the teacher in the classroom, it selects a different observation procedure. The IEP team carefully considers the questions to be answered by the observations in order to define and observe meaningful factors.

Cohen and Spenciner (2003) identify several guidelines for planning profitable observations: (a) clearly state the question to be asked and answered by the observation, (b) define the behavior in specific terms to be measured and observed, (c) observe the particular behavior across settings and over several different periods of time, (d) select the recording method best suited to the particular question, (e) ensure the observer's skill in terms of both setting up and recording the observation, and (f) determine the best method for using the data obtained from the observation with other assessment results.

A behavioral observation must be conceived ahead of time to be meaningful. Two steps concerning the use of observations in authentic assessment become critical in the decision-making process (Venn, 2004).

First, the IEP team must identify a specific behavior amenable to intervention and independent measurement (Walker, Shea, & Bauer, 2004). For example, when answering the question "Is Maria on task during story time?" several specific behaviors could be measured through observation.

The IEP team selects which behaviors to target over the course of the academic year. The teacher or observer then documents these behaviors using a variety of observational methods approved by the team. The documentation occurs over time, across settings, and examines specific behaviors.

Second, the decision-making process for behavioral observation ensures that observation methods actually provide more conclusive data than other techniques do (Venn, 2004).

Defining the target behaviors and observation procedures represent only two considerations the IEP team must contemplate when determining when to use observation. Bondurant-Utz (2002) lists several other areas of student functioning also in need of exploration through observation.

- Physical characteristics of the student noted by the observer provide the IEP team with a glimpse into the student's rate of development and health.
- Issues such as fine and gross motor development and the ability to perceive stimuli accurately lead the IEP team to consider the need for additional evaluation for related services, such as physical and occupational therapy or more intense vision or hearing evaluation.
- Information concerning the student's temperament or behavioral style lead to a better understanding of how the student approaches tasks in the daily environment.
- Communication patterns and the ability to interact measured through observation provide the IEP team with valuable information regarding the student's actual performance beyond academic development.
- Problem-solving skills and adaptive behavior noted in observations determine the extent to which generalization occurs and how well the student achieves independence.

Whether the IEP team desires an observational system to compare the student's daily behaviors with some expected norm, to observe exact behaviors to note growth, or to obtain more global, qualitative observations to consider other aspects of a student's functioning, the team must plan carefully for the experience. In the next section, the different types of behavior observation procedures are discussed.

TYPES OF BEHAVIORAL OBSERVATIONS

There are two types of observation: qualitative (unstructured) observations and quantitative (formal, systematic) observations. In addition, functional behavioral analysis, while a quantitative method, represents a distinct behavior observation system. Quantitative observation includes duration, latency, frequency, and amplitude, which are some of the most frequently used measures. **Duration** refers to the length of time behavior lasts. **Latency** refers to the length of time between request and compliance. **Frequency** describes the number of times a discrete behavior occurs. **Amplitude** refers to the strength of the intensity of the behavior. The IEP team also may elect to use functional behavior assessment for specific situations. Choosing the most appropriate characteristic helps to pinpoint the type of observation needed for the student (Salvia & Ysseldyke, 2004).

Qualitative Observation

Qualitative observation uses descriptive information rather than an examination of pre-selected behaviors. Qualitative observation provides the IEP team with a broad-based illustration of the student's daily behavior in the classroom. The three types of qualitative observation methods are ethnographic, participant–observer approach (Salvia & Ysseldyke, 2004), and anecdotal recording.

Ethnographic Observation   Ethnographic observation, or running records, requires the observer simply to watch and record all behaviors over a long period of time. The observer does not interact in classroom activity and records only behaviors seen without judgment. Ethnographic observations describe the sequence of events in the classroom. Figure 4.1 presents an example of an ethnographic running record observation.

Participant–Observer   In the participant–observer approach, the observer actually takes part in classroom activities and makes field notes regarding what takes place. The student initiates the activities, and the observer joins in to gain a better understanding of the student's functioning (Denzin & Lincoln, 2000). The observer acts primarily as a recorder but engages in some interaction during the session (Glesne, 1999). Glesne delineates the following questions to direct this type of observation: (a) What is happening? (b) Am I seeing what I hoped to see? and (c) Am I refraining from making judgments about the observation? Figure 4.2 presents an example of a participant–observer record.

Figure 4.1   Sample of an Ethnographic Running Record

Tyler was observed for 30 minutes in a general education reading classroom. He gets up from his seat within the first 2 minutes of class and moves to another corner of the room. He engages a student in a conversation. When class starts a minute later, the teacher redirects him to his seat. She asks him to pay attention and calm down. For the next 5 minutes, he sits in his seat and follows the direct instruction. The teacher then divides students into groups to analyze a story. Tyler moves all over the room for 1 minute. He talks about which group he would rather be in. The teacher stops him and assigns him to a group. He states that it is not the group he wants. Once he is seated with his group, he shows them some sort of toy he brought to school from home for the next 2 minutes. The teacher comes over to his group, removes the toy from him, and works with the group momentarily to get the students started. Tyler begins to complete the group work. They discuss the questions to complete. He listens, responds, and maintains eye contact with the group members for the next 13 minutes. The conversation remains focused on the assignment. During the last minute of class, he is concerned about what time it is and asks to have his toy back from the teacher. The class moves on to the next class period.

Figure 4.2 Sample of a Participant–Observer Record

Louis was observed in his resource reading classroom where we were working on the
differences between b and d. Louis and I were working one to one. I demonstrated for
him how his hands show him the difference between b's and d's. He told me no one
has ever mentioned this before and said he was excited about this new discovery.
I modeled the strategy and then he repeated it. He began using it immediately. We then
wrote a sentence on the board containing words with the letters b and d. I modeled
using the strategy each time I came to a word with the letter b or d. I told him to do it
with me, and he did. Then I told him to use it each time he came to a letter b or d. We
wrote a series of words with the letters b and d and used the strategy as he wrote
them on the board. We then wrote a sentence using the letters. Using the strategy,
Louis identified every letter as b or d correctly and was able to write words in isolation
on the board.

Anecdotal Recording   Anecdotal recording involves the documentation of short
occurrences of behaviors observed within a specific time frame (Overton, 2006). The
teacher often serves as the observer and remains involved with the student during the
course of the observation. Anecdotal recording requires the observer to note exactly
the information seen and heard (Cohen & Spenciner, 2003). The observer must refrain
from interpreting the behaviors during the observation. For example, to say that Vanessa
turns on her music for 4 minutes would be an appropriate statement in an anecdotal
recording. To say that she turned on her music out of boredom or unhappiness provides
too much interpretation. Figure 4.3 presents an example of an anecdotal recording.

Anecdotal recording requires a small amount of specialized training, documents
unexpected behaviors, provides evidence of functioning in a natural setting, and validates other pieces of information gathered through assessments (Cohen & Spenciner,
2003). Cohen and Spenciner also note some disadvantages:

- The reliance on the memory and ability of the observer to write accurate notes
- The occurrence of bias when the observer selectively includes specific behaviors
  while ignoring others
- Descriptions lacking details needed to fully understand the student's functioning
- Problems associated with reliability and validity of a single observer
- The time-consuming nature of this technique
- The difficulty in summarizing several anecdotal records

Quantitative Observation

In quantitative observation, a variety of observation methods provide the IEP team with
different types of information. The diverse categories of quantitative observation include
event recording, time sampling, interval recording, duration recording, latency recording, and functional assessment (Overton, 2006).

Figure 4.3   Sample of an Anecdotal Record

10-15

As I observed Corina in her reading class today, she was very focused on the tasks she had to do. I recorded her behavior for 10 minutes. I was observing her ability to read directions to an assignment and independently begin the assignment. The teacher had explained how to complete the assignment. She stated that the students should check the assignment page, open the book to the correct page, and write the answers to the questions on that page. The teacher then had students check the assignment page, open the book, and put their fingers on the questions to be answered. Then the teacher reviewed each question and the class discussed some possible answers to the questions. Next, the teacher asked the students to complete their assignment. Corina looked at the assignment page on her desk. She turned the page in the book to the questions she was to answer. She appeared to read the directions on the page. Corina then picked up her pencil and began answering the questions.

10-16

I observed Corina for 10 minutes during resource reading class. Today, Corina had to complete an assignment in her workbook. The teacher simply stated that the students were to look at their assignment sheets and complete the workbook page according to the directions. Corina looked at her assignment page, found her workbook, and opened it to the correct page. She did not begin to work. She looked at the page for 3 minutes. She opened her reading book and looked through the pages for 2 minutes. She then played with her pencil for 1 minute. Next, she looked through her pencil box. Corina did not begin her work during the 10-minute observation.

Event Recording   Event recording, sometimes referred to as frequency recording, documents behaviors with a discrete beginning and ending. According to Taylor (2003), event recording consists of counting the number of behaviors happening within a specified time limit. Frequency counts typically represent event recordings through tally marks. For instance, event recording would be appropriate to monitor the number of times Eric interrupts class during reading. Event recording best records short-lived behaviors. Event recording easily documents a permanent outcome such as breaking a pencil or throwing rocks. Figure 4.4 presents an example of an event recording.

Time Sampling   In time sampling, a recording is made of the number of occurrences of a particular behavior during a designated time period. Time sampling utilizes time periods divided evenly throughout the observational period. If the behavior does not appear during the time period, a nonoccurrence occurs. For example, when charting the behavior "talking in class," the teacher would observe for a specific period of time and note the number of times the behavior occurred.

Interval Recording   Interval recording allows the teacher to observe multiple behaviors for intermittent time periods. The teacher determines the behaviors to be observed

Figure 4.4   Sample of an Event Recording for Observing Sean Playing at Desk

9-24: Reading	9:00–9:05 Beginning of lesson	9:15–9:20 Presentation of examples	9:30–9:35 Explanation of assignment
	I I I	I I I I	I I I
9-25: Mathematics	10:00–10:05	10:15–10:20	10:30–10:35
	I I I I I I I	I I I	I I I I
9-26: Social Studies	1:00–1:05	1:15–1:20	1:30–1:35
	I I I I	I I I	I I I

and not whether the behavior occurs or not during a specific time period. Interval recording consists of two types: whole interval and partial interval. Whole interval recording splits time into designated periods. Behavior performed throughout the entire interval warrants documentation. Figure 4.5 presents an example of a whole interval recording.

Figure 4.5   Sample of Whole Interval Time Sampling for Sarah for Staring

Time	March 4	March 5	March 6	March 7	March 8
1:00–1:01	X	O	O	O	O
1:01–1:02	X	X	O	O	X
1:02–1:03	O	O	X	X	O
1:03–1:04	O	O	X	O	X
1:04–1:05	X	X	O	X	O
1:05–1:06	X	O	X	O	X
1:06–1:07	X	X	O	O	X
1:07–1:08	O	O	O	X	O
1:08–1:09	O	O	X	X	X
1:09–1:10	O	O	O	X	X
X = Staring without blinking O = No staring occurring					

Figure 4.6   Sample of Partial Interval Time Sampling for Amanda for On-Task Behavior

Time	February 6	February 7	February 8	February 9	February 10
1:00–1:01	N	O	O	O	O
1:31–1:32	N	N	O	O	N
1:52–1:53	O	O	N	N	O
2:03–2:04	N	O	O	O	N
2:24–2:25	N	N	O	N	O
2:55–2:56	N	O	N	O	N
3:06–3:07	N	N	O	O	N
N = Not on task O = On task					

In partial interval recording, the period is divided into equal but not consecutive segments. A behavior notation occurs anytime within a segment. Figure 4.6 presents an example of a partial interval recording.

Duration Recording   Duration recording also proves very helpful in documenting observations. A good example of the advantage of duration recording can be seen in an observation of a student as he begins a behavioral outburst and ends it 20 minutes later. The frequency of the outburst would not indicate the strength or the length. Duration recording gives the IEP team more information about the student's combative classroom behavior. When choosing duration recording, the amount of time a student engages in a behavior concerns teachers and IEP teams. Figure 4.7 presents an example of a duration recording.

Figure 4.7   Sample of a Duration Recording for Libby for Humming

Behavior Began	Behavior Ended	Duration
11:00	11:05	5 minutes
11:08	11:11	3 minutes
11:14	11:15	1 minute
11:20	11:25	5 minutes
11:33	11:45	12 minutes
Average time per humming episode: 5 minutes Amount of total time per lesson: 26 out of 45 minutes		

Figure 4.8   Sample of a Latency Recording for Jewel for Beginning Work in Class

	12-7	12-8	12-9	12-10
Subject Area	Language arts	Math	Reading	Language arts
Time of Signal	10:15	1:07	9:42	10:11
Time Work Begins	10:19	1:14	9:55	10:23
Number of Minutes	4	7	13	12
Average number of minutes between signal and beginning of work: 9 minutes

Latency Recording   Latency recording documents student compliance. It records the amount of time occurring between a signal and initiation of the response. For example, Marquis's teacher rings a bell for everyone to return to their places after lunch. Latency recording establishes the length of time, usually in seconds, from the signal until Marquis complies with the request. Charting day-to-day behavior using a latency recording gives the teacher and IEP team some knowledge about the type of intervention that must take place in the classroom. Figure 4.8 presents an example of a latency recording.

Functional Behavioral Assessment

Functional behavioral assessment (FBA) is used to determine critical factors that trigger and maintain inappropriate behaviors (Fox, Gunter, Davis, & Brall, 2000). This IDEIA-mandated process involves an observational system required for any student with a disability considered for a 10-day or longer alternative setting placement (Taylor, 2003).

An FBA gathers information using interviews, observations, and document review of school records (Condon & Tobin, 2001). It identifies the purpose of certain student behaviors in order to create more effective and efficient behavioral intervention plans. FBAs use more than just observation to gather data; however, direct assessment proves critical to the process (Artesani, 2001). Using FBA, the IEP team determines not only the inappropriate behaviors but also develops an understanding of why a student engages in the behavior. In addition, the team identifies the context within which the behaviors occur. According to Kerr and Nelson (2002), FBAs seek to answer the following questions:

1. Where does the student spend his or her time?
2. How does he or she identify within these settings?
3. Who does the student identify as the most important people to him or her in these settings?
4. What desired and undesired behaviors occur in these settings?
5. Who sees the behavior as inappropriate?
6. What are the behavioral expectations in the environment?
7. How does the student's behavior differ from the behavioral expectations?

Artesani (2001) identifies several positive reasons to use FBA in school settings. First, FBA helps the IEP team and others to discover underlying variables contributing to inappropriate actions. Second, by identifying the targets, alternatives to replace inappropriate actions can be generated. Third, these interventions prove positive in nature and go beyond the reduction of behavior to providing a more supportive environment. By identifying alternative behaviors, the teacher addresses the student's initial reason for engaging in the inappropriate behavior and enables the student to find a more acceptable response.

FBA often includes the use of **antecedent-behavior-consequence (A-B-C) analysis** using cumulative observation techniques to identify each component of a behavioral sequence (Kerr & Nelson, 2002). In A-B-C analysis, the observer records what takes place just before the behavior occurs, documents the specific behavior, and describes what happens after the behavior ends. With this type of information, the teacher and IEP team can make informed decisions about methods for enabling the student to learn more acceptable behaviors. Figure 4.9 presents an example of an A-B-C analysis.

Determining antecedent behavior allows the teacher to pinpoint the activities that precede a particular action. Often, the teacher discovers that a simple manipulation of the antecedent stalls the behavioral response, thereby allowing the student to circumvent inappropriate behavior. Antecedents may involve another student or teacher, a particular place in the school, a recurring event, or even a certain noise. Anything represents an antecedent behavior. What makes it an antecedent for a particular student rests in the behavior that follows it. By intervening and changing the conditions

Figure 4.9 Sample of an A-B-C Analysis of Jason's Chair-Kicking Behavior

Anecdotal Observation for September 12

10:15	Jason enters the room and throws his books on the desk.
	The teacher responds by telling him to enter the room again.
10:16	Jason enters the room again without his books and sits on the floor.
	The teacher responds by telling him she wants him to sit at his desk.
10:17	Jason sits at his desk and glares at the teacher.
	The teacher responds by telling him to turn to page 11.
10:18	Jason jumps up from his desk and kicks the chair across the room.
	The teacher responds by sending him to time-out.

A (Antecedent)	B (Behavior)	C (Consequence)
Jason enters room	and throws books	enters room again
Enters room again	and sits on floor	told to sit at desk
Sits at desk	and glares at teacher	told to open book
Jumps out of desk	and kicks the chair	sent to time-out

brought on by antecedent behaviors, students may experience more success in controlling inappropriate actions.

THE MECHANICS OF OBSERVATION

Certain procedures, such as the presence of an observer and some type of recording, appear in all observational techniques; however, the goals of the observation produce changes in how each step develops. Structured observations consist of an activity preselected to allow the teacher to observe particular skills. In this way, the observer watches the student complete the task without waiting for it to occur naturally. This observation looks at direct skills, such as a student's ability to complete a page of division problems or read a book independently. More often, however, observations occur in the naturalistic setting. The observer might delineate a specific time or academic period in which to observe, but the student initiates the behavior.

Creating Unstructured Observations

Taking Running Records When developing qualitative or unstructured observations such as running records, the observer plans to record a continuous description of all events occurring in the classroom. Having an external observer come into the classroom to do this recording proves beneficial (Rao, Hoyer, Meehan, Young, & Guerrera, 2003). The observer must maintain an unobtrusive presence within the setting and have no interaction with classroom activity (Salvia & Ysseldyke, 2004). The observer arrives prior to the beginning of any session and sits away from the student to be observed while maintaining a clear view of the student's activities. Typically, the observer uses paper and pen to precisely record every behavior produced. Care must be taken to describe the conduct without interpreting or judging the actions. Factual and detailed descriptions of the events being observed prove critical to the success of qualitative observations. Occasionally, a tape recorder or video camera will be used.

Maintaining a notebook for running records and note taking improves the organization of the observations:

1. Practice note taking in classrooms with a partner to determine the factual accuracy of notes, as well as their completeness, to ensure better running record observations.
2. Date and sign each entry.
3. Create easy-to-read accounts, recording only the behavior presented in the classroom without making value judgments such as "He or she plays happily."

Constructing Participant–Observer Observations The participant–observer approach uses the basic data collection method chosen by anthropologists and later adopted by education as an important tool (Kolesar, 1998). In participant–observer observations, the participant–observer plays a dual role, participating in the interaction *and* recording the behaviors. Often participant–observers rely on video or audio taping to aid in the process. In participant–observer procedures, certain types of behavior may be pinpointed or a global approach may be maintained. The participant–observer enters the classroom and sits where the activity will occur. The participant-observer interacts within the group but does not direct the activity. A simple note-taking system can be used to collect data without creating the copious notes of the running record. Successful participant–observers have already established good rapport in the classroom. Students feel comfortable in their presence. Teachers and teaching assistants often pair up to do this type of procedure. Teachers rehearse participant–observer duties to become proficient with this type of observation.

Generating Anecdotal Records   Anecdotal records capture small episodes of behavior. The teacher may note more global behaviors or skills or monitor specific actions. The observations take place as the behaviors occur or shortly thereafter. Notes delineate specific, factual statements about the behaviors. In some cases, the teacher decides to use A-B-C analysis to help structure the anecdotal record and obtain more specific information. For example, if Shelly experiences trouble in the reading center, the teacher creates anecdotal records to determine and assess the antecedents to her behavior. Examining the social interactions of students by using anecdotal records can aid IEP teams in selecting goals and planning interventions (Miller, Cooke, & Test, 2003).

Generating Quantitative Methods

This section provides a discussion of the development of quantitative observations, including event recording, time sampling, interval recording, duration recording, latency recording, and functional behavioral assessment. Quantitative observations can be done well only by trained and properly prepared individuals. The recording systems for quantitative observations must be determined and planned before observation begins. Quantitative observations usually involve accurate definition of a target behavior. A target behavior provides a detailed description of an action clearly identified by multiple people.

Designing Event Recordings   The technique known as event recording, or frequency recording, provides an appropriate method for counting target behaviors with a beginning and ending. The behaviors must occur at a countable rate. As with all other observations, the observer must develop knowledge of the recording system. Often, this type of recording involves a simple tally system over a designated period in multiple settings. Observers usually situate themselves with the student in view; however, observers should try to be as subtle as possible while keeping the student unaware of the observer's intentions. As the student works in class, the observer makes tallies of the number of times the student engages in the target behavior. For instance, Veronica, a kindergarten student, is being monitored in her classroom. While playing in a free-choice center, Veronica pushes students when she cannot get what she wants. Sometimes Veronica uses a card to indicate that she wants to play with a certain item. The observer records the number of times that Veronica pushes or exhibits aggressive behavior instead of using a card to ask for permission to play with something another student is using.

Producing Time Sample Observations   Time sampling or interval recording provides another quantitative approach to observation. An imperceptible time signal that is audible only to the observer signals the beginning of each observational period. The observer needs to set up in an unobtrusive part of the room where it is possible to sit inconspicuously with headphones and a tape recorder. The observer makes tally marks with pencil on paper while using timing signals. Like event recording, time sampling records the target behavior at certain intervals. Usually, the observer uses a tape recorder and a tape marked at even intervals of 15 seconds (this may vary) with words such as "Record now," then a 15-second interval, then "Stop record." Then there will be a specified even break and the recorder will repeat the sequence. This type of observation continues for an indefinite period and provides a practical technique for teachers (Gunter, Venn, Patrick, Miller, & Kelly, 2003).

A couple of disadvantages occur with time sampling. First, the addition of a signaling system requires some equipment and proves hard to maintain inconspicuously. Second, behavior often occurs during nonrecording periods. One advantage to time sampling includes the elimination of observer drift; in other words, it keeps the observer on target, watching intently.

Crafting Duration Recordings   The third type of quantitative observation technique, duration recording, also maintains the need for discreet observer behavior. Using a stopwatch or a watch with a second hand, the observer measures a target behavior for the length of time that the student engages in the behavior. The observer notes the time the behavior begins. When the specific behavior ends, the observer documents the time. The observer may choose to do this during a specific time period or over the course of a week or semester. This type of recording requires constant attention, and observer drift can completely invalidate findings.

Making Latency Recordings   Latency recording monitors behaviors affected by compliance. Equipment includes a stopwatch or a watch with a second hand. After being seated in a discreet area, the observer waits for a signal to begin the observation. The signal may consist of the bell ringing for the beginning of class or an oral direction given by the classroom teacher. After the signal has been given, the observer registers the time it takes the student to comply with a target behavior. For example, Luis has trouble finding his seat. In latency recording, the time lapsed between onset of the signal and Luis's seating compliance will be monitored. The objective of the observations is to develop an appropriate intervention to prompt Luis to be seated immediately.

Functional Behavioral Assessment

FBA entails a multiphase process moving from identification of inappropriate behaviors through intervention. Kerr and Nelson (2002) state that two questions should be addressed in this phase of the FBA: (a) What does the target behavior look like? and (b) Under what conditions does the target behavior occur? This observation method serves not only to teach more appropriate behaviors but also to evaluate the environment to determine necessary supports for increasing desired actions. FBA forms the basis for the development of behavior intervention plans for students with disabilities.

Phase 1 of FBA   The first phase of FBA focuses on describing inappropriate actions in order to develop an **operational definition** to describe the behavior precisely in observable and measurable terms (Taylor, 2003). Many of the quantitative procedures can be used as techniques for determining the conditions under which the behavior occurs. Another method includes behavioral interviews (Kerr & Nelson, 2002), in which the student and others answer structured questions.

In addition, a **scatterplot** can be developed to show the presence or absence of a behavior (Artesani, 2001). The observer creates a grid with spaces for the time of day and days of the week. Observations reveal when the inappropriate behavior occurs. Artesani recommends that more intensive observations may be required after identifying the patterns of behavior. Figure 4.10 presents an example of plotting to show the presence and absence of a behavior.

Figure 4.10   Plotting Jason's Chair-Kicking Behavior

Number of Chair-Kicking Incidents per Period for 2 Weeks				
Date	Reading 9:00–9:50	Language Arts 9:55–10:40	Math 10:45–11:30	Science 12:15–1:00
10-6	3	2	2	2
10-7	4	3	1	1
10-8	6	4	2	3
10-9	5	6	1	2
10-10	2	5	1	2
10-13	4	9	0	0
10-14	9	3	0	0
10-15	6	3	1	0
10-16	2	2	0	1
10-17	8	5	1	1
Average	4.9	4.5	.9	1.02

The A-B-C analysis (described previously) is another technique used to pinpoint inappropriate behaviors. To complete an A-B-C analysis, the team develops a chart with space for each element. One column represents the antecedent behaviors, the next the specific behavior being addressed, and the final column documents the consequences following the behavior. The observer must record exactly what happens immediately before and after the behavior in order to establish behavioral pattern. Understanding these patterns aids in the design of the intervention. Antecedents represent environmental triggers that prompt particular behaviors (Artesani, 2001). Some examples include being made fun of, pushing or other physical contact, having a privilege removed, or eye contact.

All behavior serves one of two functions: to get something or to get away from something. Consequences become the reward for behavior, either reinforcing or punishing it. A reinforcing outcome maintains the action. Historically, punishment for inappropriate conduct and reward for appropriate actions have been fundamentals of typical school rules.

In FBA, the team seeks to discover why the student engages in inappropriate behavior. Consequences inform us about student behavioral choices. When the inappropriate or undesirable behavior has been performed, reinforcement follows: getting what one wants or escaping what one does not want (Artesani, 2001). Understanding these responses to behavior proves critical to intervening and planning a positive behavioral plan. Examples of consequences include getting peer attention, avoiding math class, staying away from bullies, not having to read in class, and stealing food. These examples often manifest themselves in a variety of forms for various students.

Phase 2 of FBA   The second phase of FBA involves the development of a **hypothesis** or perceived reason for the particular behavior. Analysis of the collected data identifies the antecedents, behaviors, and consequences. Based on this information, the IEP team answers questions regarding antecedents. The following questions help to probe the antecedent behaviors.

1. Where does the behavior occur?
2. When does the behavior occur?
3. When does the behavior disappear?
4. What persons are present when the behavior occurs?
5. What persons are present when the behavior does not occur?

Next, the IEP team pinpoints the specific inappropriate behaviors. Defining the behavior precisely enables the team to clearly understand the target. Subsequently, the team determines the consequences or function of the behavior. The following questions enable the team to ascertain the function of the antecedent:

1. What occurs immediately following the target behavior?
2. Do the surroundings change following the behavior?
3. How do others act following the behavior?
4. What is lost or gained in performing the behavior?

IEP teams must also look at settings where the student's behavior appears appropriate (Kerr & Nelson, 2002). Creating a hypothesis becomes the basic objective of Phase 2. Figure 4.11 presents an example of the process for developing a hypothesis for Jason.

Phase 3 of the FBA   In the third step of the FBA, the teacher collects data to support or reject the hypothesis determined in Phase 2 (Kerr & Nelson, 2002). The original data suggest that certain conditions or antecedents cause a particular inappropriate action. In this step, the observer attempts to systematically alter the situation to determine if change impacts the student's behavior. For example, by varying the classroom conditions from sitting at one desk to moving freely around the room during math class, the observer begins to see if this change makes a difference in the target behavior. This process describes a method for systematically determining a purposeful relationship between a particular behavior and the variable (Kerr & Nelson, 2002). Artesani (2001) suggests that using a prescribed direct observation form, such as the one developed by O'Neill, Horner, Albin, Sprague, Storey, and Newton (1997), proves helpful. This form allows the observer to trace on one form specific behaviors, triggers, perceived reasons for behavior, apparent function of the behavior, and the actual consequences.

Phase 4 of the FBA: The Intervention Step   After the observer becomes sure that the hypothesis or perceived reason for the behavior has been determined, the fourth step

Figure 4.11   Hypothesis Development for Jason's Functional Behavioral Assessment

1. **Where does the behavior occur?** Most often in reading and language arts class.
2. **When does the behavior occur?** During the beginning of reading and language arts class.
3. **When does the behavior disappear?** Most often in math and science class.
4. **What persons are present when the behavior occurs?** Mrs. Brown and the students in the resource room.
5. **What persons are present when the behavior does not occur?** Mr. Clark and the students in the general education classroom.
6. **What occurs immediately following the target behavior?** Jason goes to time-out.
7. **Do the surroundings change following the behavior?** Yes, he is isolated and does not work.
8. **How do others act following the behavior?** The students try to ignore him.
9. **What is lost or gained in performing the behavior?** Removal from expected work and from the other resource students.

Hypothesis: Jason is kicking the chairs to absent himself from both the expected assignments and the other resource students.

in the FBA process involves the designing of an **intervention**. The intervention details the behavior, any particular settings impacting or producing the action, antecedents that appear to trigger the conduct, and specific consequences obtained by engaging in the target (Kerr & Nelson, 2002). The IEP team begins to delineate the intervention. First, the IEP team determines any desired or replacement behaviors to be taught and identifies the criterion for achieving success or the preferred behavior. To reinforce enough to result in continued use, the replacement behaviors have to help the student achieve the consequence or outcome craved.

A **replacement behavior** will have to be taught and practiced for the student to be successful. The student needs to learn to engage in the replacement behavior in small steps while receiving reinforcement for each time he or she utilizes the steps. In addition, the student may not be able to engage in the complete replacement behavior for a long time but will work toward attainment of the desired behavior through the use of successive approximations. Successive approximations achieve small tasks that constitute a specific behavior. In many cases, the teacher uses successive approximations of a particular action to approach appropriate standards through a stepwise intervention while reinforcing incremental success.

If the target behavior needs **extinction**, the teacher should introduce a less inappropriate replacement behavior that subsequently diminishes the original behavior using the same stepwise approach. Behaviors such as hitting, biting, scratching, or wetting during a tantrum might be included in this category. Again, the use of successive approximations proves suitable.

Phase 5 of the FBA   In this final phase of the FBA, the IEP team must evaluate the effectiveness of the intervention. To create a successful FBA, the IEP team determines ahead of time the criteria for success. Data collection occurs to verify the student's progress toward attainment of the desired behavior. Interview data provide an opinion about a student's behavior change, but direct observation supplies a more exact description (Taylor, 2003). The ultimate criterion, however, becomes the student's continuous and intrinsically reinforced success in a naturalistic setting (Kerr & Nelson, 2002).

Development of a Behavior Intervention Plan

FBA allows the teacher to intervene prior to the escalation of problem behaviors in the classroom. Intervention plans to circumvent inappropriate actions encourage a proactive approach to challenging behavior. By intervening through FBA, the teacher addresses issues, whether behavioral or academic, prior to them reaching a crisis point.

FBA also forms the foundation for IDEIA's 2004 mandated Behavior Intervention Plan (BIP), which stipulates the crisis intervention plan for use with individuals with disabilities exhibiting seriously inappropriate behavior. When such a behavior occurs, a **manifestation determination IEP** meeting must take place. Before removal from the current placement, a manifestation determination seeks to answer the following questions: (a) Does the behavior interfere with the learning of the student or others within

Figure 4.12   Types of Graphs Available to the IEP Team

Type	Reasons to Use
Bar graph	Easy to understand; encourages student participation
Cumulative graph	Adds information about each day to the document
Frequency polygon	Numerical; most commonly used type of graph
Progress graph	Provides a look at the time it takes for mastery
Performance graph	Shows progress on a single task

the classroom or school? and (b) Does the behavior represent an inability of the student to control his or her actions because the disability impedes the student's understanding or restraint? (Artesani, 2001). However, the IDEIA 2004 revision allows the student's removal for not more than 45 days in the case of violations of drugs, weapons, or infliction of serious bodily harm. IEP goals continue in force during this period of removal. A BIP results from an FBA conducted by the IEP team. The FBA identifies the target behavior and intervention strategies to be used by the school.

SUMMARIZING OBSERVATIONS

The IEP team needs to have ready access to the results of observations in order to make decisions about completion of IEP goals. Individual observations reveal a good deal about a student at one point in time, but they do not provide a look at the student's progress over time. Graphs or charts motivate students and supply the IEP team with more concise information regarding progress. Graphs show functional relationships and represent shorter or longer periods of time. Typically, a graph deals with only one replacement behavior at a time. Figure 4.12 presents a chart that displays the different types of graphs identified by Kerr and Nelson (2001).

What Do Behavioral Observations and Functional Behavioral Assessment Contribute to IEP Development?

- They supply information useful in planning proactive approaches for student support.
- They determine the antecedents present in behavioral episodes.
- They create opportunities to intercede before problem behavior escalates.
- They add to the documentation of teacher observations through tallying and recording events.
- They establish consequences that can be used to create a positive behavioral environment

USING THE OBSERVATIONAL DATA IN THE IEP

The IEP team uses the data collected during behavioral observations for a variety of purposes. The most obvious includes the use of behavioral observations to complete an FBA for a student who faces removal from the current setting due to unacceptable behavior. In this case, the steps outlined in the preceding section guide the IEP team through data collection and intervention. Sometimes the original BIP fails to teach replacement behaviors. In that case, the IEP team may want to reconsider the BIP and engage in an additional FBA to gain a better understanding of what the student does and to determine why the student engages in a particular behavior.

In addition to the FBA, the IEP team considers the use of behavioral observations to gather information about other areas of classroom functioning beyond the realm of sociobehavioral conduct. Information about the student's on-task responses provides valuable insight into the reasons for academic failure on a given assignment. Recognizing patterns of task avoidance after instruction has been completed and assignments given helps the teacher to guide the student into more meaningful use of time. IEP teams want to know about a range of behaviors interfering with student learning opportunities, including those specific to the student, his or her peers, and the teacher. Defining behaviors in specific, observable, and measurable terms remains critical to the success of the FBA.

The IEP team applies the data gathered from behavioral observations to suggest specific changes in the classroom. These changes include the addition of modifications or accommodations to improve the student's functioning, the inclusion of specific technology to increase the student's performance, or the selection of IEP goals to more closely match the student's observed abilities. IEP teams rely on observational data to validate the results of standardized testing as required by IDEIA to provide information about achievement, progress, student characteristics, and behaviors (Cohen & Spenciner, 2003).

BEHAVIORAL OBSERVATIONS AND ASSESSMENTS AND TECHNOLOGY

Technology records observations conveniently and accurately. Basically, a timing device, a counter, and a graph form the tools of observation (Salvia & Ysseldyke, 2004). Software used to develop graphs and charts may be very sophisticated. Handheld data collectors, including counters and timing tools, prove quite useful. These often provide an interface with computer programs that can receive the observational data and produce a graph with the input. While these systems prove convenient, they may be costly and require some training for reliable results.

Software and hardware for observing and documenting behavior aid observation. With the common use of laptop computers, observations on many different behaviors can be recorded and stored by teachers. These data are used to immediately generate a graph or chart. However, Kerr and Nelson (2002) list the following disadvantages of using computer-based observational techniques:

1. A laptop computer can be obtrusive.
2. Not all teachers have access to a laptop in the classroom.
3. The laptop requires the observer to be seated.
4. For some individuals, the use of technology represents another time-consuming step for the observer to perform to document behavior.

The advantages of using technology may far outdistance these disadvantages. Accuracy and the ability to chart or graph instantaneously provide significant advantages. New technology becomes available daily. Handheld devices require little training and increase the accuracy of observations. Making recording easier and less obtrusive encourages teachers to readily create and utilize observations. New technology should be purchased by examining observation needs and matching it with the observational tool. Equipment may require replacement periodically as new sophisticated technology becomes available.

SUMMARY

- Behavioral observation consists of watching and recording actions of an individual student.
- Issues of cultural and linguistic diversity must be addressed by the examiner to ensure unbiased observation techniques.
- Behavioral observations provide the IEP team with an array of information concerning daily functioning, outlined in precise detail, leaving little room for doubt about a student's routine.
- Quantitative observations isolate specific inappropriate actions and note exactly how the behaviors take place. In addition to the behavioral observations used to identify troublesome academic or social behaviors, the IEP team uses FBA to pinpoint difficult behaviors, identify replacement actions, and provide intervention.
- Summarized information from behavioral observations or functional behavioral assessments provides the IEP team with a clearer understanding of the student's actions.
- Whether the IEP team employs behavioral observations to change classroom behaviors or FBA to address more challenging behaviors, observation becomes a valuable asset for improving the classroom environment for students with disabilities.
- The use of technology in behavioral observations and functional behavioral assessments aids the IEP team in organization and data management.

COMPREHENSION CHECK

1. Explain the differences between qualitative assessment and quantitative assessment. Provide some examples of situations appropriate for using each type of assessment.
2. Explain the following techniques: event recording, time sampling, interval recording, duration recording, and latency recording.
3. Describe functional behavioral assessment, and list the steps required to complete one.

ACTIVITIES

1. Select a student who would benefit from a charting exercise to demonstrate growth or change. Create the chart with the student and monitor daily his or her ability to keep the chart. Interview the student regarding the effectiveness of the chart and the effect on the student's behavior.
2. Choose a student to observe in a school setting. Isolate a target behavior and select an appropriate method of evaluation to evaluate this target behavior.
3. Perform two of the methods of evaluation described in the chapter with an individual in class to demonstrate how to collect the data in an organized fashion.

REFERENCES

Achenbach, T. M. (1986). *Child behavior checklist: Direct observation form* (rev. ed.). Burlington: University of Vermont Center for Children, Youth, and Families.

Albert, L. R., Mayotte, G., & Sohn, S. C. (2002*).* Making observations interactive. *Mathematics Teaching in the Middle School, 7*(7), 396–401.

Artesani, A. J. (2001). *Understanding the purpose of challenging behavior: A guide to conducting functional assessment.* Upper Saddle River: NJ: Merrill/Prentice Hall.

Baca, L. M., & Cervantes, H. T. (2004). *The bilingual special education interface* (4th ed.). Upper Saddle River, NJ: Merrill/Prentice Hall.

Bondurant-Utz, J. (2002). *Practical guide to assessing infants and preschoolers with special needs.* Upper Saddle River, NJ: Merrill/Prentice Hall.

Cohen, L. G., & Spenciner, L. J. (2003). *Assessment of children and youth with special needs.* Boston: Pearson.

Condon, K. A., & Tobin, T. J. (2001). Using electronic and other new ways to help students improve their behavior. *Teaching Exceptional Children, 34*(1), 44–51.

Denzin, N. K., & Lincoln, Y. S. (Eds.). (2000). *Handbook of qualitative research* (2nd ed.). Thousand Oaks, CA: Sage.

Fox, J. J., Gunter, P., Davis, C. A., & Brall, S. (2000). Observational methods in functional behavioral assessment: Practical techniques for practitioners. *Preventing School Failure, 44*(4), 152–157.

Glesne, C. (1999). *Becoming qualitative researchers: An introduction* (2nd ed.). New York: Longman.

Gunter, P. L., Venn, M. L., Patrick, J., Miller, K. A., & Kelly, L. (2003). Efficacy of using momentary time samples to determine on-task behavior of students with emotional/behavioral disorders. *Education and Treatment of Children, 26*(4), 400–412.

Hunt, P. Soto, G., Maier, J., & Doering, K. (2003). Collaborative teaming to support students at risk and students with severe disabilities in general education classrooms. *Exceptional Children, 69*(3), 315–332.

Kerr, M. M., & Nelson, C. M. (2002). *Strategies for addressing behavior problems in the classroom* (4th ed.). Upper Saddle River, NJ: Merrill/Prentice Hall.

Kolesar, R. (1998). Participant observation: A research and assessment approach for multiple disabled populations. *McGill Journal of Education, 33*(3), 253–264.

Kubiszyn, T., & Borich, R. (2002). *Educational testing and measurement: Classroom applications and practice* (7th ed.). New York: John Wiley and Sons.

Maag, J. W. (2004). *Behavior management: From theoretical implications to practical applications* (2nd ed.). Belmont, CA: Wadsworth.

Miller, M. C., Cooke, N. L., & Test, D. W. (2003). Effects of friendship circles on the social interactions of elementary age students with mild disabilities. *Journal of Behavioral Education, 12*(3), 167–184.

O'Neill, R. E., Horner, R. H., Albin, R. W., Sprague, J. R., Storey, K., & Newton, J. S. (1997). *Functional assessment and program development for problem behavior: A practical handbook* (2nd ed.). Pacific Grove, CA: Brooks/Cole.

Overton, T. (2006). *Assessing learners with special needs: An applied approach* (5th ed.). Upper Saddle River, NJ: Merrill/Prentice Hall.

Rao, S., Hoyer, L., Meehan, K., Young, L., & Guerrera, A. (2003). Using narrative logs: Understanding students' challenging behaviors. *Teaching Exceptional Children, 35*(5), 22–29.

Salend, S. J. (2000). Strategies and resources to evaluate the impact of inclusion programs on students. *Intervention in School and Clinic, 35*(5), 264–270, 289.

Salvia, J., & Ysseldyke, J. E. (2004). *Assessment in special and inclusive education* (9th ed.). Boston: Houghton Mifflin.

Sattler, J. M. (2001). *Assessment of children: Cognitive applications* (4th ed.). San Diego, CA: Jerome M. Sattler, Publisher, Inc.

Strain, P. S., & Joseph, G. E. (2004). Engaged supervision to support recommended practices to young children with challenging behavior. *Topics in Early Childhood Special Education, 24*(1), 39–50.

Taylor, R. L. (2003). *Assessment of exceptional students: Educational psychological procedures* (6th ed.). Boston: Pearson.

Venn, J. J. (2004). *Assessing students with special needs* (3rd ed.). Upper Saddle River, NJ: Merrill/Prentice Hall.

Walker, J. E., Shea, T. M., & Baver, A. M. (2004). *Behavior management: A practical approach for educators* (8th ed.). Upper Saddle River, NJ: Merrill/Prentice Hall.

PORTFOLIOS

5

- Define portfolio assessment.
- Describe the benefits and disadvantages of using portfolios.
- Depict methods for highlighting cultural and linguistic diversity through portfolios.
- Illustrate when to use portfolios.
- Clarify the different types of portfolios and their uses.
- Explain portfolio evaluation techniques, including self-evaluation.
- Discuss methods for summarizing portfolio data.
- Identify methods for using portfolio assessment data in the IEP process.
- Describe the role of technology in the development of portfolios.

Chapter Focus

Portfolios provide the IEP team with an opportunity to observe a student's progress over an extended period. In addition, they involve the student in the assessment process and teach valuable self-evaluation skills. Portfolios include a variety of products, including written, oral, electronic, or other artifacts. Methods for addressing diversity issues and the inclusion of cultural aspects within the portfolio reflect the unique character of each student. In order to produce a clear picture of the student's achievement, IEP teams must clearly stipulate the rationale for the portfolio and the annual goals to be measured. This chapter provides information about advantages and disadvantages concerning portfolios, as well as a rationale for when and why to use them. It also clarifies the steps for creating portfolios. The role of technology in the development of electronic portfolios completes the chapter.

WHAT ARE PORTFOLIOS?

According to Losardo and Notari-Syverson (2001), a **portfolio** acts as a clearly planned assessment tool to evaluate specific criteria, as well as to increase a student's active involvement in the learning process. It provides a picture of a student's achievement that includes both the products and a student's perception of his or her performance on the **products** (Stiggins, 2001). The portfolio highlights not only what the student has done but also their capabilities (Salvia & Ysseldyke, 2004). The portfolio requires both the student and teacher to be involved in the **holistic evaluation** process of the student's accomplishments (Lewis & Doorlag, 1999).

According to Hartmann (2004), portfolios have long been used to document proficiency in several professional areas, including architecture, art, and music. They serve to display professional expertise and accomplishment, as well as to assess entry-level skills. Portfolios provide both formative and summative evaluations.

A portfolio consists of a collection of work accumulated over time using such student products as drawings, audio and video recordings, written work, classroom assignments, or projects. An electronic portfolio incorporates the same products captured electronically and stored on a CD or DVD. In some cases, photographs display elements of projects not easily scanned and captured by electronic media. Work samples contained within a portfolio simply reflect one skill area or provide a broader view of student accomplishment.

BENEFITS OF USING PORTFOLIOS

Using portfolios to evaluate student progress provides flexible and individualized documentation of student growth. Portfolios involve a multimethod and multidimensional, culturally sensitive approach (Losardo & Notari-Syverson, 2001). Many advantages accompany the use of a portfolio system. Losardo and Notari-Syverson identify the following:

- Portfolios provide a direct link to classroom curriculum.
- Portfolios allow for ongoing assessment across environments.
- Portfolios passed from teacher to teacher or grade to grade supply information to ease a student's transition.
- Portfolios provide a way to examine a student's performance from a variety of perspectives.
- Portfolio assessment improves **self-advocacy** for students by encouraging their participation in the selection of products and communication about their work.

Venn (2004) describes the following advantages to using portfolios:

- Portfolios promote **critical thinking** through the **self-evaluation** process.
- Portfolios make it possible to evaluate achievement based on genuine samples as an accurate measure of performance.
- The portfolio system allows latitude for selecting methods to demonstrate mastery.
- The portfolio system places joint responsibility on the student and the teacher to provide and evaluate the products to indicate achievement.

Stiggins (2001) explains additional advantages to using portfolios for assessment:

- Portfolios create a detailed and complex representation of a student's mastery over time.
- Portfolios promote student motivation by helping students see improvement through a self-reflective process.
- Portfolios document student progress as mandated by district and state standards.

Several additional reasons for using a portfolio assessment system are these:

- Portfolios provide a tangible and accessible product with which the teacher can identify and highlight small steps in a student's progress.
- Portfolios utilize real-life examples, as opposed to contrived ones.
- Portfolios enhance a student's **self-monitoring skills** by involving them in constant evaluation of their own products.
- The techniques encourage students to learn **self-evaluation skills** that reflect state-mandated or IEP-determined standards.
- Portfolios support the development of **self-determination** skills, including the ability to set learning or performance goals by engaging the student in continuous reflection concerning the quality of his or her work.

Figure 5.1 presents the differences between portfolio products and standardized test scores.

DISADVANTAGES OF PORTFOLIOS

The disadvantages of portfolios include a variety of factors that must be considered in order to make using a portfolio a viable and efficient assessment tool in the classroom. Without careful planning, portfolio assessment requires too much time (Venn, 2004). Because portfolios are bulky and difficult to manage and store (Venn), IEP teams must

Figure 5.1   Differences Between Standardized Test Scores and Portfolio Products

Standardized Test Scores		Portfolio Products
Test computation	88	Work samples
Number sense	84	Chapter tests
Geometry	80	Checklists
Time and money	90	Homework
Problem solving	85	Self-evaluations
Show the way the student ranks in a standardized pool on a given day.		*Show progress, problem-solving skills, actual class work over time.*

consider the use of electronic portfolios to circumvent this problem. Conferencing with students may be considered to be time-consuming (Venn); however, weaving the conference format into daily instruction circumvents this issue. These methods should not be used in isolation but rather combined with the results of other assessment data to document growth (St. Maurice & Shaw, 2004). Portfolios omit traditional, standardized evaluation tools (Losardo & Notari-Syverson, 2001); therefore, the IEP team must consider the inclusion of standardized scores to complete the assessment picture.

CULTURAL AND LINGUISTIC DIVERSITY CONSIDERATIONS

Portfolios serve as a lens through which to view a student's growth and development (Strudler & Wetzel, 2005). For culturally and linguistically diverse students, cultural perspectives guide the portfolio evaluation process. The individualization of portfolios provides the opportunity for evaluation to be based on work generated by individual students rather than by comparing performance to others. The scoring or rating of the products contained within the portfolio should be responsive to the needs of diverse learners. Focusing on specific goals in the portfolio diminishes issues of bias in this form of assessment. The use of well-constructed **rubrics** for assessment tied to IEP goals also helps lessen bias. By using portfolios, the teacher can construct assignments that focus on the student and include cultural preferences, rather than simply assigning a similar task to all students. In addition, the teacher can help the student to identify particularly relevant cultural topics, activities, or dates to include within the portfolio for assessment.

DECIDING TO IMPLEMENT PORTFOLIOS

IEP teams use portfolio assessment for the following reasons:

- To form a picture of a student's progress over time
- To obtain realistic data rather than a comparison to a preselected group criterion
- To look within the academic development of each student's progress
- To assess progress over a period of time, rather than through a snapshot as in standardized assessment

Other considerations include the need for greater individualized assessment that matches the student's placement in special education. A student who requires more intensive supports, such as full-time aides, one-to-one instruction, hand-over-hand techniques, or a specialized communication system, will be more accurately assessed by a portfolio system that evaluates individual skills and characteristics. For example, a standardized checklist can be used to evaluate a student's compliant behavior, and by considering the evidence collected in the portfolio the IEP team can understand how she complies over time and in different situations and how well she understands the reasons for compliance. Students also complete portfolios to satisfy outside evaluators (Strudler & Wetzel, 2005).

TYPES OF PORTFOLIOS

A variety of reasons support the use of an assortment of portfolio styles. Nitko (2004) identifies five different types of portfolios:

1. Best work
2. Educational growth
3. Most favorite work
4. Process through a long-term project
5. Composite picture compared to a group of students

Each of these portfolios is planned ahead of time to represent the particular aspects being assessed. As with all performance assessments, the evaluation component of the portfolio does not lie in the materials collected but rather in the use of a prescribed scoring rubric or scoring sheet (Losardo & Notari-Syverson, 2001). The evaluation occurs across the portfolio and involves both the student and the teacher in the assessment procedures. Assessment includes regularly scheduled portfolio review conferences that include both the student and members of the IEP team (Losardo & Notari-Syverson). Portfolios provide the student and the IEP team with the opportunity to evaluate progress together by bringing the student into the evaluation process through self-evaluation and review.

Taylor (2003) differentiates between working and show portfolios. He indicates that a working portfolio includes daily work samples while a show portfolio presents only selected products used for conferences and more formal evaluation purposes, such as an annual IEP team meeting. Swicegood (1994) describes five purposes for a portfolio that determine the specific contents needed to fulfill the goal:

- To produce an exhibit of the student's best work and development
- To acquire a multidimensional collection of products over time
- To document an actual view of the student's range of abilities
- To create a tool to enhance student and teacher reflection about progress and learning mastery
- To improve dialogue and communication between the student and IEP team members

Chang (2001) identifies five major items included in portfolios or electronic portfolios:

1. Student-selected learning results
2. Student reflections
3. Clearly defined goals
4. Sample of completed work
5. Tangible examples of growth

These items appear in all types of portfolios to provide a complete representation of the student's skills. In the following sections, the portfolio types described by Nitko (2004), as well as others, are presented.

Best Work Portfolios

Best work portfolios represent a collection of work samples or other products deemed by the student and teacher to highlight the student's most effective indicators of mastery. The contents of the portfolio include predetermined elements. The student then selects samples that best represent mastery (Nitko, 2004). In the general education setting, the best work portfolio helps the student to display his finest efforts even though many trials were necessary to accomplish the goal. Students with disabilities need direct help in determining when a work sample or other product actually meets the criterion of best work. Through this process of conferencing to self-evaluate work, the student gains a greater understanding of indicators of mastery and becomes more proficient at evaluating other aspects of performance.

Educational Growth

A portfolio describing a student's educational growth or progress focuses on the learning and thinking processes. It also documents difficulties and directs the student in identifying new learning strategies (Nitko, 2004). The student continues to be directly involved in the development of the portfolio by selecting work samples or other products. This type of portfolio contains examples of the student's work across time. Work samples represent *beginning, intermediate, and final* products (Nitko). Also, the IEP team and student decide to include work samples, such as rough drafts, that substantiate the student's understanding of the process rather than just the end product. Educational growth portfolios may incorporate work samples that represent different time periods, such as the beginning, middle, or end of a semester or year (Nitko). Figure 5.2 presents an example of an educational growth portfolio.

Most Favorite Work

An IEP team might select a most favorite work portfolio to document a student's ability to self-evaluate progress, as well as to document improved work habits when the student engages in the creation of products that represent areas of interest. A most favorite work portfolio includes work samples or other products, as well as student reflections about the work and a rubric for scoring. Once again, establishing the rubric early in the portfolio process enables the student to select items that actually reflect the goal of the IEP team. In addition, the rubric encourages the student to evaluate the product in an appropriate manner. This experience in self-evaluation increases a student's ability to examine progress with a more discerning eye. Participation in self-evaluation benefits all students; however, the teacher must plan carefully to allow it to occur. Self-evaluation prepares students for lifetime learning and decision making based on facts rather than passive acceptance of others' decisions concerning situations. Figure 5.3 presents an example of a self-reflection from a student's most favorite work portfolio.

Process Through a Long-Term Project

Using the portfolio to observe target skills and skill development over time proves particularly effective. IEP team members provide structure, including verbal encouragement

Figure 5.2   Madeline's Educational Growth Portfolio

Each selection includes the first draft and final draft.

1. *Madeline's written language sample critique from the beginning of the year:*

I really like this story. It is my first story for the year. I love to go to football games because I want to be a cheerleader. This story is written about what I like. It is not very long. I could have told more details and used color in my pictures. I forgot to use the spell check and grammar check.

2. *Madeline's written language sample critique from the middle of the year:*

My middle of the year selection is about the Christmas trip my family went on. It is longer than my first. I used spell check and wrote about many details. I put together 3 good paragraphs. My teacher liked my drawing. I think that my story sounded exciting. My teacher says it is good to write about what you find fun and exciting.

3. *Madelines's written language sample from the end of the year:*

My best story was written close to the end of the year. My teacher had put a list on my desk to remind me of the steps I needed to take to write a story. I followed each step. It took me several tries to get the story the way I wanted it. My mom took me to a cheerleader class at one of the high schools. I made notes about what I liked. My story was about the day with all of the cheerleaders. My story has two good pictures with lots of detail. I had five paragraphs that told lots of detail. Detail is what makes my stories better. My teacher hung my story on the wall. I know that I had done a good job. She gave me an A. I used the spell check and grammar check. I used my best handwriting. I liked the story best from all I have done. I worked hard on this story.

and oral evaluation, to help the student move the project toward mastery (Losardo & Notari-Syverson, 2001). Engaging in portfolio development using a long-term project allows the team members to collect information to reflect the student's ability in higher-order thinking skills, such as research and synthesis. In addition, a long-term project portfolio provides an opportunity to report on the student's incremental progress. Understanding how the student moves toward mastery remains as important as viewing the finished product, subsequent evaluations, and reflections. Figure 5.4 presents an example of a list of items to be included in a long-term project portfolio.

Figure 5.3   Caleb's Self-Reflection

Using the computer, Caleb is able to describe his feelings about his favorite portfolio entry. The following entry was recorded by Caleb using word prediction software.

I really like writing on the computer! I have fun with it! Everyone wants to read my stories. The computer helps me choose words.

Figure 5.4 Long-Term Project Portfolio for Kendra

The following list of items will be placed in Kendra's portfolio to demonstrate mastery and long-term growth during the academic year. Each story in Kendra's portfolio will be developed through the following stages:

- Rough draft of a story
- List of strengths in her story by Kendra, her peers, and her teacher
- List of needed changes by Kendra and her teacher
- Lists of details to expand rough draft
- Copies before and after spell/grammar check
- Copy with editing by Kendra
- Copy with editing by teacher
- Final copy

Composite Picture Compared to a Predetermined Standard

For some IEP goals, using a portfolio system to compare the student's achievement with a composite picture of the desired skill produces valuable information. Nitko (2004, p. 275) cites an example of E. L. Thorndike's 1910 handwriting scale to compare a student's handwriting samples with a variety of samples ranked for accuracy. These comparisons identify a match between the Thorndike levels and the student's work to determine the student's level of mastery. Using this type of process, a composite-picture portfolio relies on an external dimension or standard for the evaluation process. The student and the IEP team collect multiple samples over time to engage in the comparison. The student learns to score the samples. The student reflects on the analysis according to a specific reflection criterion. In many cases, the composite portfolio allows for evaluation of a specific level of criteria over time. Figure 5.5 presents an example of a scoring sheet from a composite portfolio.

Subject Area: Specific Versus General

Portfolios guided by annual goals and learning outcomes for the student provide specific information concerning achievement (Gronlund, 2003). This type of portfolio concentrates on a specific subject area or presents a more general look at a student's mastery over several subject areas. The decision to select one focus or several depends upon the assessment needs. For example, an annual goal focusing on a student's ability to improve written language skills might be very specific and focus on one type of writing, such as story writing, according to the goals to be assessed. However, if the goal involves more generalized skills, such as improvement to a specific grade level, then a variety of products becomes necessary. Sometimes the IEP team may determine that a student's written language development could be more thoroughly explored through an electronic language portfolio. Examples of drawings with accompanying descriptions will form the content of such portfolios. Figure 5.6 presents an example of Lee's language entry in her portfolio.

Figure 5.5 Using a Composite Approach to Sophie's Portfolio

Sophie will score her portfolio according to its effectiveness in answering the following:

1	2	3	4	5
Never	Seldom	Sometimes	Frequently	Always

My portfolio helps me to:

#1. pick jobs that I can do.

1	2	3	4	5

#2. remember to be happy.

1	2	3	4	5

#3. use my schedule book.

1	2	3	4	5

#4. be proud when I finish.

1	2	3	4	5

#5. ask when I don't understand.

1	2	3	4	5

Theme Oriented

For the student captivated by a particular area of interest, the development of the portfolio around that theme helps to guide appropriate instruction and motivate. Theme-oriented portfolios can be centered around science or social studies topics, such as sharks or culture. Each entry demonstrates progress toward an IEP goal based on the shark theme.

Figure 5.6 Laura's Language Entry in Her Portfolio, with Her Teacher's Commentary

March 12

   Laura's drawings are the beginning of her language portfolio. At the present time, Laura draws a picture and I, her teacher, record her verbal description of the drawing. I complete simple sentences with Laura's words. Laura then uses the script and picture to read and expand her knowledge of language and written symbols.

I love cats. They are fun to pet. My cat's name is Daisy.

Art- and music-based portfolios include fewer written products but emphasize the student's interest in songs, music, or other sound. Electronic portfolios include digitized music recordings or artwork. In addition, they represent the student's growth in the area of artistic expression and include a variety of paintings or drawings or, perhaps, photographs of these items. As with other portfolios, reflections by both the student and the IEP team provide critical feedback through a specified evaluation process.

Personal Knowledge

Another type of portfolio includes information based on a student's personal knowledge in the areas of self-esteem, cooperative learning skills, citizenship, or **social skills** (Cohen & Spenciner, 2003). This type of portfolio fits with IEP goals that are less academic in nature. The contents of the personal knowledge portfolio include drawings representing student feelings, teacher feedback notes concerning student progress in the personal knowledge area, student reflections concerning progress or group relationships, or a listing of activities undertaken to strengthen personal skills. The evaluation component of this type of portfolio includes regular reflections from both the student and the IEP team concerning progress, as well as direction, for continued growth.

Personal knowledge portfolios used in conjunction with social skills programming serve as a measure of change in a student's self-determination skills. Abilities such as explaining needs, desires, and feelings to others empower the student to self-advocate and become valuable traits as the student moves through school. The ability to self-advocate and determine the future impacts a student's success in the long run. Research emphasizes the importance of self-advocacy and self-determination in the lives of successful individuals with learning disabilities (Gerber & Reiff, 1994). Figure 5.7 presents an example of a social skills portfolio entry for Rocky.

Figure 5.7   Rocky's Social Skill Portfolio Entry

> I have trouble following the school rules. It really is no big deal. Everybody makes it a big deal. When I do something wrong, everybody gets bent out of shape. I don't know why. If they didn't make me so mad I wouldn't hit them. Sometimes, I think that kids come to school just to make me mad. I want to win at all the games. I want to win at school. If they would just get out of my way I could win. I want to be good. Why do they make me mad? I don't ask for it.
>
> My Social Skills Development
>
> Skill   Completion of Skill
>
> 1. See another's point of view
> 2. Acknowledge the role of rules
> 3. Express desire for compliance
> 4. Relate the reasons for rules
> 5. Talk instead of hit

Goal-Directed Individual Education Programs

Portfolios using IEP goals as the foundation provide the IEP team with specific information about the student's progress toward mastery. IEP goals describe specific observable and measurable behaviors. The IEP team must, however, decide exactly how the portfolio assessment documents the student's growth (Losardo & Notari-Syverson, 2001). Agreeing upon both the evaluation criteria and methods for IEP team members to collect the data remains essential. In addition, Losardo and Notari-Syverson specify that progress toward mastery includes information concerning the student's use of strategies, an analysis of errors, and the effectiveness of the supports in the classroom to facilitate the student's mastery. The IEP team can use the portfolio method to evaluate a student's progress on an annual goal. The team also can determine a variety of products for inclusion in the portfolio to demonstrate mastery. Figure 5.8 presents an example of a work sample from Greg's product portfolio.

Vavrus (1990) describes five principles to follow in determining the appropriate type of portfolio to develop:

- Determine both the physical and conceptual structure of the portfolio.
- Decide on the purpose of the portfolio and its contents.
- Agree on how and when to use the contents of the portfolio.
- Establish the **scoring criteria**, as well as the procedures for evaluation, including both the IEP team and student evaluation phases.
- Clarify the future use of the portfolio by the student and IEP team.

THE MECHANICS OF PORTFOLIOS

Many issues impact the IEP team as it decides to include a portfolio assessment system in its evaluation strategy for a student with disabilities, including these:

1. The selection of the type of portfolio
2. Decisions about the contents of the portfolio and how that content will accurately reflect progress on the IEP goals

Figure 5.8   A Sample from Greg's Portfolio

Area for Assessment: Language Arts

Work Sample from Greg's Portfolio:

Make a sentence with each word: fish, live, children, park, and sleep.

I love to fish with my grandfather.

I live at 511 Meadowbrook Lane.

The children on my street like to play with me.

I have a great park near my house.

My dogs like to sleep in my room.

---

3. The organization of the portfolio and the portfolio container
4. Determination of a selection process for the work samples or products to be included in the portfolio
5. Development of a quality evaluation system for both student reflection and assessment, as well as IEP team member appraisal

In the following sections, specific suggestions for addressing each of these matters are addressed.

Selecting the Type of Portfolio

As described, selection of the appropriate type of portfolio depends upon answers to the questions posed by the portfolio evaluation. While the student plays an important role in the selection of the items contained within the portfolio (Stiggins, 2001), the IEP team decides the purpose for the portfolio, how it serves to evaluate progress on IEP goals, and the specific elements comprising the rubrics or evaluation system. Also, the team discusses what support the student needs to effectively engage in self-evaluation and reflection about the portfolio entries and summary.

In an IEP-directed portfolio, the IEP team wants to answer the following questions posed by Gronlund (2003) concerning the selection of the specific type of portfolio to be used:

• What knowledge and skills should result from the development of the portfolio?
• What performance tasks provide the best evidence of student progress?
• Who will use this portfolio, when will they use it, and how will it impact the student's school programming?

The conceptual framework of the portfolio remains a vital concern of the IEP team. This framework, guided by the IEP goals, serves as the road map for the student's development. In some cases, the IEP team chooses to focus the portfolio on only one classroom goal, but often a range of behaviors appears along wth mastery of the IEP goals.

The **conceptual framework** determined by the IEP team should be clear and concise so the portfolio can be easily developed and evaluated. The team also wants to determine who will administer the portfolio, gather and store the contents, and interact with the student concerning reflections and evaluations. Finally, the IEP team must clearly identify the exact goals to be assessed. The IEP team can address these matters by developing a guiding conceptual framework for a student's portfolio assessment. Figure 5.9 presents an example of a conceptual framework developed for Leann's portfolio.

Decisions About Portfolio Content

The second step identified by Taylor (2003) in the development of a quality portfolio assessment concerns the determination of the contents. Taylor suggests the following aspects be established:

Figure 5.9   Leann's Conceptual Framework for Her Portfolio

---

1. *Areas for Assessment*
   a. Oral reading fluency
   b. Reading comprehension
2. *Who will administer Leann's portfolio?*
   Ms. Kessler, her classroom teacher in the general education classroom
3. *Who will gather and store contents?*
   Ms. Price, the special education teacher, and Ms. Kessler, the classroom teacher
4. *Who will interact with the student?*
   Ms. Kessler; Ms. Price; Ms. Herman, the teaching assistant; Ms. Mecham, the speech pathologist

---

1. The purpose of the portfolio
2. The intended audience
3. The needs of the audience
4. The type of entries to demonstrate progress

The Organization of the Portfolio

Taylor (2003) reports the need for certain critical elements in a portfolio:

- A completed table of contents using the student's preferred mode of communication
- A written or dictated letter to the reviewer describing the portfolio and its contents
- Seven to 10 entries that represent the goal being addressed
- The student's name, date of the product, and a title for each entry
- The student's weekly schedule describing student activities, opportunities to select activities, and interface with nondisabled peers
- A sample of the student's current modes of communication
- A letter from a family member or another person who works closely with the student authenticating the contents of the portfolio

Taylor's (2003) suggestions for the contents of a portfolio require the IEP team to plan the following. In the first step, the team must determine both the physical and conceptual structure of the portfolio. Figure 5.10 presents options that the IEP team can consider for the physical structure of portfolios.

The Selection Process for the Products

According to Taylor (2003), the fourth step involves the determination of a selection process for the work samples or products to be included in the portfolio. IEP goals, as

Figure 5.10   Options for the Physical Structure of the Portfolio

- Use an expandable file folder.
- Use a briefcase with flaps, pockets, and attached bands or strings.
- Use a cardboard or plastic file box.
- Use a flat-bottom shopping bag.
- Use a notebook.
- Arrange entries by sections with a table of contents.
- Date and label each entry in the portfolio.
- Include sections for entries, student reflections and evaluation, teacher evaluations, documentation of growth, and summaries.

well as the type of information the team seeks, become impacted by this process. The IEP team may be interested in documenting the student's learning over time with work samples that demonstrate early and final products, along with the student's reflections about the learning process.

The Development of Evaluation Criteria

The fifth step of Taylor's (2003) portfolio development scheme is the development of evaluation criteria, including the establishment of the rubric and summary sheets. According to Venn (2004), teachers develop impressions concerning student performance (a) as the student completes the entries for the portfolio, (b) as they engage in conferences with the student, and (c) as they review the portfolio for evaluation. These impressions do not accurately appraise the student's development.

The Management System   Venn (2004) recommends the establishment of a management system prior to the inception of the portfolio, including both a management checklist for use by the teacher and a student portfolio checklist. Each checklist serves as a mechanism for recording the expansion of the portfolio and enables the teacher and student to clearly focus on the IEP goals being assessed. A management system involves the determination of meaningful feedback. This feedback occurs between the teacher and student or simply involves self-monitoring by the student.

Self-monitoring includes decision making concerning the completion or quality of a product, as well as the ability to represent achievement either orally or by visual symbols. The self-management chart becomes a part of the management checklist.

Self-Reflections   Self-reflections provide evaluation criteria used in portfolios in which the student describes learning processes and accomplishments (Cohen & Spenciner, 2003). This evaluation criterion becomes critical for two reasons: (a) it provides a glimpse into the student's view of the learning process through the student's description and (b) it encourages the student to take responsibility for learning and promotes the use of thinking strategies and abilities used in the real world (Nitko, 2004). Self-assessment entails a variety of different activities: (a) reviewing the completed portfolio, (b) examining in-progress products and discussing possible revisions, (c) selecting two work samples that demonstrate growth, or (d) evaluating a work sample independently (Taylor, 2003).

Many students with disabilities need specific instruction about how to effectively self-evaluate work and engage in quality self-reflections. Teachers may want to provide the students with specific questions at the beginning of the process to use during self-reflections. Another method uses direct contact between the student and teacher during the reflection time in the classroom. The teacher orally directs the student by commenting on change and asking the student to respond to the comment (Taylor, 2003). Having students compare two work samples and evaluate their likes and dislikes about the products also helps to focus the student's self-reflective activities (Taylor).

Conferencing with the Teacher   Conferences in which the teacher guides the discussion and helps the student record responses also provide effective methods for improving a student's self-evaluation skills (Nitko, 2004). The record of the discussion provides a joint evaluation of the student's progress and the level of agreement on that progress between the student and teacher. Teaching this type of evaluative skill provides opportunities for the student to engage in higher-level thinking and self-critique.

Rubrics   A rubric describes a set of criteria, assigns a numerical value to the student's performance, and is usually indicated from lowest to highest (Gronlund, 2003). Rubrics rate the student's completion or mastery of both the details and the finished project. Taylor (2003) suggests the following procedures for developing a rubric:

- Make a list of the most important features of the IEP goals.
- Determine the rating scale (for example 1 = unacceptable through 5 = outstanding), being careful to avoid scales that involve more than six points.
- Write a descriptor for each and every component.

The best rubrics tie directly to specific criteria for evaluation (Venn, 2004). Tying the rubric to the IEP goal with its measurable and observable behavior certainly helps to stabilize this process and strengthen the rubric's reliability or ability to measure a specific set of standards. Salvia and Ysseldyke (2004) suggest that even the best rubrics present problems in interpretation and reliability. These include issues concerning the following:

1. The specific meaning of the scoring descriptors (What does "excellent" really mean?)
2. Score generalizability (How many products are required to really represent mastery, or under what conditions can acceptable results be obtained?)
3. An inability to compare student performance with others' performance
4. Questions about how self-reflections really impact the portfolio process

Issues of reliability include problems with consistency of scoring over time, often due to a lack of interscorer reliability or the instability of scoring among different evaluators. Salvia and Ysseldyke (2004) caution the developers of portfolio evaluation systems to be aware of these problems and to create scoring systems that are clear, concise, and agreed upon by members of the IEP team. In addition, they suggest that all members engaged in the assessment process receive training to clarify the scoring procedures.

Rubrics generally use one of two types of scoring systems: **analytic scoring** or **holistic scoring** (Cohen & Spenciner, 2003). Analytic scoring provides for an independent score for each element of the rating scale on the rubric. Rubrics use both a numerical value and a descriptive word to help evaluators to use the same levels of achievement when scoring. Cohen and Spenciner (2003) also report that these descriptors allow the IEP team to have a more thorough understanding of the student's achievement, rather than just a cursory look at the numerical values. Analytic scoring does, however, provide the opportunity to add together all the scores from the components to obtain one overall score (Taylor, 2003).

Holistic scoring occurs by assigning one overall score for the entire portfolio rather than several scores for each component part. Holistic scoring also includes written descriptors assigned to each number to further clarify the meaning of the number. Taylor (2003) suggests that holistic scoring works when scoring large numbers of portfolios. For smaller groups and individual portfolios planned by the IEP team, analytic scoring remains appropriate and provides the most detailed picture of the student's progress.

IEP teams sometimes elect to utilize published rubrics for scoring a student's progress. These rubrics can be adapted to fit the student's needs (Gronlund, 2003). Published rubrics have the advantage of including a variety of subskills to help the IEP team determine the exact elements required for demonstration of mastery. In addition to published rubrics, some schools or school districts include portfolio assessment as part of the review of student progress in school. Fuchs and Fuchs (1996) recommend that the IEP team consider using published inventories in combination with portfolio assessment to strengthen the reliability of the assessment process. In many cases, the school or district develops a basic rubric for assessing the student with disabilities and allows specific information to be added (Cohen & Spenciner, 2003).

Using small group or peer conferences for students to evaluate the strengths and weaknesses of each other's portfolios provides another method for the IEP team to consider (Taylor, 2003). Students with disabilities benefit from this type of conferencing system by learning appropriate methods for giving and receiving feedback from others. Conferencing methods expose students to a variety of levels of mastery within the group and allow them to develop a more realistic understanding of the required quality.

In step five, Taylor (2003) describes the procedures for using portfolio data by the IEP team. For the portfolio to yield useable documentation, the IEP team needs access to information in a summary format. As mentioned, simple numerical ratings lose some assessment value. The development of both numerical and descriptive summaries produces more understandable results. Summary sheets produce a wide variety of information;

however, the IEP team must determine the data necessary to make decisions about the student's progress prior to the development of the portfolio. Gronlund (2003) proposes one type of summary sheet that lists the skills to be evaluated and then provides a numerical rating scale to indicate the student's level of mastery. Written descriptors explaining the numerical ratings also appear.

Documentation of the student's use of learning strategies, as well as typical errors, rounds out the assessment picture (Losardo & Notari-Syverson, 2001). In addition, knowledge of the effectiveness of modifications as demonstrated during portfolio development remains critical.

While summary sheets provide data useful for making decisions about mastery of IEP goals, care should be taken when using the portfolio in high-stakes testing situations (Cohen & Spenciner, 2003). The facts, records, and other types of assessment data gathering done through portfolio assessment allow the IEP team to make informed decisions about high-stakes testing.

USING THE PORTFOLIO ASSESSMENT DATA IN THE INDIVIDUAL EDUCATION PROGRAM

As discussed, the summarization of the information obtained from the portfolio must be available for the IEP team to efficiently and effectively understand the role that the portfolio plays in documenting student mastery. How does the team use the summary data, and what formats prove most helpful? The team can choose to use the data presented in the portfolio summary sheets in several ways. First, the team must look at the information presented in the summary sheets and determine their match with other progress indicators. For example, if a student works on improving his spelling skills, the team looks at all measures of spelling skills development. If weekly tests and criterion-referenced assessment show little improvement, the team looks to the portfolio. If the summary sheets do not indicate progress, the team begins to explore other avenues. If the summary sheets indicate progress on written work done over time and self-reflective information indicating the student's understanding of accurate spelling requirements, the IEP team investigates additional strategies or modifications, such as the use of a mnemonic strategy to remind the student to look for misspellings.

A second consideration for the IEP team includes the examination of products within the actual portfolio that more clearly indicate movement toward mastery than typical classroom assignments or tests do (Taylor, 2003). Portfolios contain a variety of products that reveal a student's learning. Drawings, photographs, tape recordings, and other tangible examples may produce a different picture of the student's growth.

Fuchs and Fuchs (1996) indicate that it is important for the IEP team to look at three aspects of portfolio assessment for students with disabilities:

1. Consider the level of acquisition of the skill.
2. Look for evidence of skill completion in a real-life situation.
3. Document the successful use of learning skill strategies.

What Do Portfolios Contribute to IEP Development?

- They give meaning to a group of work samples/products selected by the student and the teacher as progress markers.
- They enable students to self-evaluate and contribute to IEP team planning.
- They offer tangible evidence of the progress of the student.
- They allow the IEP team to look firsthand at the progression of the student during the year.
- They reflect many efforts of the student gathered over a period of time.

IEP teams use these three elements in the portfolio summary to clarify not only mastery but generalization.

PORTFOLIOS AND TECHNOLOGY

Many educators utilize "electronic containers" to prepare, store, and present electronic portfolios (Taylor, 2003). Word processing used in both traditional and electronic portfolios provides students with tremendous assistance. Specialized software—such as multimedia presentation, graphic design, digital photography, music, and outlining or mind-mapping software—aid the student with disabilities to create an electronic portfolio that expresses individuality.

The inclusion of video footage of class activities, presentations, student–teacher conferences, or other products such as plays allows the teacher and student to capture quality pieces of the school experience (Male, 2003). Electronic portfolios allow for easy portability to share their contents with family members and other team participants, as well as serving as a permanent historical record (Pecheone, Pigg, Chung, & Souviney, 2005).

At the present time, many teacher preparation programs use electronic or Web-based portfolios to document student progress through the standard-based curriculum. This familiarity with the use and production of electronic portfolios by new teachers promises to filter into the classroom rapidly. Chang (2001) identifies the following benefits of electronic portfolios:

- Demonstration of student growth
- Encouragement of student goal setting
- Presentation of documented effort
- Display of student performance
- Enhancement of self-assessment and self-monitoring skills
- Exhibition of more in-depth understanding of student skill levels
- Improvement in student self-confidence and self-determination

In addition to enhancing or changing the paper-and-pencil tasks of the traditional portfolio, the use of technology as an aid in accessibility is critical. Use of speech-recognition, text-to-speech, word-prediction, translation, and basic grammar and spelling checking programs enhances development opportunities for many students with oral and written language deficits. In addition, accessible hardware, such as adaptive keyboards, a specialized mouse, touch screens, or switch-activated mechanisms support many students with physical or sensory impairments.

Two final considerations with regard to the role of technology include the advantages of using the computer to maintain neat, readable, and easy-to-find records. Students and teachers utilize the computer with little trouble to maintain records in individual folders specific to each student. Finally, when the portfolio is complete, a CD or DVD can be burned as a permanent record for the student and teacher of the student's accomplishments.

SUMMARY

- Portfolios provide a method for IEP teams to gather systematic information about a student's progress over time and in the naturalistic environment.
- Portfolios must be planned and implemented as culturally sensitive, relevant classroom assessments to gain a complete understanding of the student.
- These methods promise to expand opportunities for students with disabilities to demonstrate achievement in a variety of media.
- A quality portfolio begins with a specific description of the goals to be assessed. It also contains a specialized plan for how the products will be evaluated, including both student and teacher assessments.
- The IEP team benefits in decision making from information obtained from portfolios.
- Technology enhances portfolios through new methods for gathering student data.

COMPREHENSION CHECK

1. Explain the five purposes for developing a portfolio. What would be the advantages of using a portfolio in an IEP setting?
2. Discuss the importance of teacher and student evaluation of the components of a portfolio. What does the student learn by engaging in self-evaluation?
3. In what ways does portfolio assessment honor cultural diversity? What specific components would you include in a portfolio to create a culturally sensitive evaluation system?

ACTIVITIES

1. Describe the different types of portfolios. Create a chart depicting annual goals best evaluated by each type of portfolio.
2. Develop a rubric for scoring one product from a student portfolio.
3. Generate a table of contents suitable for documenting your growth as a teacher throughout this course.

REFERENCES

Chang, C. C. (2001). A study on the evaluation of the effectiveness analysis of web-based learning portfolios. *British Journal of Educational Technology, 32*(4), 435–458.

Cohen, L. G., & Spenciner, L. J. (2003). *Assessment of children and youth with special needs.* Boston: Pearson.

Fuchs, L. S., & Fuchs, D. (1996). Combining performance assessment and curriculum-based measurement to strengthen instructional planning. *Learning Disabilities Research and Practice, 11*(3), 183–192.

Gerber, P. J., & Reiff, H. B. (1994). *Learning disabilities in adulthood: Persisting problems and evolving issues.* Boston: Andover Medical Publishers.

Gronlund, N. E. (2003). *Assessment of student achievement* (7th ed.). Boston: Allyn & Bacon.

Hartmann, C. (2004). Using teacher portfolios to enrich the methods course experiences of prospective mathematics teachers. *School, Science and Mathematics, 104*(8), 392–407.

Lewis, R. B., & Doorlag, D. H. (1999). *Teaching special students in the mainstream* (5th ed.). Upper Saddle River, NJ: Merrill/Prentice Hall.

Losardo, A., & Notari-Syverson, A. (2001). *Alternative approaches to assessing young children.* Baltimore, MD: Brookes.

Male, M. (2003). *Technology for inclusion: Meeting the special needs of all students* (3rd ed.). Needham Heights, MA: Allyn & Bacon.

Nitko, A. J. (2004). *Educational assessment of students* (4th ed.). Upper Saddle River, NJ: Merrill/Prentice Hall.

Pecheone, R. L., Pigg, M. J., Chung, R. R., & Souviney, R. J. (2005). Performance assessment and electronic portfolios: Their effect on teacher learning and education. *The Clearing House, 78*(4), 164–176.

Salvia, J., & Ysseldyke, J. E. (2004). *Assessment in special and inclusive education* (9th ed.). Boston: Houghton Mifflin.

St. Maurice, H., & Shaw, P. (2004). Teacher portfolios come of age: A preliminary study. *NASSP Bulletin, 88*(639), 15–25.

Stiggins, R. J. (2001). *Student-involved classroom assessment* (3rd ed.). Upper Saddle River, NJ: Merrill/Prentice Hall.

Strudler, N., & Wetzel, K. (2005). The diffusion of electronic portfolios in teacher education: Issues of initiation and implementation. *Journal of Research on Technology in Education, 37*(4), 411–433.

Swicegood, P. (1994). Portfolio-based assessment practices. *Intervention, 30*(1), 6–15.

Taylor, R. L. (2003). *Assessment of exceptional students: Educational and psychological procedures* (6th ed.). Boston: Pearson.

Vavrus, L. (1990). Put portfolios to the test. *Instructor, 100*(1), 48–53.

Venn, J. J. (2004). *Assessing students with special needs* (3rd ed.). Upper Saddle River, NJ: Merrill/Prentice Hall.

CONTEXTUAL MEASURES OF ASSESSMENT FOR EDUCATIONAL INTERVENTION

INTERVIEWS AND QUESTIONNAIRES

6

Chapter Focus

One of the most parent-friendly techniques in authentic assessment utilizes the questionnaire or interview. These two tools offer valuable information regarding parent goals, classroom insights, and attitudinal data. Using questionnaires and interviews to provide powerful observations into a student's daily functioning provides the assessor with direction in classroom planning and daily instruction. The acquired information also adds to the knowledge base concerning the student's performance and attitudes concerning learning tasks. Questionnaires and interviews help complete a holistic picture in a naturalistic setting.

LEARNER OBJECTIVES

- Define interviews and questionnaires.
- Explain the benefits of and concerns about using interviews and questionnaires.
- Relate the importance of cultural and linguistic sensitivity when using interviews and questionnaires.
- Recognize opportunities to use interviews and questionnaires as vehicles for obtaining important assessment data.
- Describe the types of interviews and questionnaires.
- Express the steps for creating interviews and questionnaires.
- Convey the different methods for summarizing data from interviews and questionnaires.
- Articulate the ways in which the IEP team uses interview and questionnaire results to inform decision making.
- State the contribution of technology to the interview and questionnaire process.

WHAT ARE INTERVIEWS AND QUESTIONNAIRES?

Questionnaires and interviews consist of **contextual** measures used to collect the perspectives of a variety of people concerning a student's strengths and needs (McLoughlin & Lewis, 2001). While the two measures obtain similar results, they utilize two different strategies for acquiring data to reflect a student's daily life. Questionnaires and interviews aid the assessor in (a) creating a historical and developmental view, (b) improving diagnostic precision, and (c) planning more relevant intervention strategies (Sattler, 2001).

Questionnaires

Questionnaires provide a convenient method for acquiring personal information difficult to achieve by other means (Stiggins, 2001). These written measures elicit data by asking questions relevant to the student or parent (McLoughlin & Lewis, 2001). The format of a questionnaire varies from the highly structured checklist style to a more objective form, such as multiple-choice or true–false questions. Less-structured questionnaires feature open-ended questions requiring the student or parent to provide more detailed responses (McLoughlin & Lewis, 2001). Questionnaires allowing the examiner to engage the individual in a reflective process encourage the communication of desires or skills (Bauer & Shea, 2003).

Interviews

According to Chatterji (2003), interviews depend upon orally articulated, open-ended, and untimed responses. They provide a means for respondents to give more detailed explanations regarding their original answers, increasing the validity and accuracy of such responses to improve the quality of the interaction. This opportunity to redirect the interview either to obtain information or refocus the conversation represents a particular strength of the interview process (Bauer & Shea, 2003). **Viva voce** examinations or interviews involving face-to-face meetings that provide a more effective and flexible means of acquiring relevant data (Spinelli, 2006).

Interviews eliminate **literacy barriers** by removing the need for caregivers to respond in written format and allow respondents to thoughtfully answer interview questions (Spinelli, 2006). The respondent concentrates on conveying oral answers rather than developing a more formal written response. In addition, interviews provide the student with reassurance or encouragement to produce the most accurate replies (Spinelli).

BENEFITS OF USING QUESTIONNAIRES AND INTERVIEWS

Questionnaires and interviews prove particularly appropriate for accessing responses from very young children and students in special populations (Chatterji, 2003). These individuals require extensive observation and authentic data collection to obtain reliable and valid pictures of their abilities. Benefits and disadvantages exist for both the questionnaire and interview.

Interviews and questionnaires supply rich sources of information. Although qualitative in nature, the information provides a foundation for probing curriculum areas and using observation skills to determine strengths and needs. Ideally, the team takes these comments and places them in a contextual framework to pinpoint and verify the need for further assessment. By using many sources of data, the team increases its ability to problem solve.

Questionnaires and interviews offer the teacher a variety of benefits, including the following:

- They allow the examiner to sample a broad range of information in a short time (Chatterji, 2003).
- They provide different perspectives from a variety of individuals (Bauer & Shea, 2003).
- They permit the teacher or examiner to gain insight into the student's life beyond the classroom (Spinelli, 2006).
- They promote home–school partnerships by involving the parents and other family members or friends in providing in-depth information about the student's daily living situation (Spinelli, 2006).
- They help acquire social, familial, and medical histories about a student (Spinelli, 2006).
- They help verify previously collected information from other assessment sources (Sattler, 1998).
- They provide insight into the role of culture in the student's daily living settings (Sattler, 1998).

DISADVANTAGES OF USING QUESTIONNAIRES AND INTERVIEWS

The disadvantages of questionnaires and interviews include the issue of literacy. First, written responses become barriers to collecting good information from respondents with minimal literacy skills (McLoughlin & Lewis, 2001). When a person with inadequate literacy skills tries to fill out a lengthy questionnaire, the questionnaire becomes an instrument for evaluating the writing skills rather than a data source concerning the student. Second, language competency presents a viable concern, and misunderstandings based on the different cultural values of ethnic groups prove common (Baca & Cervantes, 2004). For example, some cultural groups value dependence on family while others place more importance on independent behavior. The interpretation of material acquired from questionnaires and interviews should be matched with cultural traditions so that misinterpretation does not occur (Sattler, 2001).

Another disadvantage of questionnaires and interviews relates to the need for privacy. Information acquired from all sources must be considered confidential. A failure to ensure confidentiality results in an inability to convey sensitive material for fear of being misquoted or misconstrued (Stiggins, 2001).

According to Chatterji (2003), the disadvantages of the interview process include issues of time and teachers/examiners. Interviews require a good deal of time to plan, administer, analyze, and interpret. In addition, teachers and examiners must be trained in interview techniques, such as appropriate active listening and recording skills. The ability to analyze interviews requires practice and reflective thought. Training in the evaluation of interviews also requires extensive time and practice.

CULTURAL COMPETENCE IN USING QUESTIONNAIRES AND INTERVIEWS

Valuing differences in cultures and their impact on communication becomes a critical component for successful service delivery for students with disabilities. When developing and using a questionnaire or interview, the teacher must acknowledge his or her personal biases and the needs of the individuals being interviewed. The following suggestions for acknowledging cultural and linguistic differences promise to improve the questionnaire and interview process:

- Use this technique to place parents in an active role in the education of their child (Baca & Cervantes, 2004).
- Establish a relationship built on trust prior to asking parents to engage in a questionnaire or interview (Garcia, 1994).
- Demonstrate that parent information is credible and valuable through using questionnaires and interviews (Baca & Cervantes, 2004).
- Enhance collaboration by using the information from questionnaires and interviews to plan for daily instruction (Garcia, 1994).
- Place an emphasis on common sense in the process (Baca & Cervantes, 2004).
- Make sincere efforts to include parents as true partners by being respectful of their language, culture, and socioeconomic status (Baca & Cervantes, 2004).
- Incorporate attributes of the local culture identified through questionnaires and interviews into the classroom curriculum (Garcia, 1994).

DECIDING TO USE QUESTIONNAIRES OR INTERVIEWS

Questionnaires and interviews represent one of the most common tools for informal assessment (Polloway, Patton, & Serna, 2005). They are used to gather information from parents, family members, teachers, and service providers to allow their input to influence decisions. For young children and their parents, interviews often provide the best opportunity to gather critical information sometimes missed in the questionnaire format (Westling & Fox, 2000). The following list provides a summary of reasons to select the questionnaire or interview process:

When to Use a Questionnaire	When to Use an Interview
Need global information	Need to probe
Have little time	Require details

Want written information	Want to circumvent literacy barriers
Require formal setting	Want informal contact
Seek simple facts	Desire to establish rapport
Specific answers are desired	Seek detailed discussions

TYPES OF QUESTIONNAIRES AND INTERVIEWS

Several types of questionnaires and interviews exist, including those addressed to parents and teachers, teachers and students, special education and general education teachers, and teachers and other professionals. Each of these relationships reflects unique perspectives captured by various questionnaires or interviews.

Parent and Teacher Questionnaires

Questionnaires are helpful tools with which teachers can gather information from parents when seeking understanding of a student's functioning outside the classroom. Information such as the student's interests, favorite activities, parental concerns, and attitudes toward academic tasks comprise typical, beginning-of-the-year questionnaires (Spinelli, 2006). Questionnaires provide **baseline information**, such as documentation of the family's homework practices.

In the IEP process, questionnaires provide data about the student's progress at home on IEP goals. The teacher also can obtain information concerning recent changes in the child's physical and emotional development. This tool allows the teacher to collect the same information for each student and to follow up with an interview when necessary. Figure 6.1 presents a sample parent–teacher questionnaire for Jennifer.

Figure 6.1   A Sample Parent–Teacher Questionnaire

Homework Questionnaire for Jennifer

Please respond with a true or false to the following questions:

_____1. My student should have homework every day.

_____2. My student completes homework independently.

_____3. My student complains about homework.

_____4. My student needs me with him or her to do homework.

_____5. My student loses homework often.

Please respond to the following questions in writing:

1. Do you feel that homework is beneficial for your student?

2. How long does it usually take your student to finish homework assignments?

3. How do you want us to communicate about your student's homework?

4. Does your student understand his or her homework?

Interviews with Family Members

Interviews support family participation in school by helping to maintain a positive partnership through increasing opportunities to ensure familial input (McLoughlin and Lewis, 2001). Interviews also elicit quality information regarding progress toward IEP goals. Encouraging parents to tell their student's story enhances the connection between the parent and teacher by providing an outlet for emotions, desires, or needs helping to decrease parental isolation (Bauer & Shea, 2003). In addition, interviews provide a mechanism for collecting information to personalize the IEP process and increase individualization.

The interview brings the parent into the school–home partnership by strengthening communication. In order to promote student growth in the home environment, Spinelli (2006) promotes the use of interviews as a vehicle for enabling parents to reflect on the student's progress more often than at the yearly IEP team meeting.

Questionnaires or Interviews with the Student

Interviewing or using questionnaires with students provides the teacher with insights not obtainable from other sources. These techniques allow the teacher to assess both student performance and **disposition**, such as fears, emotions, or preferences. For example, in an interview, the student reveals his dislike for completing lengthy tasks; without this information, the teacher assumed a lack of competence rather than understanding the student's frustration with the length of an assignment.

For another example, Morgan, a student with mental retardation, expresses her feelings about her job. Although Morgan lacks an extensive vocabulary, she communicates her likes and dislikes through facial expressions, communication cards, and her ability to respond to yes/no questions that impact decisions about her future. In response, the teacher implements changes on the job site as needed, and the IEP team adjusts goals to help Morgan fulfill her desires.

Questionnaires and interviews explore both current and past experiences and perceptions to understand a student's functioning (Spinelli, 2006). They provide a window into a student's attitudes, study skills, and work habits in a particular subject area (McLoughlin & Lewis, 2001). Students also express opinions concerning particular instructional procedures in terms of both ease of use and ability to make progress.

Questionnaires become suitable for students who demonstrate the ability to read, comprehend written information, and convey their thoughts in writing (McLoughlin & Lewis, 2001). To discover the student's **problem solving process**, a questionnaire may guide the student through a written analysis of his or her thinking. Sentence completion tasks (Mercer & Mercer, 1998; McLoughlin & Lewis, 2001), such as answering the following questions, provide a good example of this technique.

1. The first thing I do when I look at a word problem is . . . .
2. When reading a word problem, I . . . .
3. If I don't understand the order of the word problem, I . . . .

Figure 6.2   A Sample Student–Teacher Interview for Diane

---

1. *What is the COPS writing strategy?*

It is a strategy I use to help me remember what to look for after I have written a story. It helps me to see if it is written right.

2. *How does using COPS help you?*

It helps me remember the things that the teacher wants when I write. Like capitalizing, using periods, and checking the spelling with spell check.

3. *When do you use COPS?*

I use it after I write a story. Sometimes I use it during the writing, like when I am about to make a mistake.

4. *Tell me how COPS makes you better at writing.*

COPS gives me four things to look for after I have written my story so that I fix them if I need to.

5. *How do you feel about your stories when you have used COPS?*

I am happier with my stories and feel like the teacher will be happy, too. I can write more and then I know what to go back and look for when I am finished. Also, my teacher will help me correct things if I can tell what mistakes I am looking for. So does the computer.

For students with **auditory processing** problems, the questionnaire proves beneficial. Auditory processing problems circumvent the student's ability to provide quality information in an oral interview. Questionnaires allow the student to create a rich response in writing. Eliminating the immediacy of an oral response through written answers provides the student with time to think. By completing the same questionnaire at regular intervals, the assessment analyzes cumulative skills over time.

Interviews may take place immediately after a student completes a task (McLoughlin & Lewis, 2001) or at selected times to obtain verification of skill mastery in a specific subject area. Such interview questions focus on the learning process by clarifying indecisiveness in the student's earlier performance. For example, the interview question "What do you do when you don't know how to solve a math problem?" elicits comments on the effectiveness of a particular strategy. This question provides information about the student's skill base for the strategy and helps to evaluate student satisfaction with the strategies commonly used. The interview also serves as a discussion point related to the student's strategy usage. The interview also provides documentation of any need for further support in strategy building. Figure 6.2 presents a sample student–teacher interview for Diane.

Questionnaires and Interviews with Other Professionals

Many individuals within the school setting provide useful information through the questionnaire or interview format. Former teachers can supply historical data concerning a student's progress, experiences, and attitudes. Teaching assistants can offer many valuable insights and details to document through questionnaires and interviews and, subsequently, to add to the IEP process. Teachers of nonacademic classes, therapists, and counselors also can contribute their experiences to data collected on a student.

The questionnaire provides an opportunity for sharing data from a student's therapy session that might otherwise be disregarded or overlooked. Because teachers and therapists often pass each other in the classroom but seldom have a mechanism for an indepth conversation, it is especially important for the teacher to share data with all other therapists and the IEP team. This can strengthen the approach of all team members when planning and implementing service delivery. In addition, the teacher can monitor and address issues highlighted in the questionnaire in the classroom. The questionnaire also provides an additional form of documentation. Figure 6.3 presents a sample questionnaire with an instructional assistant.

USING DATA FROM QUESTIONNAIRES AND INTERVIEWS

Data from questionnaires and interviews must be summarized or condensed to produce understandable and useable results. Graphs and charts are often used to display information accrued from questionnaires and interviews without the confusion possible with

Figure 6.3 A Sample Questionnaire with Another Professional About Sarah's Communication Device

---

Name: Mrs. Hartman   *Position:* Instructional Assistant

Underline your response.

1. Appears to know how to use the communication device.

Never   Sometimes   Always

2. Uses the communication device to get what she wants.

Never   Sometimes   Always

3. Uses the communication device independently.

Never   Sometimes   Always

4. Uses the communication device with prompts.

Never   Sometimes   Always

5. Has technical problems using the device.

Never   Sometimes   Always

6. Has physical problems using the device.

Never   Sometimes   Always

Comments: Sarah seems to use the device with help from me. She does not pick it up without a prompt. When she does, she can use it, depending upon how shaky she is at the moment. Sometimes she looks like she wants to use the device but isn't confident about her ability to pick it up.

Figure 6.4 A Sample Summary Graph for the Family Questionnaire for Jackson

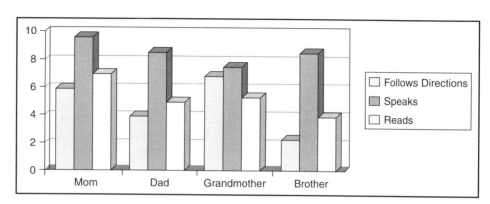

a narrative. For example, during the interview process the interviewee may list the strengths of the student and family. Charting the strengths and linking them to IEP goals enhances opportunities for generalization of skills to the home setting. In addition, frequency counts and scatterplots provide a pictorial representation, for example, of the number of times a subject gets mentioned so priorities can be established in instructional goals. Also, summaries depicted in figures deliver information to the IEP team more directly and efficiently than written text. Figure 6.4 presents a chart of the results of a family questionnaire for Jackson concerning student strengths.

A second method for presenting and utilizing the results of questionnaires and interviews involves the **analysis of themes** to pinpoint progress. The themes become recommendations taken directly from the responses of written questionnaires and interview **transcripts**. By analyzing reoccurring themes, the IEP team determines areas in need of support or attention. The frequency of these emerging themes helps the team to focus on the most critical aspects of the instructional process. Figure 6.5 presents themes emerging from a family interview concerning Leslie, a student.

Graphs, charts, and lists of themes that summarize the questionnaire and interview data for the IEP team make decision making more objective. Summarizing the results into a concise format tells the story of the student and allows the IEP team to make personal, individualized choices based on relevant data. These tools also allow input from the student, parent, and others in a time-efficient manner to increase participation in

Figure 6.5 A Sample Summary of Themes from an Interview with Leslie's Family

The following themes emerged:
1. Need to focus on the daily living skill of dressing.
2. Concern about Leslie's ability to read common signs.
3. Interest in pursuing Leslie's interest in music.
4. Unease about Leslie's lack of progress in recognizing the value of money.

What Do Interviews and Questionnaires Contribute to IEP Development?

- They allow for multiple perspectives to be considered in the aggregation of data.
- They provide opportunities for the team to look for themes that emerge for determining priority needs.
- They permit many perspectives on the identification of student strengths.
- They document data that are often regarded as opinions or hearsay.
- They create opportunities for problem solving, especially when looking at several interview results or a group of questionnaire responses.

the IEP process. By summarizing the data from accumulated questionnaires and interviews, the IEP team can look across time and settings for data that suggest needed changes and adaptation of goals. The team also discovers information based on the context that surrounds the student and his learning rather than on a simple indicator, such as a test score.

DEVELOPING QUESTIONNAIRES AND INTERVIEWS

Questionnaires and interviews utilize both qualitative and quantitative methods. The method selected should match the behaviors or conditions to be investigated (Chatterji, 2003). When determining whether to use qualitative or quantitative data collection, one must isolate the results to be obtained, know the point to which the inquiry has already progressed, and understand the desired outcome from the interaction. Complex questions—such as how a student functions, or measures of intensity, or death of responses—require the use of qualitative data (Denzin & Lincoln, 2000).

Describing Interviews

Interviews typically use qualitative techniques. The interview should not be confused with an ordinary conversation. The assessment interview differs in several aspects. Sattler (1998) makes the following suggestions regarding the difference between interviews and conversations:

1. The interview employs a planned sequence rather than a naturally occurring conversation.
2. The interviewer accepts the information acquired in the interview without challenge, focuses on the interactions, and accepts without emotional reaction the substance of the conference.

3. The interviewer and interviewee maintain a **prescribed relationship**. The interviewer asks the questions and the interviewee answers.
4. The interviewer probes deeply to acquire information.
5. The interviewer follows guidelines pertaining to confidentiality.
6. The interviewer collects the information and usually places it into a written format.

Using the interview proves particularly useful for expanding responses through open-ended questioning techniques. Ambiguity and confusion concerning classroom problems are more readily investigated with qualitative measures.

Interview Development and Procedures

The development of the interview represents an important phase in the process. Chatterji (2003) suggests the following considerations:

1. Interviews must be structured to fit the assessment goals through the creation of interview questions that directly reflect instruction and school-related functioning by linking the questions to a targeted area.
2. A sufficient number of questions related to the desired results must be asked to achieve a measure of reliability.
3. The interview questions must be clear and focused.
4. Plenty of time must be allowed for the interviewee to express his or her thoughts.
5. Responses must be respected, without disagreement.

During the interview, certain procedures positively improve the outcome. The interviewer must explain the purpose for the interview at the beginning of the conference. He or she should state that note taking ensures that details of the conference are accurately recorded. However, participants should be allowed to refuse permission for the notes to be taken (McLoughlin & Lewis, 2001). The notebook should be kept in full view throughout the interview. Multipart carbonless paper or photocopying should be used to allow the respondent to keep a copy of the interview (McLoughlin & Lewis).

Start with comfortable, non threatening, open-ended, easy-to-understand, and relatively easy-to-answer questions to establish rapport. Respect the time constraints of the people involved by scheduling the interview at an appropriate time and ending it at the specified time. At the end of the interview, read aloud the responses to validate or correct the person's answers and ask "Is this what you mean?" or "Let me see if I understand what you are saying." Avoid times when the respondent feels too rushed or fatigued for an interview.

Factors to Think About when Interviewing

According to Sattler (1998), three components directly impact the quality and success of the interview as an assessment device, including (a) interviewer/interviewee characteristics, (b) the climate of the interview, and (c) the message component. Attending to these elements during the development of the interview produces stronger and more useable results in the assessment process.

Interviewer/Interviewee Characteristics Interviewer/interviewee characteristics include the following:

1. Establishment of sufficient empathy or rapport
2. Ability to listen
3. Persistence
4. Patience to probe
5. Insight to remain objective (Sattler, 1998)
6. Integrity
7. Humor when appropriate
8. Thinking toward the future (Polloway, Patton, & Serna, 2005)

A quality interview requires the interviewer to separate one's internal view of reference in order to comprehend and appreciate the world from the interviewee's point of view (Turnbull & Turnbull, 1997).

The Conditions of the Interview The conditions surrounding the actual interview impact the results obtained. Selecting an appropriate and convenient time of day, avoiding distractions during the interview, arranging the furniture in a comfortable setting, and providing for eye-to-eye contact between the interviewer and interviewee positively impact the climate of the interview (Sattler, 1998). Even the interviewer's physical appearance and body language impact the quality of the interview. Issues such as facial expressions, choice of clothing, and volume, pitch, and rate of speech will influence the interview in some manner (Sattler).

Turnbull and Turnbull (1997) explain that both eye contact and physical closeness affect the interview process. The interviewer must be aware of differences in cultural expectations, such as amount of eye contact in a conversation due to differences in cultural norms. For example, White, middle-class people avert their gaze from the listener 50% of the time when talking but establish eye contact approximately 80% of the time while listening; African Americans make greater eye contact when speaking and less when listening.

Personal contact perimeters also differ according to cultural norms. The ideal interview distance for Whites would be 1.5 to 4 feet; Hispanic, African American, and several other cultures favor a closer distance (Turnbull & Turnbull, 1997). American Eskimos sit side by side when discussing personal information; in typical U.S. culture, the parties sit face to face at or around a table or across a desk. The interviewer must be aware of these cultural differences and respond appropriately.

The Message Component The message component of the interview consists of the principles of excellent communication. Bos and Vaughn (2002) describe these principles as mutual respect and trust, acceptance of the interviewee's message, effective listening, plain language, appropriate questioning, positive encouragement, focus, and collaboration. Figure 6.6 presents active listening skills.

Figure 6.6   Active Listening Skills to Use During Interviews

1. Focus on what the interviewee is saying.
2. Be ready when the interviewee speaks.
3. Communicate your interest to the speaker by your posture and expressions.
4. Avoid interruptions.
5. Put your personal feelings aside.
6. Remain objective and control your emotions.
7. Restate the response back to the speaker.
8. Respect the interviewee's cultural background.
9. Watch for nonverbal communication changes.
10. Determine if more questioning is needed to obtain specific information.

Barriers to effective oral communication in an interview situation include the following (Pugach & Johnson, 1995):

1. Giving advice
2. Providing false reassurances
3. Asking questions that are unrelated to the topic or do not provide specific information
4. Allowing the subject to wander during the interview
5. Permitting disruptions or interruptions in the conversation
6. Offering clichés during the interview

Minimizing the feelings of the interviewee severely impacts feelings of trust and respect (Bos & Vaughn, 2002). In addition, jumping to conclusions without listening to the message of the interviewee leads to inaccurate or incomplete information.

Practical Issues for Interviews   Practical issues impacting the quality of the interview include child care, transportation, time constraints, and inflexibility of the interviewer (Bauer & Shea, 2003). As with all personal interactions, cultural norms and differences, feeling unappreciated, language barriers, and issues with authority inhibit quality communication (Bauer & Shea).

Methods Used in Questionnaires

The questionnaire often utilizes quantitative data collection. Standardized questionnaires produce useable information for the IEP team, provided they match assessment goals. Questionnaires that employ **numerical counts, tallies of behaviors**, or rating scales of actions provide more objective information (Smith, Polloway, Patton, & Dowdy, 2000). A quantitative questionnaire utilizing rating scales or frequency counts provides efficient and effective data (Bechhofer & Paterson, 2000).

The questionnaire format aids the teacher in answering questions concerning how much or how often a student engages in a particular behavior. Percentages or tallies presented in table or graph formats facilitate the use of the data in the classroom (Thomas, 1999). Quantitative data collection through questionnaires reduces the **socially desirable responses** often obtained in face-to-face interviews (Bechhofer & Paterson, 2000). By using a combination of questionnaires and interviews, a teacher acquires a clearer picture containing both facts and opinions about the student's progress.

Constructing Questionnaires

The interpersonal characteristics of the questionnaire depend upon well-constructed questions targeting specific behaviors in a nonthreatening manner. Several key issues must be addressed when using questionnaires:

1. Questionnaires used on a periodic basis serve to establish a positive working relationship between the school and home and allow opportunities for the parent to become engaged in the student's education (Bauer & Shea, 2003).
2. Questionnaires require both written and oral directions for completion.
3. The teacher must ensure that the questionnaire appears in the respondent's native language.
4. If the respondent requests help, the teacher may sit with the person during completion of the questionnaire to offer assistance, aid in comprehension, or answer general questions. The teacher must refrain from influencing the respondent's answers.
5. Some respondents want to complete the questionnaire at home but may appreciate the opportunity to ask questions and receive assurance before they return the questionnaire.

Other steps for creating a questionnaire include these:

1. Ask specific questions that tap into the respondent's feelings and attitudes about school-related issues that provide data for more accurate interpretation (Stiggins, 2001).
2. Respect the confidentiality of the questionnaire results.
3. Make envelopes and stamps available, if necessary, for participants to return the questionnaires. (Remember, this information must be treated as confidential.)
4. Give the respondent a due date for returning a written questionnaire.
5. Determine the person responsible for collecting questionnaires from teachers or parents. This person usually compiles the information from questionnaires for the next team meeting.

The Climate of the Questionnaire   The question format establishes the climate of the questionnaire. Selecting an appropriate response format enables the respondent to produce quick, accurate information in a timely manner. Bauer and Shea (2003) list five types of questions typically found on a questionnaire:

1. Open-ended
2. Multiple choice

3. True–false
4. Response form
5. Fill-in-the-blank

Open-ended questions allow the respondent to share their opinions and express any concerns or ideas. In addition, this type of question encourages the respondent to take time to answer the questions and reflect thoughtfully on each one. Multiple-choice formats reduce the amount of writing required for each response and help to narrow the respondent's focus into a distinct area. True–false questions require less time to answer and encourage the respondent to objectively consider each statement to isolate explicit areas of progress. In a response form, the respondent marks an appropriate icon or picture that indicate his or her perception of student functioning. Fill-in-the-blank formats guide the respondent to answer particular indicators conveniently and efficiently. A space should be supplied for the respondent to give additional comments if the question elicits a new idea or some related information.

Stiggins (2001) describes some other possible question formats for questionnaires, including those that do the following:

1. Indicate agreement or disagreement with specific statements
2. Identify how the respondent values the particular skill
3. Reveal the respondent's interest in a subject area
4. Pinpoint the frequency of a particular behavior

The Message Component   The message component of the questionnaire revolves around both the quality of the directions and the clarity of the questions (Thomas, 1999). Directions must include clear and concise explanations of the methods for responding, as well as the behaviors being evaluated. Questions should reflect the specific behaviors and types of responses needed for the assessment. Figure 6.7 displays a description of suggestions for writing clear directions.

Figure 6.7   Writing Clear Directions for Questionnaires

1. Let the respondent know the format for responses (e.g., circle, write a sentence).
2. Give plenty of explicit and simply written directions.
3. Arrange the directions and questions in an easy-to-follow format.
4. To ensure clarity, ask someone to proof the directions before administering the questionnaire.
5. Proof the directions again for spelling or typographical errors.
6. Provide the directions on each page of the questionnaire.
7. Discuss the directions with the respondent and ask for questions.
8. Supply an example response to help guide the respondent.

The formatting of the questions establishes a positive message in the questionnaire process. The creator of the question must generate a sufficient number of questions related to the specific assessment goals established prior to the development of the questionnaire (Chatterji, 2003). Next, care must be taken to phrase the questions to produce pertinent facts about the assessment goals (Stiggins, 2001). Quality questionnaires present easy-to-understand questions and avoid questions answered in one or two words, particularly with yes or no responses. Questions requiring affirmative responses should be coupled with a request for further information. Plenty of space should always be provided for answers. To gather specific information, precise wording will enhance the instrument's ability to focus on particular aspects of the assessment.

The Technical Aspects   Attention to a few technical aspects of questionnaire development helps to create a stronger assessment device:

- Arrange the complete question on one page, avoiding splitting questions and responses.
- Make the questions readable while avoiding difficult, technical vocabulary or jargon.
- Format items to contain only one idea.
- Avoid overlapping choices in response formats, such as multiple choice.
- Eliminate the word "and" to avoid combining two thoughts in one question.
- Break lengthy questions into shorter segments to aid readability.
- Single space within the item but provide for double spacing between items.

QUESTIONNAIRES, INTERVIEWS, AND TECHNOLOGY

Technology provides many time-saving advantages when using questionnaires and interviews. It makes the process accessible and less laborious for some; however, the teacher must ascertain the ability of the respondent to successfully use technology. If **computer literacy** appears inadequate, technology becomes a barrier. Consider the following suggestions when using technology in interviews and questionnaires.

- Place repeated questionnaires (i.e., those done once a month) online for accessibility.
- Identify a computer in the school library and train library workers to assist parents in using the computer to complete the questionnaire.
- Tape record interviews with parents (obtain permission first) to avoid having to write during the interview.
- Archive interviews and questionnaire data for use as a measure of change.
- Video tape interviews (obtain permission first) and create a story about the student's progress over the year for the IEP committee.

SUMMARY

- Questionnaires and interviews provide in-depth information about a student's performance and attitudes through data collection from students, family members, and those who work with them.
- Cultural and linguistic issues reflected in interview and questionnaire questions help to obtain valuable information about a student.
- Questionnaires and interviews are used to obtain important information from a variety of people to add to assessment data.
- Questionnaires and interviews utilize both qualitative and quantitative data collection methods to formulate results.
- Using charts, graphs, written text, and other summary methods allows the IEP team to peruse the data efficiently and effectively for annual goal or programmatic decision making.
- The IEP team selects the most appropriate method for the appraisal by determining the specific assessment questions and considering how the data impact future decisions.
- Technology aids in the organization and collection of data to increase access for all members of the IEP team during the assessment process.

COMPREHENSION CHECK

1. List the advantages and concerns about using questionnaires and interviews.
2. How do data from questionnaires and interviews help to monitor changes in student progress?
3. When is written communication, such as a questionnaire, more effective than an interview? When is an interview more effective?

ACTIVITIES

1. This chapter contains many examples of ways to use a questionnaire or interview. Describe a plan for using technology to improve these techniques.
2. Create a questionnaire to investigate a particular student achievement issue.
3. Role-play an interview with a teacher and one with a family member to explore a social skills issue.

REFERENCES

Baca, L. M., & Cervantes, H. T. (2004). *The bilingual special education interface* (4th ed.). Upper Saddle River, NJ: Merrill/Prentice Hall.

Bauer, A. M., & Shea, T. M. (2003). *Parents and schools: Creating a successful partnership for students with special needs.* Upper Saddle River, NJ: Merrill/Prentice Hall.

Bechhofer, F., & Paterson, L. (2000). *Principles of research design in social sciences.* New York: Routledge.

Bos, C. S., & Vaughn, S. (2002). *Strategies for teaching students with learning and behavior problems* (5th ed.). Boston: Allyn & Bacon.

Chatterji, M. (2003). *Designing and using tools for education assessment.* Boston: Allyn & Bacon.

Denzin, N. K., & Lincoln, Y. S. (Eds.). (2000). *Handbook of qualitative research* (2nd ed.). Thousand Oaks, CA: Sage Publications.

Garcia, E. (1994). *Understanding and meeting the challenge of student cultural diversity.* Boston: Houghton Mifflin.

McLoughlin, J. A., & Lewis, R. B. (2001). *Assessing students with special needs* (5th ed.). Upper Saddle River, NJ: Merrill/Prentice Hall.

Mercer, C. D., & Mercer, A. R. (1998). *Teaching students with learning problems* (5th ed.). Upper Saddle River, NJ: Merrill/Prentice Hall.

Polloway, E. A., Patton, J. R., & Serna, L. (2005). *Strategies for teaching learners with special needs* (8th ed.). Upper Saddle River, NJ: Merrill/Prentice Hall.

Pugach, M. C., & Johnson, L. J. (1995). *Collaborative practitioners, collaborative schools.* Denver, CO: Love Publishing Company.

Sattler, J. M. (1998). *Clinical and forensic interviewing of children and families: Guidelines for the mental health, education, pediatric, and child maltreatment fields.* San Diego, CA: Jerome M. Sattler, Publisher, Inc.

Sattler, J. M. (2001). *Assessment of children: Cognitive applications* (4th ed.). San Diego, CA: Jerome M. Sattler, Publisher, Inc.

Smith, T. E. C., Polloway, E. A., Patton, J. R., & Dowdy, C. A. (2000). *Teaching students with special needs in inclusive settings.* Boston: Allyn & Bacon.

Spinelli, C. G. (2006). *Classroom assessment for students with special needs in inclusive settings* (2nd ed.). Upper Saddle River, NJ: Merrill/Prentice Hall.

Stiggins, R. J. (2001). *Student-involved classroom assessment* (3rd ed.). Upper Saddle River, NJ: Merrill/Prentice Hall.

Thomas, S. J. (1999). *Designing surveys that work! A step-by-step guide.* Thousand Oaks, CA: Sage Publications.

Turnbull, A. P., & Turnbull, H. R. III. (1997). *Families, professionals, and exceptionality: A special partnership.* Upper Saddle River, NJ: Merrill/Prentice Hall.

Westling, D. L., & Fox, L. (2000). *Teaching students with severe disabilities* (2nd ed.). Upper Saddle River, NJ: Merrill/Prentice Hall.

CHECKLISTS AND RATING SCALES

7

Chapter Focus

This chapter focuses on the use of checklists and rating scales to document student progress. These instruments utilize predetermined standards to rate or document the behavior being assessed. Two types of checklists and rating scales form the tools for this method: standardized or published instruments and nonstandardized devices formulated to evaluate specific aspects of a student's classroom performance. While checklists and rating scales prove helpful for all students, they provide detailed evidence of levels of mastery and generalization for individuals engaged in life skills programming. The use of checklists and rating scales to gather data from a variety of sources in numerous settings provides the IEP team with quality information regarding progress on IEP goals.

LEARNER OBJECTIVES

- Define the role and uses of checklists and rating scales in the authentic assessment process.
- Identify the advantages and disadvantages of using checklists and rating scales in the IEP process.
- Explain ways in which checklists and rating scales reflect culturally and linguistically diverse approaches to assessment.
- Determine the appropriate uses of checklists and rating scales in the assessment process.
- Describe the types of standardized and nonstandardized checklists and rating scales.
- Explain how to create summary sheets to inform the IEP team about results from checklists and rating scales.
- Illustrate the role that checklists and rating scales play in the decision-making process of the IEP.
- State the ways in which technology aids in the process of checklists and rating scales.

WHAT ARE CHECKLISTS AND RATING SCALES?

Checklists and rating scales provide contextual measures of behaviors using an **informant** to provide details about performance not obtained during a direct observation (McLoughlin & Lewis, 2001). They supply a tool for evaluating a student's abilities according to a set of predetermined standards. Checklists contain a sequencing of skills or steps to monitor student growth (Overton, 2006). Rating scales provide a **standardized** method to quantify behavior, feelings, and dispositions (Salvia & Ysseldyke, 2004). Developed by teachers to specifically reflect behaviors or performance in the classroom, they also supply useful information to the teacher and IEP team. Checklists and rating scales represent an inexpensive, efficient, qualitative, and global-in-nature technique for obtaining information about a student's progress (Bondurant-Utz, 2002). They are of two types: standardized and **nonstandardized** (McLean, Wolery, & Bailey, 2004).

Standardized checklists and rating scales examine specific **domains** and include a scoring mechanism to determine at-risk students. Nonstandardized checklists and rating scales also include items grouped into domains and attempt to obtain information from informants concerning how the item impacts them, rather than to identify potential areas of concern. Teacher-made checklists and rating scales constitute another type of nonstandardized technique for acquiring information from a third party, such as the teaching assistant or teacher, rather than through direct observation. They lack established validity but reveal the existing behaviors in the classroom setting (Gallagher, 1998).

BENEFITS OF USING CHECKLISTS AND RATING SCALES

Checklists and rating scales share some advantages over other assessment techniques. First, as compared to many other direct observation measures, ease of use characterizes checklists and rating scales. Second, checklists and rating scales are quick to administer. Third, they provide an easy-to-score method of assessment. A lesser amount of training for raters to become proficient is another benefit. In addition, some published checklists and rating scales provide normative scores to allow the student's performance to be compared to his or her age or grade group.

McLean, Wolery, and Bailey (2004) report that the predictive validity of some rating scales provides a better look at later behavior than other types of observations do and that the results remain more stable over time. Also, published rating scales supply the IEP team with a global look at a student's skills, particularly in the behavioral or social realm, that can be used to screen or measure a student's progress in an area. Checklists and rating scales prove especially useful when used in combination with other types of assessment data (Cohen & Spenciner, 2003). They work equally well with an individual or a group of students.

Bondurant-Utz (2002) reports that while checklists and rating scales appear highly subjective in nature, they add to the depth of information available about a student if ratings occur at regular intervals. Also, obtaining data from several different sources and in a variety of settings increases the reliability of this method. Checklists and rating scales capture the **breadth and depth** of student achievement over time (Prestidge & Williams-Glaser, 2000) by achieving the following:

- Comparing a student's current functioning with desired behaviors
- Fostering progress on IEP goals
- Providing a readable format for easily completing the form
- Encouraging student participation by including the student in the rating process
- Defining areas of needed improvement with specific data
- Supplying information on a frequent basis, sometimes daily
- Supporting the parental role in collecting information about student progress
- Supplying an avenue for collaboration between parents and teachers
- Offering a convenient method for documenting improvement over time
- Focusing student and teacher on current goals

DISADVANTAGES OF USING CHECKLISTS AND RATING SCALES

Several disadvantages are inherent when using checklists and rating scales. First, the technical adequacy of these devices has been questioned for a number of reasons, including interrater reliability (Taylor, 2003), which refers to the consistency of ratings between two individuals scoring the same student at the same time. Second, checklists and rating scales provide inadequate information if they do not contain clear and specific descriptions of the behavior to evaluate or the scale used to rate the behavior (Bondurant-Utz, 2002).

Third, commercially available checklists and rating scales often lack detail to make them useful for planning, so teachers must create their own versions to obtain the necessary information. In addition, use of many of them requires specific graduate education in administration and interpretation. Fourth, Sattler (2001) reports subjectivity of the observer as a typical problem with checklists and rating scales. For example, when both a parent and teacher rate a student with widely varying results on the student's behavioral responses, both parties' subjectivity comes into question.

For another example, in a study examining the differences in ratings between mothers and fathers of 12-year old twins, results indicated that the parents' ratings differed—but not due to a problem with the rating scale. The disparities in the ratings resulted from the parents' assessment of different perspectives concerning the student's behavior rather than a measurement error within the actual rating scale (Bartels, Hudziak, Boomsma, Rietveld, Van Beijsterveldt, & Van Den Oord, 2003). Gathering further assessment data using a variety of other techniques to support the findings circumvents this problem.

Logical errors describe a fifth disadvantage of checklists and rating scales. These errors arise when the rater makes a connection between behaviors and scores the student based on that belief (Nitko, 2004). An example of logical error occurs when a teacher rates a student low on all items because of the student's identification as a special education student without basing the ratings on the student's actual performance. A sixth disadvantage occurs when the evaluator ignores additional information not listed on the checklist or rating scale, thereby overlooking critical data (Cohen & Spenciner, 2003).

Error arises when the examiner does any of the following:

- Bases ratings on what is expected rather than what is observed
- Subjects students to inappropriate checklists and rating scales
- Uses difficult directions or vocabulary
- Creates an instrument requiring extensive time to complete
- Selects unobservable behaviors
- Requires judgments based on attitudinal or perceived information
- Chooses situations unavailable to the rater
- Bases placement decisions on positive or negative opinions rather than on factual ratings
- Utilizes a rating scale with too few or too many choices
- Employs a rating scale without specific descriptors for the ratings
- Treats the data obtained from checklists or rating scales in isolation
- Disregards other informants' results
- Disallows for emerging skills by rating incomplete mastery as "never"
- Leaves off an indicator of "no opportunity to observe" from the rating scale

Additional types of errors can occur in the administration of checklists and rating scales:

- **Observer bias** takes place when the rater wishes either consciously or subconsciously to rate the student favorably (Gallagher, 1998).
- The **halo effect** happens when the rater's feelings about the student influence responses on checklists or rating scales.
- The **generosity error** arises when the rater lacks specific information about the student's skill on a particular item but marks that item more favorably than another item.
- The **leniency error** transpires when the rater scores everyone on the high end of the rating scale.
- The **severity error** occurs when everyone falls on the low end of the rating scale. Teachers with only generalized knowledge about hearing impairments, for example, may misperceive students' behaviors and evaluate them more severely than those with specific training on the impact of hearing impairments on social skill development (Cartledge, Cochran, & Paul, 1996).
- The **central tendency error** happens when the rater uses only the middle portion of the scale (average range) due to a lack of knowledge about the student or a desire to avoid making extreme judgments.
- Personal bias takes place when criteria such as race, gender, disability, or socioeconomic status factor into the rater's scoring of a student's abilities (Nitko, 2004).

In their study of student/teacher ratings in science education general education settings, Carlisle and Chang (1996) suggest that teachers tend to have a negative view of the abilities of students with learning disabilities. The study findings remain unclear as to whether this view results from realistic or excessively negative judgments or from actual data known by the teachers in the study pool.

In a study of the relationship between self-ratings of students with sensory impairments and the ratings of their vocational teachers, results indicated that the lack of consistency between the sets of ratings might be due to personal bias (Loeding & Greenan, 1999). The vocational teachers rated the students without specific knowledge of the students' mathematics, communication, interpersonal, or reasoning skills and appeared to base their ratings on scores on standardized tests and their awareness of the students' disabilities.

Nikto (2004) identifies two disadvantages of checklists and rating scales that occur when a person unfamiliar with the student and classroom creates the ratings. First, **rater drift** occurs when raters begin to apply different standards to the original items while forgetting initial instructional experiences. Second, reliability decay occurs as time passes from the original training and raters begin to mark items differently and with less consistency. In both cases, retraining of raters and monitoring of their ratings for consistency provide better results.

CULTURAL AND LINGUISTIC DIVERSITY CONSIDERATIONS

Issues of cultural and linguistic diversity also impact checklists and rating scales. McLean, Wolery, and Bailey (2004) caution that information gathered through checklists and ratings scales may not match the family's vision for their child and, therefore, the IEP team must use the findings with caution. Specific judgments about programming and instruction require family input and deliberation about the impact of such decisions on the family's desires.

The inherent role of bias in checklists and rating scales must also be considered by IEP teams when evaluating the results of these devices. The appropriateness of items with regard to culture influences the findings, as do the responses of the rater. In fact, all the informant errors previously mentioned as disadvantages must be considered by the committee. The results of checklists and rating scales always must accept and reflect differences due to cultural and linguistic abilities.

For example, Wilder and Sudweeks (2003) studied the reliability estimates of the *Behavior Assessment System for Children-2* (BASC-2) (Reynolds & Kamphaus, 2004) to determine whether consumers (specifically graduate students using the BASC-2 for dissertation research) indicated awareness of and reported these estimates with respect to various subpopulations of students from different cultures in their studies. The authors point out that the reliability estimates provided by the BASC-2 fail to include culturally and linguistically diverse students in the normative sample. If other reliability estimates, including culturally and linguistically diverse students, fail to be developed, then the researcher ignores the possibility that scores might be different for students from subpopulations not included in the original sample.

The use of commercially published checklists and rating scales with normative samples that exclude or do not report scores for students in culturally or linguistically diverse subpopulations remains problematic. First, a specific level of training prior to administration and interpretation remains critical and the examiner must be specifically trained to administer and interpret this type of checklist. Second, prior to using data gathered from any standardized checklist or rating scale, the IEP team must consider as a serious disadvantage the lack of normative data that include culturally and linguistically diverse students.

Third, the linguistic abilities of the rater have an effect on the ratings by an individual. If the language on the checklist or rating scale proves too difficult to understand, the impact affects the ratings. Unfortunately, reading the checklist or rating scale to the individual or marking the results through a third party sometimes results in manipulation through observer bias. IEP teams must make every effort to create an atmosphere and opportunity for every rater to provide information free from cultural and linguistic issues.

DECIDING TO IMPLEMENT CHECKLISTS AND RATING SCALES

Checklists and rating scales provide valuable information to the IEP team to produce a snapshot of a student's abilities on selected outcomes or to investigate the process of learning in the student (Gallagher, 1998). These tools provide documentation of progress in academic, developmental, and functional skills, as stated in IDEIA 2004. In addition, they prove extremely valuable for evaluating the small but incremental progress characteristic of students in life skills programs.

Checklists and rating scales also contribute information valuable for making individualized educational decisions (Pemberton, 2003). Nitko (2004) reports that checklists allow the team to understand whether the student accurately completes all the subtasks required to master a skill. These tools also indicate whether the student accomplishes the subtasks in the required order, and rating scales provide for judgments about the quality of the student's performance.

The IEP team decides to use checklists or rating scales to obtain information about a specific area of student functioning from a variety of individuals. For example, a checklist of student progress in the area of eating provides a detailed assessment of a student's ability to complete the many tasks needed to use a cup successfully. In addition, the checklist allows the teacher and IEP team to determine both where mastery occurred and the steps needed to facilitate generalization. The simplicity of checklists and rating scales, the limited training needed, the quick administration time, and the ability to compare the results across individual perceptions permits the IEP team to gain a variety of perspectives with little effort. Checklists and rating scales present the IEP team with another source of data to support the findings gathered from other assessment information.

Checklists and rating scales afford the team with general screening measures opportunity to indicate the student's ability and direction for further diagnostic study (Venn, 2004). Furthermore, checklists and rating scales supply records of the student's functioning at a specific time or can be the culmination of the rater's impressions over a longer period (McLean, Wolery, & Bailey, 2004). Checklists and ratings apply both to specific student behaviors and the products the student produces (Cohen & Spenciner, 2003).

The flexibility of the checklist or rating scale encourages the IEP team to use either tool for a variety of assessment needs. In addition, checklists and rating scales present the IEP team with the opportunity to look across responses from individuals acquainted with the student and determine if the team is missing a valuable perspective concerning the student's progress and functioning (Bondurant-Utz, 2002).

TYPES OF CHECKLISTS AND RATING SCALES

A variety of types of checklists and rating scales provide data about student progress. The IEP team selects the checklist or rating scale that most appropriately fits the required data. Often the team chooses a commercial checklist or rating scale as an early indicator of student performance but may determine the need for more specialized and individualized devices to be developed in the classroom.

Standardized Checklists and Rating Scales

Standardized checklists and rating scales provide generalized screening measures to indicate an overall look at the student's functioning rather than a specific diagnosis (Venn, 2004). Standardized checklists and rating scales often evaluate problem behaviors in the classroom and home, identify social skills issues, or supply a screening method for attention deficit disorder or autism (Taylor, 2003). Many of these instruments require advanced graduate preparation in administration and interpretation. IEP teams must be aware of these constraints and ensure that the individuals responsible for the evaluation demonstrate proper credentials.

Nonstandardized Checklists

Checklists allow the informant to indicate the presence or absence of particular behaviors that appear on a predetermined standards or curriculum-imbedded list, thus providing a record of the student's skills based on the informant's perceptions (Cohen & Spenciner, 2003). They include specific, easily observable activities organized in a logical manner (Nelson & Nelson, 2001). Checklists also use verbs for **observable behaviors**. Well-defined, clearly written curricular standards comprise the most desirable checklists (King-Sears, 2001). Figure 7.1 presents a sample nonstandardized checklist.

Nitko (2004) identifies the following four types of checklists:

1. A *procedure checklist* examines the student's ability to complete a task entirely by noting the specific skills successfully completed.
2. A *product checklist* assesses the student's ability to complete something by looking at a list of critical, final components and evaluating the completion of these components.

Figure 7.1   An Example of a Nonstandardized Checklist for Carrie Writing a Paragraph

Items	Scoring		
	Yes	No	Comments
Begins with a topic sentence			
Includes five details related to topic			
Indents the topic sentence			
Capitalizes each sentence			
Uses appropriate punctuation			
Selects a variety of descriptive words			

   3. A *behavior checklist* consists of a list of actions necessary for adequate per-
      formance that supply the evaluation criteria for determining the student's
      performance.
   4. A *self-evaluation checklist* presents an inventory of skills that a student uses to
      rate the success of a particular assignment or project.

Procedure Checklist   The procedure checklist permits the rater to document
whether the student completes all steps in the correct sequence to successfully accomplish a task. Procedure checklists include the required steps and additional elements
that might be impeding the student's progress. Figure 7.2 presents an example of a procedure checklist.

Product Checklist   The product checklist evaluates the characteristics of a student's
work in terms of quality. These products include but are not limited to papers, projects,
models, drawings, and any other results from the classroom. The informant evaluates
the product using a predetermined set of criteria and indicates their presence or absence. Students use product checklists to self-evaluate projects. Figure 7.3 presents a
product checklist.

Behavior Checklist   A behavior checklist consists of behaviors often grouped to
provide a picture of a student's functioning in a particular setting and provides the IEP
team with another method for obtaining information. Although many commercial behavior checklists exist, an IEP team or teacher can also construct a behavior checklist
to focus on a particular behavior rather than obtaining a more general impression
(Taylor, 2003). Behavior checklists produce information about behavioral functioning

Figure 7.2   An Example of a Procedure Checklist

Observing Jenny's Subtraction Skills for Two-Digit Problems			
	Number correct	Number Incorrect	Comments
Copies problem from book			
Maintains numbers in the correct column			
Begins with the right-hand column			
Determines the need for regrouping			
Writes regrouping procedure			
Regroups correctly			
Subtracts first column correctly			

Figure 7.3   An Example of a Product Checklist

A Checklist of Skills for Oral Reporting				
	Mastered	Not Mastered	Needs Improvement	Comments
Stands still				
Makes eye contact				
Describes the topic				
Provides five details				
States two new ideas learned				
Explains how the information was obtained				
Cites favorite part of the report				
Reports for at least 5 minutes				

Figure 7.4 An Example of a Behavior Checklist

	Present	Absent	Comments
Sits in chair			
Feet on floor			
Looks at teacher			
Opens book			
Volunteers to answer			
Answers when prompted			
Answers when called on			
Refrains from talking			
Uses manipulates			
Looks at overhead			
Waits for next step			
Stays on task			

in the setting. When employing a checklist to document the presence or absence of a behavior, the informant simply indicates yes or no responses to items on the list of predetermined behaviors. Often, this type of checklist conveys data useful in diagnostic settings (Tombari & Borich, 1999). However, behavior checklists sometimes fail to supply the most effective method for observations requiring more detailed and student-oriented results. Figure 7.4 presents a sample of a behavior checklist.

Self-Monitoring Checklist A self-monitoring checklist creates an opportunity for students to examine their own progress. In many cases, the self-monitoring checklist engages a student in reflection about personal abilities and the need to focus on particular developmental issues. It also offers a useful method for teaching the student the criteria necessary for success, as well as how to evaluate personal work in relation to the criteria. Self-monitoring checklists also provide a structured opportunity for the student to develop self-evaluation skills.

Self-monitoring checklists support the student to make decisions about which products to include in a portfolio and increases ownership of and responsibility for assignments. Teachers require the student to complete the checklist, which indicates the presence or absence of particular skills. The checklist responses can be converted into a grade with points assigned to the tasks that figure into the student's final grade average (Corcoran, Dershimer, & Tichenor, 2004). Figure 7.5 presents an example of a self-monitoring checklist.

Figure 7.5   An Example of a Self-Monitoring Checklist

	I Did It!	**Whoops, I forgot!**	**Next time I'll . . .**
Put heading on paper			
Used a title			
Skipped a line			
Wrote the words I know			
Wrote the words I don't know			
Checked my favorite word			
Underlined the hardest word			
Wrote one sentence			
Completed checklist			

Nonstandardized Rating Scales

Rating scales afford the informant the opportunity to indicate the degree to which a particular behavior or skill presents itself, rather than simply noting its presence or absence (Gronlund, 2003). Rating scales typically use descriptors, such as "below," "at," or "above" grade level, to allow the rater to mark the student's ability level (McLoughlin & Lewis, 2001) and appear in a variety of formats.

Likert-Type Rating Scales   Most rating scales, however, utilize a **Likert-type scale** in which raters select from a list of descriptors ranging from "never" to "always" or 1 to 5 to pinpoint their perception of the student's proficiency on a particular skill or behavior (Bondurant-Utz, 2002). Such scales reflect the frequency with which a particular behavior occurs (always, sometimes, never), rate the general quality of the performance, use indicators such as "below average," "average," or "above average," or examine the degree of acceptability in the performance (slowly completes, completes on time, completes ahead of time) (Gronlund, 2003). Rating scales that use Likert-type scales require the informant to select a number to describe the student's performance that is tied to a particular descriptor, such as those identified here. Figure 7.6 presents a sample of a Likert-type rating scale.

Numerical, Graphic, and Descriptive Rating Scales   In addition to Likert-type rating scales, three additional types of rating scales include numerical, graphic, and descriptive rating scales (Nitko, 2004).

In numerical rating scales, the examiner independently rates the student's performance on a set of predetermined skills from 0 to 10. The total of these ratings supplies an overall numerical score. When using this type of rating scale, teachers often provide

Figure 7.6   An Example of a Likert-Type Rating Scale

Use the following numbers to tell how you feel about these questions.	Never	Sometimes	Always
1. Math is my best subject.	1	2	3
2. When I work on adding, I feel that it is easy.	1	2	3
3. Addition problems make me excited.	1	2	3
4. Using the adding reminder page makes the problems easy.	1	2	3
5. I would like more help understanding how to add.	1	2	3
6. I like to do lots of adding problems.	1	2	3

specific descriptors for each numerical value to increase the student's understanding of the quality of the project.

Numerical rating scales are the most common type and involve the use of a numerical system to indicate the different levels of achievement on a particular characteristic. The stages of development range from one extreme to another, from a complete inability to perform the task to an excellent ability to perform it. The informant rates the student's performance along this numerical continuum. In addition to the numerical continuum, each number matches a written descriptor to explain what the number means. Figure 7.7 presents an example of a numerical rating scale.

Graphic rating scales use a line graph with verbal indicators spaced on the line to allow the rater to show where the student's performance falls on the line. Graphic rating scales supply a line graph that represents the student's achievement. Instead of numbering the different levels of achievement, the line graph uses points on the scale defined with written descriptors. Graphic rating scales, however, allow the informant to mark

Figure 7.7   An Example of a Numerical Rating Scale

Rating Latisha's Text Reading Comprehension Skills	
Rating	**Skills Demonstrated**
5	Uses what is read to create new thought connections about what was read
4	Analyzes and evaluates the selection to make judgments about what was read
3	Uses what was read to infer the meaning of the text
2	Recalls the major details, sequence of events, and characters in the text
1	States the main idea of the text

anywhere along the line graph to indicate the student's performance. The informant selects the point on the line graph that best represents the student's functioning, therefore allowing for more flexibility in the ratings.

Descriptive rating scales employ the same type of presentation on a line graph but replace the single word descriptors with more detailed explanations. Stanford and Siders (2001) indicate that these detailed explanations convey more complete meaning for the teacher and learner. These semantic descriptions explain desired learning outcomes more thoroughly.

Descriptive graphic rating scales offer more information concerning each level of achievement by replacing the single word descriptors with phrases to represent the points on the scale. These more detailed explanations increase the consistency among raters by improving their understanding of the levels of achievement represented on each scale.

CREATING CHECKLISTS AND RATING SCALES

Checklists and rating scales employ similar developmental steps. Both need an easy-to-read, organized list of criterion to be evaluated. Rating scales go beyond checklists to include a scale used by the informant to evaluate the level of the student's performance.

Turner, Baldwin, Kleinert, and Kearns (2000) studied the process of developing a rating scale to assess writing ability in a secondary setting. Their results indicated that careful planning and discussion of the variables or tasks to be included on the rating scale produced a positive impact on the reliability of the scale and the usefulness of the information it provided.

Munson and Odom (1996) reviewed parent–infant interaction rating scales. They determined the following important characteristics for developing quality checklists and rating scales:

- Readability
- Appropriateness for populations of various cultural, ethnic, religious, and linguistic backgrounds
- Reliability
- Validity, or a way to show that the device measures what it purports to measure

The next section describes specific steps for developing quality checklists and rating scales to enable the reader to create effective and efficient devices.

Producing Checklists

Checklists consist of a list of items or behaviors arranged in a logical order to represent achievement of a goal or objective. Cohen and Spenciner (2003) describe the following guidelines for developing a quality checklist:

- Create easy-to-understand, consistently sequenced items.
- Group items into categories to help the informant more easily assess the presence or absence of the particular behavior.

- Use a specific method for noting each behavior including yes–no responses or checkmarks.
- Utilize positive language for each behavioral descriptor, emphasizing the student's abilities rather than deficiencies.
- Ensure parallel word construction (including word order and subject/verb agreement) to increase readability of the checklist.
- Avoid repeating items on the checklist.
- Enhance continuity by arranging the items on the checklist in the order in which they naturally appear within a behavioral sequence.
- Provide enough items to develop a detailed picture of the student's abilities in a non-judgmental fashion.

Nitko (2004) recommends that IEP teams or teachers complete a detailed analysis of behaviors or goals prior to the development of a checklist. A task analysis often works well for this procedure (Kerr & Nelson, 2002). Once the analysis has been completed, the steps become the elements of the checklist and allow the informant to describe the student's performance in terms of the critical steps needed to complete the particular behavior. By using task analysis as the basis for the checklist, the IEP team ensures the collection of detailed data for decision making, particularly for students learning life skills.

Using Task Analysis   **Task analysis** represents a process for dividing a larger task into its component parts. The parts of the task appear sequentially in the list and form the basis for the checklist or rating scale (Polloway, Patton, & Serna, 2005). The lists of individual steps appear in some commercial material, or teachers create the list based on their knowledge of the components needed for mastery of the larger task. Often a task analysis results from the teacher's experimentation with the steps to determine exactly what must be done to actually complete the activity. The importance of task analysis for examining incremental but minor improvement in student progress cannot be overlooked. Advancement in students working in life skills programs sometimes seems non-existent. Using task analysis checklists, important development is noted and used to determine appropriate goals for future learning. Figure 7.8 presents an example of a task analysis for toothbrushing.

For example, telling someone to make a peanut butter and jelly sandwich while leading them through a detailed task analysis of that activity highlights the need to state each individual step sequentially and with specificity. If the person relies only on the teacher's directions and does not use prior knowledge, the teacher may accidentally lead the student to create, for example, a sandwich with peanut butter on the outside of the bread.

Other Helpful Suggestions   Paraphrased items on the checklist provide an aid to the observer concerning the behavior to be assessed and increase the amount of observation time (Gallagher, 1998). Gallagher also stresses the need for positive wording for the items to be assessed so that a mark in the "yes" column represents positive behaviors. This technique eases interpretation once the checklist has been completed. Clustering items into particular categories also simplifies the task for the observer and

Figure 7.8   An Example of a Task Analysis

A Task Analysis for Sean for Toothbrushing				
	Independently	With Visual Prompts	With Oral Prompts	Not Mastered
Selects his own toothbrush				
Gets the toothpaste				
Puts toothpaste away				
Wets brush				
Squeezes ¼ inch on toothbrush				
Moves to mirror				
Brushes bottom left teeth for 30 seconds with timer				
Brushes bottom right teeth for 30 seconds with timer				
Brushes bottom middle teeth for 30 seconds with timer				
Brushes upper left teeth for 30 seconds with timer				
Brushes upper right teeth for 30 seconds with timer				
Brushes upper middle teeth for 30 seconds with timer				
Does not swallow toothpaste				
Rinses mouth using cup				
Spits in sink				
Rinses and replaces brush in holder				
Dries hands and face with paper towel				
Dries countertop with paper towel				
Throws paper towels away				

assists in the final understanding of the results of the checklist. Comment sections present the occasion for the informant to explain why a particular item was rated as a "no," or negative performance.

Developing Rating Scales

The development of a rating scale involves a two-step process: establish (a) the criteria to be evaluated and (b) a method for rating each criterion during the development of the rating scale (Gronlund, 2003). The rating method usually involves a 4- or 5-point scale with each rating representing a spot on a continuum between two extremes (Gallagher, 1998). Rating scales use both a numerical rating system and a descriptor to clarify the meaning of the numerical ranking.

In some cases, a teacher chooses to produce a rating scale that uses only written descriptors for the ratings to simplify the rating process (Gallagher, 1998). Another method used to increase the dependability of the rating scale involves the use of descriptors to provide more detailed information about the levels on the rating scale (Cohen & Spenciner, 2003). Descriptors using sentences to more fully explain each level supply more information about the intent of the rating and enhance the consistency of the ratings.

The IEP team improves the usefulness of rating scales in the classroom by having several teachers work together to create the scales and review them for viability. Training prior to the administration of the rating scales provides another assurance that everyone understands the rationale for the rating scale.

Nitko (2004) includes the following elements to ensure the quality of rating scales developed by teachers or IEP teams:

- Emphasize the most important components of the IEP goals.
- Ensure that the rating scale is understandable.
- Create rating scales that match the tasks required for overall attainment of the IEP goals.
- Develop rating scales that both target the attainment of particular skills and analyze the student's process in the learning cycle.

SUMMARIZING DATA FROM CHECKLISTS AND RATING SCALES

Checklists and rating scales provide quality information to the IEP team, particularly when combined with other assessment data (Cohen & Spenciner, 2003). Enhancing their usefulness through summary tables provides the IEP team with an efficient and effective method for utilizing the information to make plans for the students. In addition, relating data from checklists and rating scales to other sources of information can augment the IEP team's understanding of trends and issues concerning the student's performance.

The Written Report Method

The written report represents the most common summary format. In the written report, the data collector looks at a single checklist or rating scale or across related checklists or rating scales and determines the presentation of salient features that describe the student's strengths and needs. Copies of the original checklists or rating scales placed after the written summary allow the IEP team to inspect individual entries. Figure 7.9 presents an example of a written report summary.

The Grouping Method

Another method for summarizing the results obtained from checklists and rating scales uses grouping to condense the data. Using the grouping method, the data collector clusters similar skills or behaviors to provide a picture of the student's functioning in the broader category. For example, a checklist that contains items to examine a student's self-help skills might include a section on personal grooming, eating, dressing, and attitudes toward independence.

The grouping method summary analyzes these behaviors to supply the IEP team with an overall synopsis of the student's abilities. Once again, the individual checklists or rating scales allow the IEP team to peruse individual responses. Figure 7.10 presents an example of a summary using the grouping method.

Averages Included in a Written Report

Summarizing numerical rating scales by averaging the responses across categories presents an additional method for analyzing rating scales. Rating scales examining behaviors across a group of behaviors allow the data collector to determine a numeric average for

Figure 7.9   An Example of a Written Report Summary

Summary of checklist results for Denise from 9-15 through 11-20:
- Identifies equation as addition problem 57/60 times
- Adds from right to left 55/60 times
- Points to the starting point 58/60 times
- Regroups to the 10s place 45/60 times
- Writes the regrouped number above the 10s place 45/60 times
- Correctly adds the digits in the 10s place 30/60 times

Denise needs to continue working on the process of regrouping the digits from the 1s to the 10s place.

Figure 7.10 An Example of a Summary Using the Grouping Method

Sylvia's Self-Help Skills Summary				
	Independent	Visual Prompts	Oral Prompts	Not Mastered
Personal Grooming 1. Combs hair 2. Brushes teeth 3. Washes hands				
Eating 1. Uses spoon 2. Uses napkin 3. Chews food				
Dressing 1. Puts on shoes 2. Puts on coat 3. Zips pants				
Independence 1. Puts things in cubby 2. Uses picture schedule 3. Asks for help				

the actions. The IEP team uses these averages to support other assessment information. Once again, copies of the actual rating sheets should be made available to permit for a more thorough study. This method also studies the differences in raters and highlights their perceptions about a student's performance from a variety of perspectives.

The Developmental Summary Method

If the student's IEP goals require documentation of continuous growth over a long time, the data collector selects the developmental summary method to reflect the student's progress over the year or reporting period. The developing skills summary method (Thurman & Widerstrom, 1985) provides the IEP team with a task analysis or a detailed, sequential listing of all the skills needed to complete a particular task, the date the student demonstrates the skill, and the level of proficiency from emergent to mastery across time. The developing skills summary method presents the IEP team with a look across the student's progress on one review form.

Figure 7.11   An Example of a Summary Across Assignments

A Metacognitive Skill Summary for Kenosha

This summary represents Kenosha's development in higher-order thinking metacognitive skills, reflecting her reading checklists and rating scales over this semester.

Task Reflecting Level of Thinking	Average Score
1. Recognizes and recalls information	8/10
2. Summarizes and paraphrases information	8/10
3. Generalizes and connects facts	6/10
4. Identifies problems to be solved	5/10
5. Identifies similar and different parts of a problem	6/10
6. Uses critical thinking to solve a problem	4/10
7. Evaluates or discriminates between ideas	3/10

Summarizing Across Assignments

Another method for summarizing the results of data gleaned from checklists or rating scales looks across student assignments. This method changes the focus from specific skills demonstrated by the student to the attitudes or critical thinking behaviors used by the student across activities in the classroom (Nitko, 2004). For example, in a critical thinking skills summary, the data collector assembles the data from several checklists or rating scales by selecting specific items that reflect the student's progress using critical thinking skills in addition to the development of particular subject-related skills. Figure 7.11 presents an example of a summary from across assignments.

Summarizing Performance on a Set of Tasks

Summarizing a set of performance or procedure checklists in which the informant directly observes the student's progression through a set of required steps to complete a particular task enhances the IEP team's understanding of the rate of student learning, as well as possible obstacles to mastery. A summary page for gathering the results of several performance or procedure checklists begins with a task analysis or detailed listing of the steps to be completed. The informant then notes actions that occur during the sequence that do not aid the student in completing the task. Several columns for the informant to

Figure 7.12   An Example of a Summary on a Set of Tasks

A 6 Week Summary of Handwashing for James				
Task	**Independent**	**Oral Prompts**	**Hand Over Hand**	**Does Not Complete**
Turns on water	✕			
Pumps soap in hand	✕			
Rubs hand and soap together	✕			
Continues for 30 seconds		✕		
Rinses hands until clear			✕	
Picks up paper towel		✕		
Dries hands			✕	
Turns off faucet with towel			✕	
Exits restroom using paper towel				✕
Throws used towel in trash		✕		

indicate the sequence of actions across multiple lessons provide the IEP team with an indication of the student's progress toward mastery. Figure 7.12 presents an example of a summary on a set of tasks.

USING CHECKLIST AND RATING SCALE DATA IN THE INDIVIDUALIZED EDUCATION PROGRAM

Checklists and rating scales provide the IEP team with valuable information to reinforce and further support assessment results obtained using a variety of other instruments. While checklists and rating scales would not be used as a single measure in the decision-making process of the IEP team, they allow the team to verify these findings and more carefully determine appropriate plans for the future. Checklists focus on evaluating specific items to determine a student's competence, while providing a convenient and realistic method for recording those judgments (Gronlund, 2003). This focus provides critical information for students with low-incidence disabilities. Rating scales determine the degree of mastery in particular skill sets and generally indicate the frequency of a particular behavior, the quality of the student's performance with the behavior, or the degree to which the behavior meets acceptable standards.

Including a Variety of Perspectives

The IEP team can employ information from several perspectives. Checklists and rating scales present the team with an opportunity to collect data from multiple individuals and to assess a student's performance from among these varying perspectives. By using multiple perspectives and condensing these individual viewpoints, the IEP team makes decisions based on data to more closely match the student's needs.

Determining Missing Skills

IEP teams apply the results of checklists and rating scales to analyze assessment data and determine the missing segments of skills, the reason for incomplete mastery with the omission of certain steps, or the lack of quality performance on particular skills. Missing skills often impede the progress of students, particularly those with severe disabilities. Determining the unmastered skill allows the IEP team to focus on the specifics to be learned, such as scrubbing of the hands in a hand-washing routine.

In practice, a procedure rating scale is devised to list the steps, in sequence, for a student to complete in order to demonstrate mastery of a particular task. These steps, whether determined by a detailed listing or a more in-depth task analysis, divide the task into its component parts. IEP goals address the missing components and allow the team to focus on the skills necessary to learn the task completely.

Increasing Shared Decision Making

IEP teams consider the usefulness of checklists and rating scales as methods for increasing sharing and decision making by families in the IEP process. Bailey and Blasco (1990) and McClean, Wolery, and Bailey (2004) report that parents rated a variety of checklists and rating scales as highly effective methods for helping them to share information with professionals. They also report that eliciting their input using these written formats added to their sense of inclusion in the decision-making process. Best practice requires multiple perspectives concerning the functioning of the student and emphasizes the need to include the parents' views (Hundert, Morrison, Mahoney, Mundy, & Vernon, 1997).

As IEP teams search for methods that allow them to include families in the educational decision-making process, the use of checklists and rating scales for gathering perceptions, attitudes, and information can provide a vital linkage.

Noting Progress Through Standardized Scales

In addition to checklists and rating scales developed by the teacher or IEP team for specific data collection, the IEP team may choose to include the results of standardized checklists and rating scales as a means of evaluating the student's progress with respect to a standardized sample. Standardized behavior rating scales assess student behavior

What Do Checklists and Rating Scales Contribute to IEP Development?

- They elicit information from various sources regarding target behavior or areas of strength and needs.
- They provide tools to garner information and different perspectives from various stakeholders.
- They rely on input from others in a summary type of technique.
- They provide information from different sources and multiple perspectives.
- They offer opportunities for varied stakeholders to interpret student academic or social behavior.

in the school setting, at home, or in the community. Some of these measures may be used as assessment devices in specialized treatment programs for students in residential treatment centers (Venn, 2004). Often, these devices provide screening and initial evaluation information; however, an IEP team may choose to utilize the data in other manners.

An IEP team might select the Behavior Rating Profile-2 (BRP-2) (Brown & Hammill, 1990) to examine the results of a sociogram in conjunction with other nonstandardized rating scales to determine improvement in a student's social acceptance. The IEP team combines the results of the BRP-2 with other assessment data to establish the need for IEP goals dealing with social skill behaviors for the student.

Establishing the Intensity of the Behavior

While many assessment devices examine the presence or absence of a particular skill or behavior, rating scales supply the IEP team with a method for examining the degree to which a student accomplishes individual components of a task. This examination creates an understanding both of the process the student uses to attain mastery over a task and the extent to which the student generalizes the task. IEP teams often seek information to guide them in determining future plans for a student. Rating scales fill in some of the gaps concerning the level of student achievement.

CHECKLISTS, RATING SCALES, AND TECHNOLOGY

Checklists and rating scales most often utilize a written format in which the informant must read and record responses in writing. However, tape recorders and text-reading software programs facilitate their inclusion in the data collection process of persons experiencing reading difficulties. Web sites such as Alta Vista's Babel Fish (http://www.

babelfish.com) provide translations of English checklists and rating scales into a variety of languages (Male, 2003). Care should be taken to ensure that translated English wording avoids offensive phrases. This can be achieved by having a fluent person read and reword the document before it is given to the family.

Technology for Documentation and Recording

Using the computer to record changes on developmental checklists becomes particularly helpful when maintaining records on a number of students. A document for each student that delineates the specific skills in the task serves as the foundation for the developmental checklist. The informant returns to the checklist often to note changes in achievement and progress toward mastery. Spreadsheets, created in Microsoft Excel, can be used to make developmental checklists.

Improving Checklists or Rating Scales

Simple clip art proves helpful when using rating scales with individuals experiencing difficulty understanding the meaning of written words. For example, a student rejects a rating scale with written descriptors. The same student participates fully in rating a behavior by using clip art pictures to delineate each level on the rating scale. The inclusion of pictorial icons on a rating scale also aids users in conceptualizing a similar dimension of scale. Checklists and rating scales such as these allow the IEP team to see beyond the performance aspects of classroom behavior into the student's perceptions of the environment and then to create better-quality programming.

SUMMARY

- Checklists and rating scales measure student progress against a sequence set of skills or standards.
- Culturally and linguistically sensitive approaches to assessment include teacher-made checklists and rating scales designed for individual differences.
- Different perspectives emerge when using checklists and rating scales to obtain data from a variety of sources.
- The two categories of checklists and rating scales are standardized and nonstandardized.
- Summary sheets allow for the emergence of themes and the opportunity to observe these themes across different raters.
- Checklists and rating scales aid the IEP team in evaluating a student from a variety of perspectives, determining missing skills, and establishing the intensity of specific behaviors.
- Technology provides a means to create checklist and rating scales to accommodate individual response modes.

COMPREHENSION CHECK

1. Discuss ways to include checklists in the classroom. What are the advantages for students, parents, and teachers?
2. How can parents be involved in collecting checklist information? What kind of checklists could parents help to develop for use at home?
3. Examine several formal checklists in a small group setting. List the pros and cons for administering these checklists to all students in a class.

ACTIVITIES

1. Using the requirements of this course, create a checklist to monitor your own assignments and progress.
2. Explore some avenues for using checklists to monitor student growth, student behavior, and teacher compliance with IEP requirements. Make a list of other suggestions for checklists.
3. Create a rating scale to evaluate the quality of the food service on campus. Summarize the results for the class.

REFERENCES

Bailey, D., & Blasco, P. (1990) Parents' perspectives on a written survey of family needs. *Journal of Early Intervention, 14*(3), 196—203.

Bartels, M., Hudziak, J. J., Boomsma, D. I., Rietveld, M. J. H., Van Beijsterveldt, T. C. E. M., & Van Den Oord, E. J. C. G. (2003). A study of parent ratings of internalizing and externalizing problem behavior in 12-year-old twins. *Journal of the American Academy of Child and Adolescent Psychiatry, 42*(11), 1351–1360.

Bondurant-Utz, J. (2002). *Practical guide to assessing infants and preschoolers with special needs*. Upper Saddle River, NJ: Merrill/Prentice Hall.

Brigance, A. H. (1999). *Brigance diagnostic comprehensive inventory of basic skills: Revised*. North Billerica, MA: Curriculum Associates.

Brown, L., & Hammill, D. D. (1990). *Behavior Rating Profile—Second Edition*. Austin, TX: Pro-Ed.

Carlisle, J. F., & Chang, V. (1996). Evaluation of academic capabilities in science by students with and without learning disabilities and their teachers. *Journal of Special Education, 30*(1) pp. 18–34.

Cartledge, G., Cochran, L., & Paul, P. (1996). Social skill self-assessments by adolescents with hearing impairment in residential and public schools. *Remedial and Special Education, 17*, 30–36.

Cohen, L. G., & Spenciner, L. J. (2003). *Assessment of children and youth with special needs.* Boston: Pearson.

Corcoran, C. A., Dershimer, E. L., & Tichenor, M. S. (2004). A teacher's guide to alternative assessment: Taking the first steps. *Clearing House, 77*(5), 213–216.

Gallagher, J. D. (1998). *Classroom assessment for teachers.* Upper Saddle River, NJ: Merrill/Prentice Hall.

Gronlund, N. E. (2003). *Assessment of student achievement* (7th Ed.). Boston: Allyn & Bacon.

Hundert, J., Morrison, L., Mahoney, W., Mundy, F., & Vernon, M. L. (1997). Parent and teacher assessments of the developmental status of children with severe, mild/moderate, or no developmental disabilities. *Topics in Early Childhood Special Education, 17*(4), 419–434.

Kerr, M. M., & Nelson, C. M. (2002). *Strategies for addressing behavior problems in the classroom* (4th ed.). Upper Saddle River, NJ: Merrill/Prentice Hall.

King-Sears, M. E. (2001). Three steps for gaining access to the general education curriculum for learners with disabilities. *Intervention and School Clinic, 37*(2), 67–76.

Loeding, B. L., & Greenan, J. P. (1999). Relationship between self-ratings by sensory impaired students and teachers' ratings of generalizable skills. *Journal of Visual Impairment & Blindness, 93*(11), 716–727.

Male, M. (2003). *Technology for inclusion: Meeting the special need of all students* (4th ed.). Boston: Allyn & Bacon.

McLean, M., Wolery, M., & Bailey, D. B., Jr. (2004). *Assessing infants and preschoolers with special needs* (3rd ed.). Upper Saddle River, NJ: Pearson/Merrill/Prentice Hall.

McLoughlin, J. A., & Lewis, R. B. (2001). *Assessing students with special needs* (5th ed.). Upper Saddle River, NJ: Merrill/Prentice Hall.

Munson, L. J., & Odom, S. L. (1996). Review of rating scales that measure parent-infant interaction. *Topics in Early Childhood Special Education, 16*, 1–25.

Nelson, L. S., & Nelson, A. E. (2001). Assessment tool for measuring progress throughout the year. *Scholastic Early Childhood Today, 16*(1), 18–20.

Nitko, A. J. (2004). *Educational assessment of students* (3rd ed.). Upper Saddle River, NJ: Prentice Hall.

Overton, T. (2006). *Assessing learners with special needs: An applied approach* (5th ed.). Upper Saddle River, NJ: Pearson/Merrill/Prentice Hall.

Pemberton, J. (2003). Communicating academic progress as an integral part of assessment. *Teaching Exceptional Children, 35*(4), 16–20.

Polloway, E. A., Patton, J. R., & Serna, L. (2005). *Strategies for teaching learners with special needs* (7th ed.). Upper Saddle River, NJ: Merrill/Prentice Hall.

Prestidge, L. K., & Williams Glaser, C. H. (2000). Authentic assessment: Employing appropriate tools for evaluating students' work in 21st-century classrooms. *Intervention and School and Clinic, 35*(3), 178–182.

Reynolds, C. R., & Kamphaus, R. W. (2004). *Behavior Assessment System for Children* (2nd ed.). Circle Pines, MN: American Guidance Services.

Salvia, J., & Ysseldyke, J. E. (2004). *Assessment in special and inclusive education* (9th ed.). Boston: Houghton Mifflin.

Sattler, J. M. (2001). *Assessment of children: Cognitive applications* (4th ed.). San Diego, CA: Sattler Publisher, Inc.

Stanford, P., & Siders, J. A. (2001). Authentic assessment for intervention. *Intervention and School Clinic, 36*(3), 163–167.

Taylor, R. L. (2003). *Assessment of exceptional students: Educational and psychological procedures* (6th ed.). Boston: Pearson.

Thurman, S. K., & Widerstrom, A. H. (1985). *Young children with special needs: A developmental ecological approach.* Boston: Allyn & Bacon.

Tombari, M., & Borich, G. (1999). *Authentic assessment in the classroom: Applications and practice.* Upper Saddle River, NJ: Merrill/Prentice Hall.

Turner, M. D., Baldwin, L., Kleinert, H. L., & Kearns, J. F. (2000). The relationship of a statewide alternate assessment for students with severe disabilities to other measures of instructional effectiveness. *The Journal of Special Education, 34*(2), 69–76.

Venn, J. J. (2004). *Assessing students with special needs* (3rd ed.) Upper Saddle River, NJ: Merrill/Prentice Hall.

Vernon, M. L. (1997). Parent and teacher assessments of the developmental status of children with severe, mild/moderate, or no developmental disabilities. *Topics in Early Childhood Special Education, 17*(4), 419–434.

Wilder, L. K., & Sudweeks, R. R. (2003). Reliability of rating scales across studies of the BASC. *Education and Treatment of Children, 26*(4), 382–399.

ENVIRONMENTAL ASSESSMENTS

Chapter Focus

Environmental assessment and intervention primarily focus on the historical and philosophical ideas that promote current inclusionary models of special education (Barnett, Bell, Gilkey, Lentz, Graden, Stone, et al., 1999). Widespread agreement for using student-centered approaches to assessment includes a mounting expectation for environmental assessment to offer significant, critical pieces of assessment-based decision making (Campbell, Campbell, & Brady, 1998). Engaging in environmental assessments shifts the evaluation spotlight from a medical model based on student discrepancies to a contextual perspective using student-centered assessment process (Overton, 2004). Environmental assessment encompasses the functioning of an individual with disability across a variety of settings. Academic need represents only one area of consideration. Evaluation must include home, school, leisure, vocational, and community environments. The central focus of these evaluations highlights the individual's ability to function in multiple environments. The examination of individual need within a myriad of settings shifts the emphasis from what people are (eligibility) to what they need (areas and extent of support) (Hamill & Everington, 2002). Environmental assessments feature the skills required immediately and in future settings. Matching the student's needs with appropriate curriculum within natural environments provides the critical component for success.

LEARNER OBJECTIVES

- Define environmental assessments.
- Describe the benefits and disadvantages of environmental assessments.
- Delineate the ways in which environmental assessments provide for cultural and linguistic differences.
- Explain the reasons for implementing environmental assessments.
- List the types of environmental assessments.
- Depict the steps to creating an environmental assessment.
- Summarize the data obtained from an environmental assessment.
- Illustrate how the IEP team uses environmental assessment data to plan.
- Identify the function of technology in environmental assessment.

WHAT IS AN ENVIRONMENTAL ASSESSMENT?

Environmental assessments examine the student's social and physical characteristics across settings (Bondurant-Utz, 2002). This type of assessment views the student and the environment as interrelated components contributing to the student's daily experiences. It seeks to discern a student's total needs within the learning environment, including home, school, vocational, and social factors (Hamill & Everington, 2002). Often, students with severe needs and/or those who are very young benefit from environmental assessments. However, environmental assessments produce effective results for a variety of students. Using an environmental view provides a richer and more resourceful type of evaluation (McConnell, 2000). Within environmental assessment, both the needs of the student in the environment and the demands placed on the student by the environment require evaluation (Maag, 2004).

Ryndak and Alper (2003) report that environmental assessments encourage family participation in the IEP process in a number of ways. First, family members contribute to the evaluation with valuable insights concerning the interaction between the student and his environments. Second, by including family members, the process informs the IEP team of progress toward positive future outcomes identified by the family. Third, environmental assessments allow the IEP team to view the student in terms of strengths rather than the deficits often identified in more formal evaluations in a variety of settings, including those exclusive to the family. Third, environmental assessments aid in the inclusionary process by identifying issues within the environment at both home and school that impact the student's ability to progress and prepare for adult living.

Environmental assessments include two different techniques: **ecological inventories** and **sociograms**. Ecological inventories seek to address three areas: (a) the student's safety, (b) the quality of the student's current environment, and (c) the need to plan and implement interventions to improve the student's functioning in the environment (Wolery, 2004). Ecological inventories gather information about a student's future environmental needs through consideration of areas of adult functioning. A description of ecological inventories follows.

Ecological Inventories

Ecological inventories determine the content of the curriculum for students who require **intermittent** and **pervasive support** (Ryndak & Alper, 2003). In this case, the ecological inventory becomes a functional or life skills assessment. However, for it to be considered ecological, it must encompass the student's natural environments and his ability to function within those environments. This type of ecological inventory assesses the student's ability to function within the domains of **community-access** and **recreation-leisure skills**. The IEP team chooses to conduct an ecological inventory for a student involved in a life skills curriculum to prepare for the student's transition to adulthood.

The essential principles of ecological inventories include six concepts: (a) **ecosystem**, (b) **natural habitat**, (c) **ecological niche**, (d) **niche breadth**, (e) **goodness of fit**, and (f) **adaptation** (Snell & Brown, 2000). First, the ecosystem represents a major component of the ecological assessment. Described as the interaction between the student and his surroundings, the ecosystem includes the home, school, and community. Second, the natural habitat represents the environment where the student lives, works, and plays. Studying a student within the natural environment provides critical information about daily functioning.

Third, the ecological niche concerns the role a student plays within the environment. For example, a student's role can be one of active participant involved in the classroom activity or silent observer simply seated within the classroom but not engaged in learning. Fourth, niche breadth refers to the variety of parts the student plays within the environment. For instance, a student may be unable to run the base paths in a baseball game. His niche breadth may be increased if a pinch runner runs for him and the student sits at the bases during the inning.

Fifth, goodness of fit involves the quality of the match between the individual and the environment. In other words, an environment suited to the characteristics of the student places him in the most optimal learning situation. Sixth, adaptation represents the ease with which a student adjusts to a new environment.

Sociometric Assessments

In addition to ecological inventories, environmental assessments examine student behavior from a people-related focus. Assessing social competence within the student's naturalistic environment supplies key pieces of information to the IEP team regarding the need for social skill training and effective interventions (Odom, McConnell, McEvoy, Peterson, Ostrosky, Chandler, et al., 1999). The sociogram provides one useful tool in determining social competence. A sociogram studies the dynamics and interactions in the classroom among the student, peers, teachers, and others in various settings (Overton, 2006). The sociogram provides a documented view of the student's social status, social functioning, and peer interaction, as well as teacher preferences. Sociogram questions can be designed for unique situations to identify issues within the social environment. Like ecological inventories, sociograms inform the teacher or IEP team regarding optimal opportunities to improve the student's environment. Miller, Cooke, and Test (2003) conducted a study using sociograms to look at social interactions of students with mild disabilities. Their findings supported the validity of using this type of environmental measure for students with high-incidence disabilities.

BENEFITS OF ENVIRONMENTAL ASSESSMENTS

Environmental assessments include some critical features beneficial to students:

1. Environmental assessments evaluate functional skills necessary throughout the lifespan. These skills form domains including home, community involvement, vocational and job-related performance, and recreational interests.
2. The level of independence and competence often increases by examining environments and making changes and adaptations. Identifying dissonant environments

saves valuable instructional time and allows the IEP team to make good choices based on student-centered information.

3. Environmental assessments increase opportunities for people with disabilities and people without disabilities to interact in natural settings (Ryndak & Alper, 2003).
4. The quality of the environment improves by the information gained from environmental assessments.
5. Environmental assessments aid in determining unsafe conditions within the classroom.
6. Environmental assessments provide key elements in improving the curriculum, intervention goals, and procedures (McLean, Wolery, & Bailey, 2004).
7. These valuable assessments identify staff training needs and document program quality, as well as the types of improvements needed in particular settings (Salvia & Ysseldyke, 2004).

DISADVANTAGES OF ENVIRONMENTAL ASSESSMENTS

Technically, environmental assessment often lacks reliability. Various factors may influence outcomes from assessment to assessment. However, these measures enjoy high validity as they employ direct connection to the student's environment. Some criticize the time needed to conduct a thorough environmental evaluation. The time taken to examine the environment often results in positive outcomes and increased implementation of the results. In addition, ecological assessment must be community referenced to be valid. The accepted activities and conditions for one community will not match those of another. Ensuring that the environmental assessment reflects the cultural norms produces an authentic evaluation tool.

CULTURAL AND LINGUISTIC DIVERSITY CONSIDERATIONS

Environmental assessments provide the opportunity for the teacher to examine both student and classroom responses to cultural and linguistic diversity. Teachers must investigate their role in creating a positive environment conducive for student learning. Families contribute to the overall effectiveness of the school program by voicing their distinct contributions and expectations for student success. In addition, by conducting community-relevant environmental assessments, the IEP team makes certain that the family's preferences in goal planning are emphasized. Finally, the use of Universal Design for Learning improves the school's ability to address the individual needs of all students.

Teacher Behavior

These techniques compel the teacher to inspect the climate of the classroom and determine how it fits the student's needs. Kea, Cartledge, and Bowman (2002) identify five areas to be evaluated to determine the cultural and linguistic status of a particular setting:

1. Environmental style or climate of the classroom
2. Interaction style or method of the teacher and students working together in the classroom
3. Instructional strategies in use
4. Cognitive responsiveness or the fit of specific strategies to particular students
5. Assessment style or method used to determine mastery

Each of these areas reveals the receptiveness of the teacher to allow for cultural and linguistic variances. They expose issues to alter when students experience difficulty.

Spinelli (2006) identifies important questions for teachers to self-assess their cultural and linguistic environmental readiness. In many cases, these questions should become part of the environmental assessment process:

- What verbal and nonverbal messages communicate high expectations for the students?
- Do verbal and nonverbal messages inadvertently communicate low expectations for some students?
- Does the classroom environment mentally invigorate all members?
- Do classroom assessments reflect the varied needs of all students?
- How does the presentation style fit the students' cultural and linguistic communication patterns?
- How do issues such as rate, questioning, and feedback change to meet individual student needs?
- What commitment to research-based practices and effective instructional procedures exists in the classroom?
- What culture has been infused into the classroom?
- Does a strength-based approach permeate the instructional practices in this classroom?

Family Awareness

Environmental assessments also allow for the inclusion of family variances in **acculturation**. These differences impact the student's success in the environment and must be taken into consideration during an environmental assessment. These topics might consist of educational background, religion, geographic location, personality, generational status, or other distinctions (Baca & Cervantes, 2004). Environmental assessments ignoring these issues lead to inaccurate or faulty interpretations and insensitive approaches to home and school partnerships.

Universal Design for Learning

Universal Design for Learning provides an adaptation to the curriculum centered around a proactive approach to learning (Haager & Klinger, 2005). Within the curriculum, universal design reflects the uniqueness of each learner rather than a one-size-fits-all traditional approach to learning. Materials include built-in accommodations for different student levels. Universal design emphasizes student strengths and considers issues of cultural and linguistic diversity as powerful elements in the learning process. Technology plays an important part in universal design and allows for cultural expression. This style of instruction utilizes three distinctive components:

1. Information presented in multiple formats
2. Choices concerning response modes
3. Various ways to participate and increase engagement in learning

Universal design embraces cultural, linguistic, and disability-related differences to enhance the educational environment.

DECIDING TO IMPLEMENT ENVIRONMENTAL ASSESSMENTS

Environmental assessments determine how the student interacts with his surroundings and what needs to be changed for the student to be more successful in the current situation. The IEP team decides to use environmental assessment when (a) information about the safety of the student's current setting needs verification, (b) questions arise about the quality of the student's existing circumstances, or (c) it needs to plan an intervention to help the student use his environment more effectively or efficiently (Wolery, 2004).

Safety Concerns   Safety issues include evaluation of the environment for potentially hazardous conditions that might result in injury or death. In addition, problems such as inadequate lighting, uncomfortable climate, or environmental matters, including black mold, might be of interest to the IEP team. Environmental topics that deal with the student's physical well-being focus on the manner in which the environment aids or suppresses the student's achievement in the classroom. The IEP team might also consider an environmental assessment when evaluating matters such as continuous school absences due to illness or repeated asthma attacks.

Quality of the Surroundings   The second rationale for using an environmental assessment highlights the quality of the surroundings. In a quality-of-the-surroundings environmental assessment, the IEP team looks for evidence regarding the appropriateness of the setting to meet the least restrictive environment mandate. The team also evaluates the student's need for additional individualized attention. In addition, the team uses environmental assessment to identify a particular curricular approach to ensure the most progress for the student.

Appropriateness of IEP Goals   A third rationale for using environmental assessments includes addressing the appropriateness and functionality of IEP goals with respect to the environment and the supports that occur in that setting. Environmental assessments help determine specific intervention practices to equip the student with skills to better maneuver in the current placement.

The IEP team also elects to use environmental assessment to document concerns about the amount of individualized time required with adult interaction that will allow the student to succeed, the supports necessary for quality functioning in the environment, and how the student and adults in the environment function together within the given setting (Wolery, 2004).

Environmental Influences on Behavior   Maag (2004) identifies several problematic actions that are caused by the environment rather than simply by student misbehavior. In these cases, the IEP team may elect to use environmental assessment to determine the causes of the inappropriate behavior prior to planning a specific intervention. The first environmental condition explores the role of conditions within the classroom that contribute to behavioral disruptions. These include a permissive environment, a noisy environment, an environment that is too regimented, or a classroom without specific rules and procedures. The student who reacts to these conditions may be perceived as problematic, but changes to the environment may, in fact, help the student to modify his behavior. A typical checklist used for behavior analysis often includes environmental factors. Looking at all pieces of assessment gives the IEP team information regarding the environment of the student during problematic periods throughout the school day (Larson & Maag, 1998).

A second issue, known as environmental dissonance, occurs when evaluating the needed changes in a student's behavior in response to different demands of an alternate setting. Often, students lack the flexibility to change a behavior or may simply not understand the need to do so. For example, a student allowed to move freely about the room in the special education resource room may have a difficult time adjusting to the more structured, seated setting of the general education classroom. Rather than looking at the differences in the two settings, teachers assume that the lack of compliance in remaining seated represents misbehavior. In fact, through environmental assessments, the teacher may realize the need for specific instruction. By planning an intervention to teach the student more appropriate conduct in the more structured setting, behavior improves and the student's success level rises.

In an environment that places high demands on a student's weak areas, the student may react with disruptive or inappropriate behavior. Maag (2004) stresses that demands for appropriate behaviors should not be waived when working with students with disabilities. Rather, through the use of environmental assessments the IEP team determines how to create an environment with a better fit to minimize disruptive behaviors while teaching the student methods for coping with areas that create problems within the desired environment. A student who has poor silent reading ability may select disruptive behaviors in lieu of reading a social studies assignment in the general education classroom. If this is dealt with as simple misbehavior, the student will not necessarily learn to control the behavior. In this example, the IEP team may elect to add the accommodation of taped texts to aid the student with reading, as well as an intervention that teaches the student to get out the book, turn on the tape, and listen to the selection rather than create a disturbance. Using interventions to circumvent undesirable environmental conditions alleviates the environmental role in the creation of disruptive behaviors brought on by responses to frustration or anxiety.

Situational Analysis   Bigge, Sherwood, Best, and Heller (2001) suggest that situational analysis techniques become useful in environmental assessments when the IEP team needs to assess the role of multiple factors in a student's environmental functioning. Situational analysis looks at the student's responses over a number of settings to discern where, why, and when certain behaviors are occurring. Situational analysis proves especially useful when a student appears successful in one environment but not another, thus impacting the team's selection of the least restrictive environment.

After the IEP team decides to use environmental assessment as a method for collecting information about a student's functioning, it needs to determine the specific environments to be assessed. The team also decides on the techniques to use, including ecological inventories and sociograms. Environmental assessments examine the environments the student currently works in or scrutinizes systems that represent future positive situations for the student. Whether the team analyzes the current location or determines future settings, gathering information through environmental assessments provides a clearer illustration of the necessary interventions.

TYPES OF ENVIRONMENTAL ASSESSMENTS

The environmental assessment process uses two evaluation techniques to gather data. The ecological inventory examines a student's total learning environment to determine how the environment contributes to success. Sociometric assessments provide information concerning the student's functioning in the social environment.

Ecological Inventories

Commercially Available Ecological Inventories   The ecological inventory includes a variety of procedures and can be purchased commercially. One example includes *Choosing Options and Accommodations for Children* (COACH) (Giangreco, Cloninger, & Iverson, 1993), which pinpoints curricular content based on the preferences and desires of the family.

Wolery (2004) identifies many types of commercially available ecological inventories, including these:

*   The HOME scales (*Home Observation for Measurement of the Environment*) (Caldwell & Bradley, 1984) evaluate the supports available within the home setting, as well as the amount of stimulation the student receives.
*   *The School-Age Care Environment Rating Scales* (Harms, Jacobs, & White, 1996) assesses the quality of care before and after school for elementary-age students.

- *Assessment of Practices in Early Elementary Classrooms* (APEEC) (Hemmeter, Maxwell, Alt, & Schuster, 2001) examines classroom quality and adherence to guidelines for developmental appropriate practices.
- *Quality of Inclusive Experiences Measure* (QIEM) (Wolery, Pauca, Brashers, & Grant, 2000) explores the different levels of learning environment using seven subscales, including program goals, accessibility to the physical environment, intervention for individuals, student participation, perception of the teaching staff, and amount of contact between students and adults, as well as peers.

Teacher-Made Ecological Inventories The IEP team decides whether these inventories provide the type of individually relevant and community-referenced data desired. If not, the IEP team develops a student-centered, individualized ecological inventory. Many of the techniques discussed in preceding chapters form the ecological inventory. These methods include narrative descriptions, such as anecdotal records, running records, specimen descriptions and jottings, sampling techniques using time and event recording, checklists, and behavior rating scales. In ecological inventories, the procedures focus on what the person needs in the current situation, they specifically describe the interaction between the student and the environment, and they also isolate factors added or rearranged to improve these interactions (Bondurant-Utz, 2003). Figure 8.1 presents a description of how these approaches are used in ecological inventories.

Figure 8.1   Components of Ecological Inventory Procedures

Anecdotal records	Gather information about reinforcers and interactions between the student and environment while looking at specific events
Running records	Obtain data over the course of time and different settings to reveal details about the student's interaction with the environment
Specimen descriptions	Collect information by way of an outside observer who watches for specific actions while recording entire episodes of behavior, including environmental concerns
Jottings	Accumulate a listing of notes concerning the student's functioning in the learning venue
Sampling techniques (time and event)	Count the number of times or the length of time that a particular behavior occurs within the classroom
Checklists	Acquire information concerning the student's developmental progress and how it impacts functioning in the environment
Rating scales	Organize perceptions of how the student is functioning in the natural environment using a numerical ranking

Sociometric Assessments

Sociometric assessments represent another procedure used in environmental assessments. These methods provide information about the student's social acceptance, social preference, and amiability (Odom, Schertz, Munson, & Brown, 2003).

Sociogram   One type of sociometric assessment, the sociogram, provides a visual representation of how a student functions within the group in the classroom (Overton, 2006). Through the use of a series of short questions, students use nomination or ratings to identify the social acceptance of students in the classroom (Bondurant-Utz, 2002). To perform this type of assessment, the student must be involved within a group. Identifying the desired attributes of the student offers insight into positive and negative factors. These attributes can be inferred through the pattern of nominations or ratings. The results of a sociogram should not be shared with individual students, particularly those recognized as socially isolated by the group. Figure 8.2 presents an example of a sociogram.

The sociogram results help the IEP team to plan for interventions such as creating a circle of friends, which arranges a peer group for an individual student and creates a positive change in the environment. Usually these results are graphed visually to provide a picture of the social connections in the environment. Figure 8.3 presents an example of a visual graph of sociogram results.

Figure 8.2   Sociogram Questions for Rick, a Student

Area for Assessment: Participate in group activities by using coping skills and reducing outbursts

Domain: Social interaction with peers

Environment: General education science class

Skill: Getting along with others in class

Directions: Complete the following questionnaire without talking with others.

1. With whom in our class would you most like to do a science experiment?
    a. _____
    b. _____
2. Who do you think is the easiest to work with in class?
    a. _____
    b. _____
3. Who do you think does the best work in our class?
    a. _____
    b. _____

Figure 8.3 A Sociogram for Rick, a Student

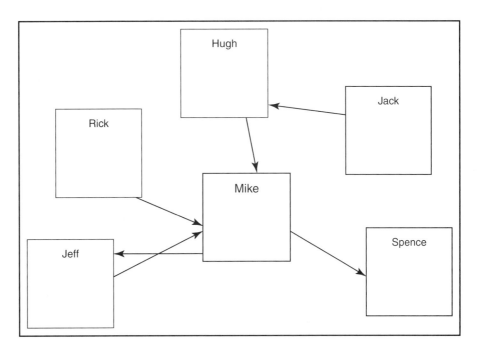

Peer Nominations Peer nominations include asking students simple questions regarding classmates who they consider to be friends or partners in work/play situations. In essence, the questions ask the students to make choices about preferences for group work, play, or friends. By collecting their responses, social and environmental concerns may be addressed. Children not selected as a peer buddy or friend by anyone, known as isolates, need additions and changes in the classroom setting to improve their social situation. Social training provides one avenue to help mediate children's social differences. Again, this information becomes useful for IEP teams to plan interventions and goals.

Peer Ratings Peer ratings represent another type of sociometric assessment pertinent to the natural environment. Examples of this type of assessment usually require students to use a Likert-like scale indicating the extent to which they enjoy interacting with another student. Pictures with varying degrees of happiness sometimes appear in place of the numbers. Typical questions for this type of assessment include "How much do you like to work in a group with _____?" In the early childhood setting, this type of interview/rating involves a process in which children sort photographs of individuals with whom they would most like to work within a group. This type of information helps IEP teams establish environmental changes to aid in creating a positive environment. Peer ratings represent a very sensitive type of assessment, and the results should only be used to help a student by creating changes in the environment and classroom setting,

Figure 8.4   Sociogram Results Presented in a Bar Graph

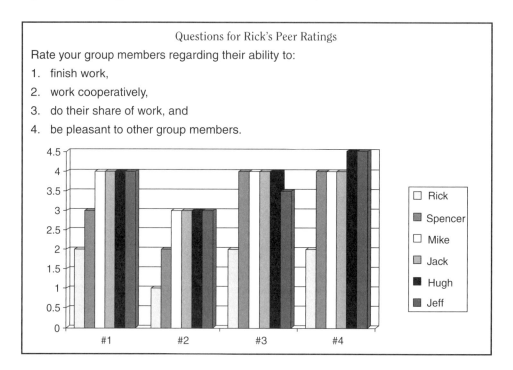

not for student confrontation. Figure 8.4 presents an example of the results of a sociogram in a bar graph.

THE MECHANICS OF ENVIRONMENTAL ASSESSMENTS

The steps necessary for conducting an environmental assessment depend upon the information the IEP team desires to obtain. Identifying the behaviors to be assessed becomes critical. By isolating the behaviors and the effects of the environment on these behaviors, the IEP team builds the best plan for the assessment.

Developing Ecological Inventories

Alper, Ryndak, and Schloss (2001) describe the components of an ecological inventory designed to determine specific curricular content, as follows. First, the team must identify the domain to be explored. The domains include home, community, vocation, community access, and recreation–leisure. Next, the team determines the environments in which the domains appear. For example, self-help dressing skills from the community domain occur in both the classroom and in the restroom. Third, the team ascertains the subenvironments or more specific places where the learning occurs. A subenvironment in the restroom might include the sink area. Then the team identifies specific activities to be undertaken in the subenvironment. This might include brushing one's teeth at the sink. Finally, a **task analysis** developed by the team evaluates the student's strengths and weaknesses.

Discrepancy Analysis   After these initial steps, the teacher conducts a **discrepancy analysis** to determine if the assessment actually measures differences among the student, the developmental functional level expected of them, and typical nondisabled peer functioning (Linehan, Brady, & Hwang, 1991). A discrepancy analysis investigates three questions: (a) What do same-age, typical peers without disabilities in general education classrooms do? (b) What is the student with disabilities able to do in the setting? and (c) What additional skills will be required in order for the student to be successful in the setting? By answering these questions, the teacher puts the student's abilities in perspective and raises the level of expectation for performance.

Identifying Curricular Match   One rationale for developing an ecological inventory revolves around the need to establish a curricular match between what the student needs to learn and how the instruction should proceed. The IEP team gathers information about the particular annual goals and determines how the curriculum needs changing to better serve the student. Figure 8.5 presents an example of an ecological inventory for a curricular match.

Identifying Opportunities for Independence   Another method for developing ecological inventories provides information about how the learner becomes more independent within a particular environment rather than focusing on a particular task (Bigge, Sherwood, Best, & Heller, 2001). In this type of ecological inventory, the team first identifies all the environments in which the learner participates. Second, the team pinpoints subenvironments. Next, the team lists all possible options available for the learner. Then, the team considers and evaluates all methods for enabling the learner to participate in each of these options. Then the team makes decisions about the best ways in which to achieve independence for the student. Figure 8.6 presents an example of an ecological inventory to investigate methods for increasing a student's level of independence.

Teacher Recollections   Teacher recollections form a third method for the IEP team to consider when developing an ecological inventory (Bigge, Sherwood, Best, & Heller, 2001). In this procedure, the teacher or IEP team uses personal knowledge of the skills necessary to complete an outcome and then keeps notes about the student's ability to meet the skills as observed in a variety of environments. For example, eating

Figure 8.5   An Ecological Inventory for a Curricular Match for Rebecca, a Student

Area for Assessment: Use of signs to indicate personal needs at the job site.

Domain: Community

Environment: Work site

Skill: Using signs to indicate the need to go to the bathroom, time for a snack, time for a drink, the desire to listen to music while working within the workshop setting.

1. What does Rebecca do when she needs a drink at work?
2. What does Rebecca do when she needs to go to the bathroom at work?
3. What does Rebecca do when she wants a snack?
4. What does Rebecca do when she wants to listen to music?
5. Does Rebecca use her signs to demonstrate the following needs?

Function			Curricular Change for Rebecca
Drink	Yes	No	Try using an empty water bottle to indicate in a functional way what Rebecca desires. Practice moving from an actual object to the signal for drinking.
Food	Yes	No	Use an empty snack bag of chips or other healthy snack to indicate in a functional way what Rebecca desires. Practice moving from an actual object to the signal for eating.
Bathroom	Yes	No	Use a roll of toilet paper to indicate in a functional way what Rebecca desires. Practice moving from the actual object to the signal for going to the bathroom.
Music	Yes	No	Use a CD to indicate in a functional way what Rebecca desires. Practice moving from the actual object to the signal for listening to music.

in the lunchroom at a table with nondisabled peers might represent an social goal for one student. The teacher knows that the student must be able to sit in his chair, not throw food, talk in a lowered voice, and refrain from touching others inappropriately. The teacher then collects data from a variety of environments that support the student's ability to use these skills or indicate that more instruction will be necessary. Figure 8.7 presents an example of an ecological inventory to examine a student's peer acceptance.

Examining Student Interests   Another procedure for developing ecological inventories revolves around evaluating the student's interests in relation to same-age peers (Bigge, Sherwood, Best, & Heller, 2001). The IEP team may want to gather information about how well the student fits in with others or to teach the student some appropriate

Figure 8.6   An Ecological Inventory to Identify Independence for Rebecca, a Student

---

Area for Assessment: Use of hand signals to indicate personal needs at the job site.

Domain: Community

Environment: Work site

Skill: Using hand signals to indicate the need to go to the bathroom, time for a snack, time for a drink, the desire to listen to music while working within the workshop setting.

After using the calendar system for Rebecca over a semester, the job coach gradually moves Rebecca's calendar box to a small photo album with pictures and then to a more independent system of signs. First, the bathroom signal is learned well. Next, the music signal is added. Food and drink follow incrementally. The following questions are answered through environmental observations and interviews:

1. What other signs does Rebecca need at the workshop?
2. What would improve her ability to work at the workshop?
3. With whom does Rebecca enjoy working?
4. Are there other jobs at the workshop that Rebecca would like to learn?
5. Does Rebecca have sufficient break time and leisure time?
6. What kind of leisure time would Rebecca enjoy most?
7. What skills does Rebecca need to learn to participate in leisure time?
8. Who would Rebecca like to join at leisure time?

Through the answers to these questions, several goals are developed that will help Rebecca become more independent and increase her level of enjoyment in the workshop setting.

Possibilities

Communication photo album with pictures in purse

Music played for everyone

Working with Chris and Jack

Learning to dance during breaks

Rewards when she uses her signs

---

behaviors or activities to help him or her be better accepted. An example of this type of ecological inventory involves the development of a questionnaire for students that indicates their interests in playground activities. All students in the peer group complete the questionnaire. The teacher then looks for patterns of interest, as well as other important clues to the student's preferred activities. The teacher develops an intervention plan to teach the student with disabilities how to engage in the activities. In addition, the teacher looks for ways to include the student with disabilities by engaging others in more inclusionary play. Figure 8.8 presents an example of an ecological inventory to identify student interests.

Figure 8.7   An Ecological Inventory that Identifies Peer Acceptance for Meredith, a
Student

Area for Assessment: Attention during circle time.

Domain: Classroom

Environment: Circle setting

Skill: Sitting with her teaching assistant in circle time without bothering others or interrupting

1. Who does Meredith like to sit by in circle time?
2. Who is a good model for Meredith to watch?
3. What kind of reward would reinforce Meredith's ability to sit quietly and participate with others?
4. What could Meredith do or hold in her hands to keep from touching others?
5. Is Meredith allowed to interact during circle time?
6. Does the teacher direct her gaze at Meredith?
7. Do other children in the room understand Meredith's communication cards?
8. Does Meredith have a specific spot with a boundary in which to sit?
9. Where is the teaching assistant seated? Is she intrusive? Is she bothering Meredith? Does the teaching assistant's presence bother the other children?
10. How can the teacher include Meredith in the classroom circle time?

Knowledge Gained from the Answers to These Questions

Meredith likes Jennifer and Nancy; they are good role models. She likes to be rewarded with stickers so that she can share them with her friends. Meredith is pleased when others understand her communication cards. Jennifer and Nancy like to work and play with Meredith. Meredith likes it best when her teaching assistant is sitting behind her so she can sit between two friends. Meredith can model after other students. The teacher increases Meredith's participation by asking her to repeat activities just performed by Jennifer or Nancy. Meredith sits on her numbered cushion just like the other children do. Her number is three. Nancy and Jennifer are her near neighbors. Meredith holds her communication card bracelet during circle time so that she can answer questions. This also keeps her hands busy. Jennifer and Nancy now play more often with Meredith. Other children notice that she can communicate and are trying to learn how to use Meredith's cards. She is also not annoying others by touching them during circle time.

Targeting IEP Goals   Hamill and Everington (2002) list several steps for developing an ecological inventory to target IEP goals. First, the IEP team identifies the instructional domains to be achieved, including home, school, leisure, community, and vocational. Next, it recommends that the student's current and future environments be explored within each domain to determine the important or critical skills. Third, the team identifies specific critical or main activities in each domain that are paramount for

Figure 8.8   An Ecological Inventory to Identify Interests for Tyson, a Student

Area for Assessment: Maintain on-task behavior
Domain: Physical
Environment: Physical education class
Skill: Change locale in the gym to participate in group activities.

1. What kinds of games do you play during adaptive P.E.?
2. Name games you play while standing or sitting still in a circle.
3. Name games you play by moving around.
4. Name your three favorite games.

success. Fourth, the IEP team assesses the student's ability to perform each of the activities to determine where intervention must proceed. Often these activities include the use of a task analysis to simplify and clarify the activity. Figure 8.9 presents an example of an ecological inventory utilizing task analysis.

Figure 8.9   Using Task Analysis for an Ecological Inventory of IEP Goals

Area for Assessment: Mastery of state-mandated knowledge and skills for geometry
Domain: School, home
Environment: Help sessions, class, or home
Skill: To ask for help with geometry problems

1. Work on geometry problems.
2. Identify that you are having trouble working a problem.
3. Go back through the problem-solving steps shown in class.
4. Recognize that you still do not understand how to solve the problem.
5. Decide the appropriate method for seeking help: raise your hand, approach the teacher, consult with a peer tutor, call the homework helpline, go to school early, or bring lunch to stay in during lunch period.
6. Complete the request for help.
7. If obtaining help requires going to school early, adjust your alarm clock.
8. If obtaining help requires staying in during lunch, pack a sack lunch and write a note to yourself to go to algebra during lunch.
9. Continue to ask for explanations until you understand exactly how to work the problem.
10. If you are not obtaining help, check these steps and identify where you are missing one of the steps.

Creating Sociometric Assessments

Sociometric assessments involve the creation of a peer rating form or questionnaire to determine a student's status in a peer group. A diagram picturing the results provides the IEP team with a quick overview of the student's social inclusion. Sociometric assessments employ the sociogram and peer rating scales to analyze the student's standing.

Sociogram   The sociogram represents one type of sociometric assessment technique using peer nomination. The sociogram results in personal information graphed in an easy-to-read format. The following steps are used to generate a sociogram constructed through the use of nominations:

1. Design questions that all students will be asked to answer. Examples include these: With whom would you like to work on a project? With whom would you like to be paired for a reading partner?
2. Distribute the questions to the students. Ask them to put their name on the paper and to answer the questions.
3. Explain the need for silence during the activity and tell students that the information will be used to plan some group activities.
4. Explain the importance of keeping selections private and emphasize the sensitive nature of the activity.
5. Ask students to think about the questions and give their best answer.
6. Collect the questionnaires for analysis.
7. Look at the unique choices shared by several students.
8. Use this information to identify groups of friends, compatible groups, and social isolates.

The teacher and the IEP team use this information to evaluate variables contributing to isolated status. A peer-rating sociogram may provide further information to clarify why students are isolated within the group.

Peer Ratings   Peer ratings form the basis for another sociometric assessment technique. The IEP team may elect to complete peer ratings in response to negative findings on the sociogram or to other environmental indicators reflecting isolation of the student. The first step in developing the peer ratings involves the selection of particular characteristics recognized as valuable to inclusion in the peer group. The team then develops a rating instrument using a Likert-like scale for each characteristic. All students in the classroom complete a rating scale for every classmate. The teacher tabulates the results with mean ratings. This information provides a description of how the particular student in question rates in comparison to the class.

SUMMARIZING ENVIRONMENTAL ASSESSMENTS

Environmental assessments focus on current and future needs to formulate effective plans. The assessment results provide the IEP team with information to extensively influence the student's functioning. Furthermore, examining the compilation of data obtained during the environment assessment allows the IEP team to investigate the results and ascertain the relevance for the student with respect to the community.

Summary Chart

One method for summarizing the data consists of a chart format to identify various domains in which the student functions. A series of questions to synthesize a holistic picture of the student's needs rounds out this process (Alper, Ryndak, & Schloss, 2001). The first step identifies the domains where the student functions. These often include home, school, vocational, community, family, peer group, and leisure activities. The teacher summarizes each piece of information gathered through the environmental assessment. For example, one student might have an ecological inventory in the school domain. Another student might have more pervasive needs and have inventories in the family, community, school, and leisure domains. A third student might have ecological inventories in the home and school domain, as well as a sociogram based on the classroom.

The next step in the summary process requires considering the following questions:

1. How many times is a particular topic mentioned across the inventories or domains?
2. What are the preferences identified by the student?
3. Which skills/activities are most important for the student now and in the future?
4. Which skills/activities will increase the student's success in the general education setting or least restrictive environment?
5. Which skills/activities can the student accomplish while receiving services?
6. Are these skills/activities generalizable across settings?

The summary chart aids the IEP team in visualizing the results of the ecological assessments. This visual representation allows the IEP team to make decisions about future plans.

Family-Focused Interview Process

Another method for summarizing the data collected from environmental assessments mirrors the family-focused interview process (Bailey & Simeonsson, 1988). This summary identifies specific goals for the future by looking at the data in a narrative fashion. The summary provides indicators of the details gleaned from the domains. The three areas include (a) summarizing high-need priorities, (b) identifying difficult skills or activities, and (c) determining critical upcoming transitions or events. The IEP team receives a document that lists the specifics for each area.

The Narrative Summary Model

The narrative summary model provides a written description of the data obtained through the authentic assessment. Narrative summaries include information about the student's environment and the skills necessary for success in that setting. In addition, a narrative summary consists of a determination of strengths and needs in particular locations. A narrative summary also reflects the skills necessary for transitioning to more complex environments.

The Box Summary Method

Summarizing an environmental assessment as a component of an assistive technology evaluation (see Assistive Technology later in this chapter) through the use of a box summary method highlights another style for providing data to the IEP team. Raskind and Bryant (2002) describe a method in which the team examines four areas of the student's functioning: the tasks, the individual, the device, and the context in which the student will use the technology. In this case, the summary describes each area in detail, using the information gathered in an environmental assessment process and placed in a box summary table. Figure 8.10 presents an example of a box summary of assistive technology needs.

Person-Centered Planning

Person-centered planning is another method for summarizing data from an environmental assessment. The synopsis for the IEP team consists of a six-part review. The first section provides information on the student's personal history. Second, the teacher describes the student's capacities and opportunities. Third, the summary lists choices that reflect independent activities and encourage self-advocacy. Fourth, the teacher identifies individual needs to enable and support the student to achieve the end goals. Fifth, the environmental assessment focuses on natural supports available in the student's

Figure 8.10   The Assistive Technology Box Summary for Marsha, a Student

Tasks	Individual
Marsha needs to communicate. She has trouble remembering visual cues not in front of her.	Marsha can use pictures to help remember what she is trying to communicate. She is interested in animals and would like to be friends with other students.
Device	**Context**
A communication board will augment Marsha's ability to talk with others. She will need the help of her speech–language pathologist and possibly the help of an AT technician. Marsha's teacher will need to learn the board alongside parents, family members, other teachers, and peers.	Marsha will use the board in all settings at school, home, and community. The use of the board will be evaluated at the end of the semester.

environment. Finally, the team works together to identify network services, from agencies and other providers, that are helpful in achieving the student's personal goals. Person-centered environmental assessments remain grounded in relationships, settings, dreams, strengths, preferences, and the individual goals of the student.

USING ENVIRONMENTAL ASSESSMENT DATA FOR THE INDIVIDUAL EDUCATION PROGRAM

Moving from summaries to the actual implementation in the IEP provides a natural step in planning for students. The IEP team uses the information described by the summaries to make decisions about planning for the next year, the least restrictive environment, and IEP goals. The results of an environmental assessment supply a view of the impact of the environmental assessment on the IEP process. The IEP team decisions and rationale accompany the environmental assessment summaries.

The IEP team is able to use the information provided in each of these summaries to examine a variety of factors obtained through the environmental assessment process. The summaries help the team to see patterns and look for overriding concerns that are based in many environments. Providing a summary to the IEP team facilitates decision making based on multiple facets regarding the student's ability to function, rather than relying on the results of one assessment device.

ENVIRONMENTAL ASSESSMENTS AND TECHNOLOGY

Technology allows teachers to quickly produce a custom-made ecological inventory for each student, including the most appropriate factors, while discarding those without value. By basing the ecological inventory on student characteristics with potential links to instructional technologies, such as exploratory activities, tutorials, drill and practice, educational games, simulations, and problem solving, the IEP team identifies student needs in the environment that can be met using these programs (Bryant & Bryant, 2003).

What Does an Environmental Assessment Contribute to IEP Development?

- It provides data regarding the most beneficial setting for the student.
- It offers information that is often neglected but may prove helpful to individuals who are experiencing learning problems.
- It examines the settings where instruction occurs across the entire school day.
- It compares the abilities of the student to work in a variety of settings.
- It considers all aspects in creating a fertile learning environment.

Virtual Reality

Virtual realty represents one such software innovation. It teaches social skills, identified in an ecological inventory, through the use of a software program (Male, 2003). The student interacts with a computer software program to experience a realistic environment via technology. Exploration of appropriate and inappropriate choices or actions allows the student to see the consequences of actions. For example, Softhaven, a virtual-reality kitchen software program, allows a student to experience cooking. It provides a series of prompts and cues to enable the student to select the appropriate tools needed to cook. With the growth of technology and virtual reality, the possibilities of experiencing settings through the computer that might otherwise present barriers to the student are endless.

Assistive Technology

The use of environmental assessments to evaluate a student's technology needs remains appropriate. Using **assistive technology** (AT) devices to help students complete tasks more independently aids the student in self-determination (Bigge, Sherwood, Best, & Heller, 2001). First, the IEP team determines the independent behavior. Then the teacher develops an ecological inventory based on the tasks needed for the student to accomplish the behavior/skill. Next, an observation of the student attempting to perform the actions occurs. The observer notes specific technological aids that help the student complete the activity. The observation provides information that helps in planning for instruction concerning the use of the AT device. Equipment ranging from no-tech devices, such as a plate with a rim, to high-tech communication systems or talking word processors should be considered (Hammill & Everington, 2002).

AT provides access to adult-living skills by helping the student use devices that impact hygiene, eating skills, and both oral and written communication. Through the use of an ecological inventory, the IEP team determines what the student needs in terms of AT in his environment, rather than simply guessing about the student's requirements (Wehmeyer, 1999). Establishing the need and function of AT remains critical to the consumer's successful usage of AT. Ecological inventories allow the IEP team to assess both need and function.

However, several commercially available AT assessments provide the IEP team with information to augment the ecological inventory. Hammill and Everington (2002) identify some such products, including the following:

- *Augmentative/Alternative Technology Assessment Tool* (Dodgen & Associates, 1997)
- *Lifespan Access Profile: Assistive Technology Planning for Individuals with Severe or Multiple Disabilities* (Williams, Stemach, Wolfe, & Stanger, 1995)
- *Augmentative or Alternative Communication Feature Match Software* (Dodgen & Associates, 1996)

The FEAT The *Functional Evaluation for Assistive Technology* (FEAT) (Raskind & Bryant, 2002) includes numerous rating scales to assist the IEP team in evaluating a student's AT needs from an ecological assessment standpoint. The FEAT Contextual Matching Inventory looks at the student's individual competencies and needs within each environment. It includes a listing of student tasks and issues related to how the student will use the AT device to perform in a variety of settings.

Several other components of the FEAT assess the student's environmental needs. The FEAT Checklist of Strengths and Limitations evaluates the student's skills in the areas of listening, speaking, reading, writing, mathematics, memory, organization, psychomotor skills, and behavior.

The final scale, known as the FEAT Individual Technology Evaluation Scale, provides a rating scale measuring the degree of proficiency possessed by a student. Areas within the scale include individual/technology match and general technology literacy, as well as other qualitative observational components.

Issues in AT Assessment   When completing an ecological assessment for AT usage, the IEP team must consider issues such as efficiency and effectiveness. In addition, the student's desire to use the device becomes paramount (McDonnell, Hardman, & McDonnell, 2003). Other considerations identified by Parrette (1997) include (a) user characteristics, such as age, devices used in the past, and training needs, (b) technology features, such as cost, ease of use, and transportability, (c) family concerns regarding the effect of the device on the family interactions and expectations, (d) cultural factors entailing compatibility and perception of the disability, and (e) service system issues, including cost, protection from theft or damage, and training. McDonnell, Hardman, and McDonnell also report that the rate of reinforcement, quality of reinforcement, amount of physical effort required to use the AT device, or response effect and the immediacy of the reinforcement all impact the student's use of AT. Investigation of each of these factors, through ecological inventories to determine appropriate AT devices and evaluate student success with the device, provides critical information to the IEP team.

Ecological inventories ensure the exploration of multiple settings to facilitate successful use of the AT device in various classroom environments, the home, and community (Bryant & Bryant, 2003). Most important, information acquired from a variety of settings and a number of different people provide the most accurate view of the student's functioning. When assessing for AT, several models determine the needs of students and the function of the AT device. Reviewing information from other sources, including families, completes the AT picture.

Cultural and linguistic diversity considerations remain embedded within the context of environmental assessments. For example, the use of AT must be evaluated based on the effect of the AT on the family (Westling and Fox, 2004). The culture and language of the family and other related aspects, such as resources, strength, styles, choices, quality of life perceptions, and other unique needs, demand consideration (Parrette & Brotherson, 1996). Environmental assessments examine the strengths and limitations of the student and are interwoven with AT needs. AT provides an integral part of helping students with disabilities adapt to their environment and improve functioning in a variety of settings.

Kemp and Parrette (2000) developed a list of questions regarding family and culture to be considered in an environmental setting. An interview provides the best format for obtaining responses to such questions:

- Is the AT device welcome in the home setting?
- Does the AT device match family needs?
- Will the AT device change the routines and schedule of the home?
- Is the family willing to accept these changes?
- Can the siblings use the AT device?
- Will the family receive training in its own language?
- Does the family think that the student needs the AT?
- What impact will the AT device have on the student with a disability?
- Will the AT device have any negative consequences?
- Will the student's community life be enhanced through the use of the AT?
- Is the family aware of the advantages of the AT device?
- Is the family aware of any disadvantages the AT offers?
- Has the culture of the student and family been considered when selecting the AT device?

The completion of an ecological inventory provides a more in-depth understanding of family culture and linguistic considerations when selecting AT. Conducting ecological inventories, including personal interviews, allows the IEP team to determine how AT devices will be used in the home and community to examine the usefulness of the technology to improve the quality of life for the student with disabilities.

Environmental assessments not only establish the need for AT devices but examine the expectations of the student with disability within a family context. IEP teams help to implement programs that honor the diversity of families through environmental assessments. The environment includes many cultural influences. By assessing the setting, the IEP team includes specific job-related tasks, or recreational tasks desired by the family. For instance, if this family enjoys music, the student might be taught to play an instrument (e.g., maracas, drum, or flute) to participate in home- or community-based activities. Understanding the student's functioning in a variety of settings will enhance the ability of the IEP team to plan for transitioning to the future.

SUMMARY

- Environmental assessments evaluate student interactions with both physical and societal surroundings. The areas assessed include home, school, leisure, vocational, and community environments.
- The numerous advantages resulting from environmental assessments revolve around increased independence and opportunities for people with disabilities. While a lack of reliability remains a disadvantage, the validity of environmental assessments remains strong due to a direct connection to the student and current functioning.

- Identification of cultural and linguistic differences through teacher, family, and curricular issues occurs during environmental assessments.
- The IEP team seeks information about the student's actual functioning rather than his or her deficiencies or lack of skill.
- The process includes the use of ecological inventories and sociometric measurements. Environmental assessments are available commercially, but preferences for individual development for each student often impact selection of appropriate inventories.
- Person-centered goals represent the end result of the environmental assessment process.
- Creating IEPs based on environmental assessments features the crafting of appropriate curriculum with natural environments critical to the success of students with complex needs.
- Assistive technology evaluations include environmental assessments as the foundation for learning about the student's ability to benefit from a particular technological intervention.

COMPREHENSION CHECK

1. What are the differences between curriculum-based assessment and environmental assessments? Give examples of the appropriate use of each type of assessment.
2. State the advantages and disadvantages of environmental assessments.
3. Explain Universal Design for Learning.

ACTIVITIES

1. Complete a sociogram for your class. Design the questionnaire and distribute it to the class. Analyze the results by constructing a drawing of the nominations received. Talk about how to use this information and the sensitivity of the results.
2. Interview the teacher of a student with pervasive needs regarding the classroom environment. After the interview, write up a summary of your findings. Discuss how you would use your findings to ensure cultural and linguistic sensitivity in the IEP planning process.
3. Create a self-assessment for teachers to assess their own performance when accommodating individual learning needs in the classroom.

REFERENCES

Alper, S., Ryndak, D. L., & Schloss, C. N. (2001). *Alternate assessment of students with disabilities in inclusive settings.* Boston: Allyn & Bacon.

Augmentative or Alternative Communication: Feature Match Software. (1996). Arlington, TX: D. Dodgen & Associates.

Augmentative/Alternative Technology Assessment Tool. (1997). Arlington, TX: D. Dodgen & Associates.

Baca, L. M., & Cervantes, H. T. (2004). *The bilingual special education interface* (4th ed.). Upper Saddle River, NJ: Merrill/Prentice Hall.

Bailey, D. B., & Simeonsson, R. J. (1988). *Family assessment in early intervention.* New York: Merrill/Macmillan.

Barnett, D. W., Bell, S. H., Gilkey, C., Lentz, F. E., Jr., Graden, J. L., Stone, C. M., Smith, J. J., & Macmann, G. M. (1999). The promise of meaningful eligibility determination: Functional intervention-based multi-factored preschool evaluation. *The Journal of Special Education, 33*(2), 112–124.

Bigge, J. L., Sherwood, J., Best, S. J., & Heller, K. W. (2001). *Teaching individuals with physical, health, or multiple disabilities* (4th ed.). Upper Saddle River, NJ: Merrill/Prentice Hall.

Bondurant-Utz, J. (2002). *Practical guide to assessing infants and preschoolers with special needs.* Upper Saddle River, NJ: Merrill/Prentice Hall.

Bryant, D. P., & Bryant, B. R. (2003). Assistive technology for people with disabilities. Boston: Allyn & Bacon.

Caldwell, B., & Bradley, R. H. (1984). *Home observation for measurement of the environment.* Little Rock: University of Arkansas.

Campbell, P. C., Campbell, C. R., & Brady, M. P. (1998). Team environmental assessment mapping system: A method for selecting curriculum goals for students with disabilities. *Education and Training in Mental Retardation and Developmental Disabilities, 33*(3), 264–272.

Giangreco, M. F., Cloninger, C. J., & Iverson, V. S. (1993). *Choosing options and accommodations for children.* Baltimore: Paul H. Brookes Publishing Company.

Haager, D., & Klinger, J. K. (2005). *Differentiating instruction in inclusive classrooms: The special educator's guide.* Boston: Allyn & Bacon.

Hammill, L., & Everington, C. (2002). *Teaching students with moderate to severe disabilities: An applied approach for inclusive settings.* Upper Saddle River, NJ: Merrill/Prentice Hall.

Harms, T., Jacobs, D., & White, E. (1996). *School-age care environment rating scale.* New York: Teachers College Press.

Hemmeter, M. L., Maxwell, K. L., Alt, M. J., & Schuster, J. W. (2001). *Assessment of practices in early elementary classrooms.* New York: Teachers College Press.

Kea, C. D., Cartledge, C., and Bowman, L. (2002). Intervention techniques for African-American learners with behavioral problems. In B. A. Ford, and F. Obiakor (Eds.). *Creating successful learning environments for African-American learners with exceptionalities.* Austin, TX: Pro-Ed.

Kemp, C. E., & Parrette, H. P. (2000). Barriers to minority family involvement in assistive technology decision-making processes. *Education and Training in Mental Retardation and Developmental Disabilities, 35*, 384–392.

Larson, P. J., & Maag, J. W. (1998). Applying functional assessment in general education classrooms: Issues and recommendations. *Remedial and Special Education, 19*(6), 338–349.

Linehan. S. A., Brady, M. P., & Hwang, C. (1991). Ecological versus developmental assessment: Influences on instructional expectations. *Journal of the Association for Persons with Severe Handicaps, 16*, 146–153.

Maag, J. W. (2004). *Behavior management: From theoretical implications to practical applications* (2nd ed.). Belmont, CA: Thomson/Wadsworth.

Male, M. (2003). *Technology for inclusion: Meeting the special needs of all students* (4th ed.). Boston: Allyn & Bacon.

McConnell, S. R. (2000). Assessment in early intervention and early childhood special education: Building on the past to project into our future. *Topics in Early Childhood Special Education, 20*(1), 43–48.

McDonnell, J. J., Hardman, M. L., & McDonnell, A. P. (2003). *An introduction to persons with moderate and severe disabilities* (2nd ed.). Boston: Allyn & Bacon.

McLean, M., Wolery, M., & Bailey, D. B., Jr. (2004). *Assessing infants and preschoolers with special needs* (3rd ed.). Upper Saddle River, NJ: Merrill/Prentice Hall.

Miller, M. C., Cooke, N. L., & Test, D. W. (2003). Effects of friendship circles on the social interactions of elementary age students with mild disabilities. *Journal of Behavioral Education, 12*(3), 167–184.

Odom, S. L., McConnell, S. R., McEvoy, M. A., Peterson, C., Ostrosky, M., Chandler, L. K., et al. (1999). Relative effects of interventions supporting the social competence of young children with disabilities. *Topics in Early Childhood Special Education, 19*(2), 75–91.

Odom, S. L., Schertz, H., Munson, L., & Brown, W. H. (2003). Assessing social competence. In M. McLean, D. Bailey, & M. Wolery (Eds.). *Assessing infants and preschoolers with special needs* (3rd ed.). Columbus, OH: Merrill Publishing.

Overton, T. (2004). Promoting academic success through environmental assessment. *Intervention in School and Clinic, 39*(2), 147–153.

Overton, T. (2006). *Assessing learners with special needs: An applied approach* (5th ed.). Upper Saddle River, NJ: Merrill/Prentice Hall.

Parrette, H. P. (1997). Assistive technology devices and services. *Education and Training in Mental Retardation and Developmental Disabilities, 32*(4), 267–280.

Parrette, H. P., & Brotherson, M. J. (1996). Family participation in assistive technology assessment for young children with mental retardation and developmental disabilities. *Education and Training in Mental Retardation and Developmental Disabilities, 31,* 29–43.

Raskind, M., & Bryant, B. R. (2002). *Functional evaluation for assistive technology.* Austin, TX: Psycho-Educational Services.

Ryndak, D. L., & Alper, S. (2003). *Curriculum and instruction for students with significant disabilities in inclusive settings* (2nd ed.). Boston: Allyn & Bacon.

Salvia, J., & Ysseldyke, J. E. (2004). *Assessment in special and inclusive education* (9th ed.). Boston: Houghton Mifflin.

Snell, M. E., & Brown, F. (2000). *Instruction of students with severe disabilities* (5th ed.). Upper Saddle River, NJ: Merrill/Prentice Hall.

Spinelli, C. B. (2006). *Classroom assessment for students in special and general education.* Upper Saddle River, NJ: Merrill/Prentice Hall.

Wehmeyer, M. (1999). Assistive technology and students with mental retardation: Utilization and barriers. *Journal of Special Education Technology, 14*(1), 48–58.

Westling, D. L., & Fox, L. (2004). *Teaching students with severe disabilities* (3rd ed.). Upper Saddle River, NJ: Pearson/Prentice Hall.

Wolery, M. (2004). Assessing children's environments. In M. McLean, M. Wolery, & D. B. Bailey, (Eds.). *Assessing infants and preschoolers with special needs.* Upper Saddle River, New Jersey: Merrill/Prentice Hall.

Wolery, M., Pauca, T., Brashers, M. S., & Grant, S. (2000). *Quality of inclusive experiences measure.* Chapel Hill, NC: Frank Porter Graham Child Development Institute, University of North Carolina.

COMMUNICATION NOTEBOOKS AND JOURNALS

9

Chapter Focus

Communication notebooks and journals improve the collection of assessment data from parents, families, teachers, and others working with a particular student. The information pinpoints small but significant indicators of student progress impacting the development and documentation of IEP progress. The IEP team benefits from parent, teacher, and student information gathered in context and filtered through each individual's perspective. This particular technique provides a time-efficient method to allow participants to respond at their convenience.

Communication notebooks and journals create a rich, contextual picture of each student with special needs. The complex nature of students with disabilities requires the in-depth examination of student-centered concerns and requirements for success. Communication notebooks and journals add to the assessment and understanding of differences in learning.

LEARNER OBJECTIVES

- State the definition for communication notebooks and journals.
- List the advantages and disadvantages of communication notebooks and journals.
- Describe how communication notebooks and journals relate cultural and linguistic aspects.
- Recognize opportunities to use communication notebooks and journals as effective mechanisms for collecting assessment data.
- Identify the various types of communication notebooks and journals.
- Explain the mechanics of developing communication notebooks and journals.
- Understand how to summarize data gleaned from various sources through communication notebooks and journals.
- Explain the contribution of information gained from communication notebooks and journals in the IEP decision-making process.

DEFINING COMMUNICATION NOTEBOOKS AND JOURNALS

Communication Notebooks

A communication notebook includes a written account of day-to-day activities, as well as **reflections**, based in a natural setting that document growth for assessment purposes. To meet the requirements mandated in IDEIA 2004 for parental input in the ongoing assessment picture, communication notebooks allow for both documentation of progress on IEP goals and increasing the home–school connection. Communication notebooks prove appropriate for all students with special needs in a variety of settings from the general education classroom through the continuum of services and placements.

The diversity of participants adds depth to the assessment information collected in the communication notebook. The notebooks contain qualitative information with supplemental quantitative data, which allows the teacher to add authentic pieces to the continuous assessment picture. Creating an in-depth description of the student's ability to generalize IEP goals in a variety of settings strengthens the assessment process and lends credibility to the unique nature of the IEP.

Journals

Stiggins (2001) reports that journals or personal writing diaries utilize the least structured format for gathering assessment data. Students respond in writing during the instructional day concerning their feelings, class work, and events occurring in their lives. Journals, written by students and read by teachers, provide an excellent method for the teacher to gain insight into the perceptions of students. They also provide a measure of academic progress in written expression. Parents and others also engage in journal writing to inform the IEP team about concerns and successes. They also provide input regarding the student's functioning in settings outside of the school day.

Similar to a handwritten journal, journaling on the computer utilizes **electronic communication** stored for future decision making. Using word processing software facilitates a student or parent's ability to convey their thoughts with conveniences such as a spelling or grammar checker. Transmitting journal or communication notebooks through e-mail allows both parties to have immediate communication concerning the contents and can affect change in the classroom to improve the student's functioning.

BENEFITS OF COMMUNICATION NOTEBOOKS AND JOURNALS

Creating communication notebooks and journals offers teachers, parents, other professionals, and learners a method for obtaining genuine assessment information. The informants record activities and reflective thoughts on a continual basis. This information provides evidence of the connection between progress on the IEP goals at school and home. Reflective components allow the notebook participants to offer insights into successes and concerns regarding student development. The communication notebook and journal emphasize the dual responsibility for student learning (Williams & Cartledge, 1997) by all participants in the system, including parents and teachers, students and teachers, general and special education teachers, and others.

DISADVANTAGES OF COMMUNICATION NOTEBOOKS AND JOURNALS

Communication notebooks and journals require organization if quality data are to be collected. In addition, many find them to be time-consuming. This method places the responsibility for data collection on the participants who must respond in a timely and consistent manner. The challenges of parenting a student with a disability present continued time commitments that may result in little opportunity for response. In addition, communication notebooks and journals necessitate a certain level of **literacy** and comfort with written language on the part of the respondents, which impacts the quality of the responses.

Some individuals may find the process intimidating, and their data may not be recorded for consideration. Individuals also may face reading/**computer literacy** or **economic barriers** to using electronic methods for data collection.

Due to the physical nature of communication notebooks and journals, the loss of these valuable records negatively impacts the authentic assessment. Recreating the information proves difficult.

Misinterpretation of written replies represents another disadvantage of communication notebooks and journals. Often a face-to-face conversation must take place to verify the meaning of particular written entries.

CULTURAL COMPETENCE IN USING COMMUNICATION NOTEBOOKS

Aspects of cultural communication must be considered and planned for carefully when developing communication notebooks and journals. Respect for families and their comfort level with a particular style of communication is paramount. The IEP team must be aware of the family's ability to fully utilize communication notebooks and journals in terms of their reading and computer literacy levels. Access to a computer impacts the usability of an electronic-based system. The following examples demonstrate ways in which communication notebooks and journals can improve communication between individuals from different cultural perspectives:

- To help eliminate the us/them between parents and schools (Baca & Cervantes, 2004)
- To display a sincere effort to help parents feel like equal partners in the school setting (Baca & Cervantes, 2004)
- To encourage the family to use its native language when responding to the school (Baca & Cervantes, 2004)
- To allow parents to speak to their knowledge of their own child in a way that is respectful of their home culture (Baca & Cervantes, 2004)
- To consider the goals of parents and the plans they have for their child's future within a cultural context (Baca & Cervantes, 2004)

- To provide translation Web sites, such as Alta Vista's Babble Fish (www. babblefish. com) to aid in the translation of languages other than English (Male, 2003)

DECIDING TO IMPLEMENT A COMMUNICATION NOTEBOOK OR JOURNAL

According to Peyton (1993), a communication notebook involves a written conversation. It promotes a clear channel of communication in an attempt to extend the contact time among participants to gather assessment data. A journal establishes a receptive, two-way communication without a planned response time, and it is intended to improve documentation for evaluation. One person expresses feelings, perceptions, or concerns while the other receives and interprets the message. Teachers consider using a communication notebook or journal system to obtain additional information for corroborating student progress on IEP goals.

By providing a vehicle for participants to record what happens in the classroom, at home, and in everyday life, this technique enhances the quality of the data by providing a holistic observation of the student's progress (English & Gillen, 2001). The communication notebook or journal includes personal, cognitive, and emotional information, in addition to educational observations. Establishing communication notebooks and journals among various participants establishes a realistic method for expanding the evaluation component of the IEP.

The communication system must match the users' abilities and access. Sometimes a paper exchange provides the easiest and most reliable method for data collection. In other circumstances, electronic opportunities, such as e-mail, increase the amount of collectible information. According to Williams and Cartledge (1997, p. 31), the secret to a successful communication notebook or journal resides with the teacher's "consistency, persistence, and caring." Figure 9.1 describes reasons for implementing communication notebooks and journals.

Figure 9.1   A Rationale for Implementing a Communication Notebook or Journal System

- To encourage the participants to be involved in the instruction of IEP goals
- To provide a permanent product that can be used for documentation of generalization
- To empower participants to become advocates for their students
- To supply participants with valuable information to increase their understanding of what the IEP goals are really teaching
- To increase participants' understanding of the student's needs and performance across settings

Source: Williams & Cartledge, 1997.

TYPES OF COMMUNICATION NOTEBOOKS AND JOURNALS

Communication Notebooks

A variety of possible partnerships exist for establishing a communication notebook system. A student–teacher communication notebook provides a self-discovery tool to encourage students to reflect, describe, analyze, and evaluate their classroom experiences (Stiggins, 2001). When used between a student and teacher, this type of activity encourages the participants to examine assignments with respect to mastery, ease of completion, questions that need exploration, or documentation of progress (Kulm, 1994). This style of communication notebook, known as a learning log or dialogue journal, allows the student to carry on a written conversation with the teacher to develop in-depth assessment information (Bos & Vaughn, 2002).

According to Stiggins (2001), the dialogue journal "captures conversations between students and teachers." A learning log, on the other hand, requires students to keep a written record of their achievements, difficulties, successful learning strategies, and questions with the intention of enabling the student and teacher to utilize the information to plan for future learning (Stiggins). Spinelli (2002) indicates that students with poor written language skills may benefit from audio taping a communication journal to circumvent written language deficits.

Parent and Teacher Notebooks   **Daily interactive journals** create bonds between parents and teachers in the assessment process (Bos & Vaughn, 2002). In such journals, parents and teachers jot down notes and share information about the student's interests, activities, and responses (Bondurant-Utz, 2002). The daily interactive journal uses a spiral-bound notebook that travels between the home and school with the student (Westling & Fox, 2000). The notebook may be organized to obtain feedback from parents on the day's activities, as well as the generalization to the home setting. **Happy notes** represent another version of the communication notebook in which the teacher and parent communicate from school to home and home to school about the positive things that happen (Mastropieri & Scruggs, 2000). Figure 9.2 features the common problems associated with parent–teacher communication.

Figure 9.2   Common Problems Associated with Parent–Teacher Communication (adapted from Jayanthi, Bursuck, Epstein, & Polloway, 1997)

Parents identified the following six problems with parent–teacher communication:
1. Neither parents nor teachers want to initiate the communication.
2. They don't communicate enough.
3. Communication does not occur with any regularity.
4. When problems first occur, communication is often lacking.
5. Parents and teachers fail to follow through with what they say.
6. Unclear communication impacts the relationship.

Using a communication notebook improves and enhances the dialogue between parents and educators. It also helps alleviate evaluation problems associated with parent–teacher communication. It should be understood that the student should not be the responsible party in the communication system. Delivery of the written data must be a partnership between the parent and teacher. This prevents the student from having direct access to the information. Figure 9.3 features an example of a parent–teacher communication notebook.

Another twist on the communication notebook is the **traveling backpack** containing books or toys and a notebook (Hill & Ruptick, 1994). The parent engages the child in the activity described in the notebook, which usually pertains to a review of classroom activities. The parent writes back a statement concerning the child's response, mastery, and generalization in the home setting. These messages must be scrutinized carefully to prevent the student from reading negative information.

For students with **assistive technology devices**, such as a communication switch, recording a message on each student's switch device provides parents and teachers with a method to communicate daily via the student with limited communication skills. The teacher should keep a running record of the daily messages and responses that add information to the evaluation of IEP goals. This real-life accounting allows the teacher to describe progress across time rather than creating only a simple snapshot of functioning obtained through standardized instruments.

Teaching Assistant and Teacher Notebooks   Using communication notebooks between teaching assistants and teachers describes yet another avenue for obtaining and documenting everyday progress toward the attainment of IEP goals. This type of documentation includes several positive results. First, it solidifies the teaching assistant's responsibility for engaging the child in purposeful activities with direct connections to the IEP. Second, it involves the teaching assistant as a full-fledged team member integrally involved in supporting the student to attain his goals. Third, it establishes a written record of continued observations and interventions that are available for documenting goal attainment. Fourth, it creates a strong link between the teaching team to provide evidence for assessment.

Teaching assistant–teacher communication notebooks need not be formal. Self-adhesive notes or note cards placed for review in a specific child's folder can be converted into evaluation data (Mastropieri & Scruggs, 2000). Some teaching teams use small spiral notebooks turned in daily from the teaching assistant and returned the following morning from the teacher. The teacher then responds to each note or entry and directs the teaching assistant in working with the child. This system offers documentation of progress and concerns where oral interactions often become hurried. The teaching assistant–teacher communication notebooks offer evaluation records, as well as a built-in system to focus the teaching team on progress, current goals, and problems that need solutions. Daily written communication often aids the participants' understanding of the student's progress and needs (Turnbull & Turnbull, 2001).

Figure 9.3   A Parent–Teacher Communication Notebook

Lilly Baker needs to practice reading and retelling at home and school. The teacher, Ms. Morgan, and Lilly's mother create a notebook system to encourage Lilly. The information from home to school monitors Lilly's practice and keeps her mother in touch with her progress. Ms. Morgan also is seeing progress with Lilly in reading and comprehension. This communication notebook will be used in documenting the progress that Lilly has made this year.

| Lilly | Bush Elementary School |
| Ms. Morgan—Sp Ed Teacher & Ms. Baker—Mother | October–December 2006 |

Area for Assessment: Reading

Directions: Please read and have Lilly retell the story.

Date	Book or reading source	Recorder
10-1	*Muggie Maggie*	Ms. Morgan
10-6	*Muggie Maggie*	Ms. Baker
10-9	*Georgie Lee*	Ms. Morgan
10-15	*Georgie Lee*	Ms. Baker
10-23	*The Cool Crazy Crickets*	Ms. Morgan
10-27	*The Cool Crazy Crickets*	Ms. Baker
10-29	*Miss Rumphius*	Ms. Morgan
11-3	*Miss Rumphius*	Ms. Baker
11-6	*The Frog Principal*	Ms. Morgan
11-10	*The Frog Principal*	Ms. Baker
11-14	*My Brother*	Ms. Morgan
11-17	*My Brother*	Ms. Baker
11-19	*Summer Party*	Ms. Morgan
11-24	*Summer Party*	Ms. Baker
12-3	*Just Plain Fancy*	Ms. Morgan
12-8	*Just Plain Fancy*	Ms. Baker

Date	Lilly's reactions to reading	Recorder
10-1	Enjoyed special reading time	Ms. Morgan
10-13	Excited about reading together	Ms. Baker
10-27	Loved the story	Ms. Baker
11-14	Identified main characters	Ms. Morgan
11-24	Happy about increase in rate	Ms. Baker
12-11	Enjoying books, more fun	Ms. Baker

General and Special Education Teacher Notebooks   Another type of note-book exists for communication between general and special education teachers. IDEIA 2004 mandates that the general education teacher in the least restrictive environment plays an integral part in the instructional and evaluative process. Establishing a communication notebook between the general and special education teachers of a child in an inclusionary setting establishes an ongoing dialogue and verifies the student's progress with written information.

The use of a communication notebook between teachers allows them to gather data and make adjustments to increase the student's progress on the IEP goal. The addition of a **physical prompt** in the special education classroom to transfer into the general education classroom aids the student in learning to succeed with on-task behaviors.

In addition, the communication notebook pulls the general education teacher into the assessment process by employing specific classroom-based data collected in general education settings. Figure 9.4 presents an example of a communication notebook between a general and special education teacher.

Related Service and Teacher Notebooks   One of the most difficult dialogues to establish and maintain exists between related service personnel and the teacher. Often each stays busy with particular students in the classroom and little time remains for sharing progress and concerns. Implementing a communication notebook to create continuous feedback on a regular basis frames the information in terms of the evaluation of the student's IEP goals. Recording progress helps to focus the connection between the two service providers concerning the student. Furthermore, it aids in the generalization of the goal and provides feedback regarding the effectiveness of the therapeutic intervention.

Journals

Journals consist of **one-sided communication** where one party writes thoughts for someone else to read. While the teacher or IEP team should act upon the information provided, no one expects two-way communication via the journal. In addition, journals may convey more emotion and elicit information more spontaneously than can a communication notebook, which may have a more structured format. Parents, students, and others completing journal entries should understand the public nature of these documents. These notes must remain **confidential** within the IEP team. While journals can be kept by teachers, including related service personnel, parents and students author most journals. Figure 9.5 features a sample entry from a journal entry from home.

Computer-Based Notebooks

Computer-based notebooks or journals allow the parent or family member and teacher to e-mail messages and observations on a routine basis. Often the messages deal with a

Figure 9.4   A Communication Notebook Between Teachers

| Ms. Andrews—Special Education | Northwood Elementary |
| Mr. Dobbs—General Education | March 3 through May 24 |

Area for Assessment: On-task behavior

Directions: Please keep a tally of Pete's on-task behaviors by making a mark at 5-minute intervals for the 15-minutes of input and modeling. Write notes about how Pete is acting during that 15-minute period.

Tally of compliance for weeks 3-3 through 3-28

Date	Placement	Recorder	Tally
3-3	Res	BA	2
3-4	GE	BD	1
3-5	Res	BA	2
3-6	GE	BD	1
3-7	Res	BA	2
3-10	GE	BD	2
3-11	Res	BA	2
3-12	GE	BD	2
3-13	Res	BA	3
3-14	GE	BD	2
3-24	Res	BA	3
3-25	GE	BD	3
3-26	Res	BA	3
3-27	GE	BD	3
3-28	Res	BA	3

Res = Resource, GE = General Education, BA = SE teacher, BD = GE teacher

Notes

- Pete seems bothered by the larger group setting. BD, 3-4
- Movement by others is distracting. BD, 3-6
- Pete calls out an answer before the teacher finishes the question. BA, 3-7
- Cueing Pete with a "go" sign for response time improved behavior. BA, 3-11
- Began using "go" sign in general education. BD, 3-12
- "Go" sign seems to help with controlling on-task behavior. BD, 3-25

specific topic or goal. The teacher collects the exchanges to create a progressive notebook or journal. Other individuals, such as teaching assistants or related service personnel, also contribute to the process. The teacher sets up different files within the student's electronic folder to address each goal in the IEP. Care must be taken to respect issues of

Figure 9.5   A Sample Entry from the Spiral-Bound Journal of Andrea's Mother

---

Areas for Assessment: Communication skills

Directions: Please describe Andrea's initiation of conversations at home by providing a short description of the conversation, the situation, and the participants.

Today, Andrea began telling me about a show she watched over the weekend. She was very interested in the cat and said that she liked him. She also talked about having a cat and wanted to know if we could have one. Andrea asked her brother, Michael, to play a game with her. She told him that she would play UNO or checkers. Then Michael and Andrea talked about which game they liked best and decided on checkers. They were in the kitchen talking together.

---

confidentiality concerning these e-mail messages. The folder should be closed after each communication to ensure privacy. When deciding to use a computer-based notebook several issues emerge:

- Access to technology is, obviously, required.
- Computer literacy and ease of use will have a tremendous effect on a participant's ability to successfully use the computer-based notebook.
- The participant's desire to use technology rather than to handwrite entries will also determine the choice of the appropriate technique.

CREATING A COMMUNICATION NOTEBOOK OR JOURNAL

Using authentic assessment techniques, such as the communication notebook or journal, to document progress on the IEP requires the teacher to collect data from a variety of perspectives. Both qualitative and quantitative methods should be considered in data collection. By including both types of information, the teacher supplies answers to both subjective and objective questions about the student's performance, increases the scope of the data collection, and obtains information from a variety of settings and sources rather than relying simply on classroom-based results. The IEP goals, the student's response modes, and the teacher's decisions about the need for supporting documentation determine which method to select.

Using Qualitative Data

The nature of a communication notebook or journal requires individuals to respond with qualitative or genuine thoughts and observations rather than simply relying on facts based on numbers. Supplemental quantitative information, such as frequency counts, offers good sources of information. However, enhancing this type of information by pairing it with a participant's perceptions and feelings frequently occurs. Communication notebooks and journals linked to observable behaviors supply the underlying nuances that typify subtle progress that is often overlooked in a more standardized assessment process. Obtaining information through a communication notebook or journal system from students, parents, and others working with students on a daily basis allows the teacher to collect a depth of information that would be lost in a typical assessment setting.

The qualitative research methods conducive to inclusion in the communication notebook or journal begin with open-ended questions (Sattler, 2001), **thick descriptions** (Geertz, 1973; Denzin & Lincoln, 2000), and **anecdotal records** (Hamill & Everington, 2002). These methods encourage participants to provide honest, sincere and reliable information to guide ongoing assessment and IEP development. While the teacher focuses the notebook or journal on particular IEP goals, qualitative data also allow other participants to include any information they deem important for the assessment. Figure 9.6 presents a description of qualitative techniques.

Open-Ended Questions   Open-ended questions target a particular IEP goal or objective to structure the communication notebook or journal while providing an avenue to pinpoint specific information. Turnbull and Turnbull (2001) report that parents and teachers tend to respond differently in a communication notebook or journal. Parents give opinions and facts, while teachers concentrate on directives and evaluations. Open-ended questions allow participants to interject their own expert thoughts and observations into the evaluation process, thus providing the teacher with information based on home performance.

Figure 9.6   Qualitative Techniques

Method	Examples of Appropriate Use
Open-ended questions	Inquiries about leisure skills, study habits, goal generalization, after-school activities, eating habits, daily living skills, likes and dislikes, parental input regarding any of the above.
"Thick" descriptions	Synthesis of information: inclusion of emotional, social, and cognitive aspects of life. Often these descriptions need to be verified by others who also see the child with frequency.
Direct anecdotal observations	Summaries of events: recordings of events as they occur in the natural setting. Events include home arrival from school, homework strategies, daily living activities, and episodes in the community setting.

For example, through data collected using open-ended questions, the teacher gained enough information to determine that a particular student needed to work on compliance in addition to extinguishing his fist-shaking behavior. The teacher began a reward system intervention to reinforce the student's compliant behaviors. This example demonstrates how communication notebooks and journals help clarify and document a picture concerning a student's behavior patterns. While the teacher and teaching assistant might have had a discussion and made this discovery by chance, the data readily provide plausible alternatives. By documenting observations and perceptions in writing, the team isolated underlying issues associated with the IEP goal and objective to improve success.

"Thick" Descriptions "Thick" descriptions use multiple entries to add tiny details and aspects that complete a bigger, more complex picture of the student. In a communication notebook or journal, participants write continuous descriptions about how the student performs. This data collection method provides details about the student's learning experience over time. Adjectives describing the feelings, appearance, level of satisfaction, discomfort, and such deepen the data collector's understanding of the whole child. A series of descriptions brings clarity to the continuous evolvement of the student's growth. For students with pervasive disabilities, the use of "thick" descriptions provides one of the few sources of information.

Direct Anecdotal Observations Direct anecdotal observations require participants to write an ongoing description of the actual behaviors related to a specific IEP goal as it occurs in the home or school setting. This type of information supplies a less interpretive and a more factual accounting of the events in sequence. Data collected by this method allow informants to describe all aspects of the behavior rather than just a simple tally of the completion of the behavior. Observations should be included to keep the parent and teacher focused on specific IEP goal and objective attainment. This practice increases the likelihood that development will occur across settings. Figure 9.7 features a sample from a direct anecdotal observation.

Using Quantitative Data

The inclusion of quantitative data in the communication notebook or journal remains tempered with the knowledge that it does not drive the process. Opportunities for participants to gather quantitative information afford a valuable supplement to the communication notebook or journal but should always be paired with additional qualitative insights. For example, gathering a tally of the number of times Sam remembers his homework assignments supplies a simple piece of factual information. By pairing qualitative information with this tally, the teacher learns that Sam's mother works for Coca Cola from 5:00 p.m. until 1:00 a.m. on Tuesdays and Thursdays and that Sam must take care of his younger siblings on those evenings. The teacher also learns that Sam gets the younger children ready for school the next morning. This qualitative information allows

Figure 9.7   Data from a Direct Anecdotal Observation

Mark's Problem-Solving Strategies

Area for Assessment: Geometry

Directions: Please write down the physical behaviors that Mark exhibits when he works on word problems.

Date	Not Using Strategy Chart	Date	Using Strategy Chart
2-11	1. Looks at book	2-11	1. Looks at book
	2. Looks at neighbor		2. Looks at neighbor
	3. Looks at another's paper		3. Twirls pencil
	4. Twirls pencil		4. I remind him to look at the word problem strategy chart
	5. Begins circling words		5. Smiles
	6. Circles many words		6. Looks at strategy chart
	7. Talks to neighbor		7. Begins to circle 3 words in problem
	8. Comes to my desk		8. Completes problem
	9. Says he doesn't understand		

the teacher to look for alternative methods to aid Sam in meeting his IEP study skill goal and completing his homework before he leaves for school.

Quantitative methods for gathering data in the communication notebook or journal include the following five techniques (described in more depth in Chapter 4): (a) **frequency counts,** (b) **duration recording,** (c) **interval recording,** (d) **latency recording,** and (e) **antecedent-behavior-consequence (ABC) analysis** (Kerr & Nelson, 2002).

The first method, frequency counts, includes the monitoring of the number of times a student exhibits a behavior. Parents and teachers often collect this data in a **reciprocal notebook.** Frequency counts present valuable bits of information used to document generalization of behaviors.

The second method, duration recording, involves noting the length of time students participate in developing behaviors. The evaluator begins timing a particular action at its inception. The timing continues until the student ends the particular event. The record enables the evaluator to determine the amount of time spent engaged in the behavior.

The third method, interval recording, adds standardization; both teachers and parents monitor the student with regularity. Interval recording proves more convenient than duration recording as it limits the amount of time used for collecting this type of data. Teaching the parent and teacher to use the same interval recording adds understanding to the data collected.

The fourth method, latency recording, allows the teacher and parent to establish the amount of time it takes a student to comply with a request. This information provides insight into the generalization of functional and academic behaviors in a variety of settings. It also gives the participants an idea of how quickly the student engages in the appropriate behavior.

The fifth method, ABC analysis, enables the teacher to ascertain the possible triggers or antecedents for particular behaviors. It promotes the use of positive interactions to eliminate the need for disruptive or nonfunctional behaviors. ABC analysis encourages positive behavioral interventions by determining the reasons behaviors occur and identifying replacement actions.

MECHANICS OF THE COMMUNICATION NOTEBOOK OR JOURNAL

When establishing a communication notebook or journal system, the teacher should consider the following suggestions (English & Gillen, 2001; Williams & Cartledge, 1997):

- Write in everyday language to increase the informality of the exchanges.
- Recognize that it takes time to develop rapport with the notebook participants.
- Strive to obtain consistent engagement of participants.
- Write in first-person language with a conversational style, and make comments positive and reassuring.

Establish a communication notebook or journal from items readily available in the classroom. The teacher can do the following:

1. Talk with the participants about the purpose of establishing a communication notebook or journal (Williams & Cartledge, 1997).
2. Establish a specific schedule for exchanging written communication in the notebook or journal (daily, after a specific activity, and weekly) (Peyton, 1993).
3. Decide with parents whether the journal will be open to all family members or restricted to parents (Turnbull & Turnbull, 2001).
4. Choose the format for the communication notebook or journal (spiral notebook, e-mail, personalized student-decorated journal) (Peyton, 1993).
5. Provide directions with a clear message about the procedures for responding and the type of data to be collected (Peyton, 1993).
6. Allow for responses that provide specific numerical counts, listings, and yes/no responses with open-ended remarks to ensure that appropriate substantiating data are collected.
7. Read and respond to the communication notebook or journal entries in a timely fashion and validate the participant's remarks (Williams & Cartledge, 1997).
8. Provide clear examples of how the communication notebook or journal adds data to the ongoing IEP evaluative documentation and gives evidence of student growth.

9. Integrate the information into assessment data by recording the dates, the name of the recorder, and the qualitative and quantitative information acquired from the communication notebook or journal.

SUMMARIZING THE DATA FROM COMMUNICATION NOTEBOOKS AND JOURNALS

Data gathered using a communication notebook or journal become valuable when members of the IEP committee have ready access to the information. A systematic approach to gathering the data from many entries helps to provide crucial information that can be used to document progress on the IEP. To structure the information, the teacher must decide what should be reported in the communication summary. This summary takes many different forms, depending upon what type of documentation the IEP goals require. First, by initially providing concise and clear directions in the communication notebook or journal the teacher creates the best opportunity for gathering relevant and specific data to be included in the summary for the IEP committee. Next, the participants document the behaviors with honest and forthright descriptions of the student's progress. Finally, a summary of the compiled data is completed for efficient use at a later date.

The Bulleted Summary

Bulleted selections that relate to specific IEP goals help to focus the data and verify the documentation of progress. These simple, concise bullet points reflect a summary of the data accrued from communication notebooks or journals. This method provides easily read and remembered documentation that supports information for IEP development. Figure 9.8 presents an example of a bulleted summary sheet.

Figure 9.8   A Bulleted Summary of Meagan's Communication Notebook

The notebook asked the parent to record information regarding the time spent reading or looking at books at home.

Area for Assessment: Reading Skills

Dates: 9-1 through 11-15

Type = Picture and early reading books

- Meagan has favorite books at home that she will look at with me.
- I always have to call Meagan to begin her reading time.
- Meagan never initiates reading at home on her own.
- I have a hard time getting Meagan to read aloud. She says she doesn't like to do that. I don't push her.
- She will look at a picture book without reading the words, or she will allow me to read to her.

Tally Summary Sheet

A tally summary sheet with specific notes concerning progress represents a second style of summarization. For example, Marla's teacher decided to include information about the amount of time Marla read during the reporting period. In addition, comments from Marla's mother provided detail about the factors affecting Marla's progress and are an additional resource for the IEP committee.

These additional insights increase the committee's understanding of Marla's progress and provide solid evidence concerning her generalization of IEP goals. The data verify the need for additional support in the home environment to enable Marla to generalize this goal. A specific list of reading materials supplied by the teacher to be read in an allotted time period might increase the chance of accomplishing the goal. The teacher might also provide a variety of other types of reading material that Marla would enjoy. Setting up a charting program to allow Marla to see her progress and perhaps earn rewards also could enhance her reading development.

Aggregated Table Summary

In the aggregated table summary format, the teacher supplies the IEP committee with information regarding a student's behavior with particular emphasis on the antecedent behaviors. The teacher summarizes the information from the communication notebook and highlights the data describing the antecedent behaviors. If only quantitative information has been presented, the IEP committee would agree that the student had achieved his IEP goal. Through the aggregated table summary, the committee also learned about the causes of the student's behavior and will implement IEP goals that focus on helping him to master these triggers. Figure 9.9 presents an example of an aggregated table summary.

Figure 9.9 Gathering Information Derived from an Aggregated Table Summary

Philip's Reactions and Inappropriate Gestures		
Area for Assessment: Social Skill Development		
Directions: Please answer the following questions by describing Philip's behavior.		
When does Philip shake his fist?		
Date	**Teacher's Comments**	**Teaching Assistant's Comments**
3-8	Philip shook his fist during reading today when I asked him to read aloud.	
3-9	Again, today when asked to start his assignment, Philip made two fists and waved them at me.	Philip shook his fist when the cafeteria aide asked him to put his milk carton in the trash.

3-10	I asked Philip to finish his work, and he shook his fist and made an angry face.	
3-11	Philip hit his fist against his desk when asked to finish his math.	
3-12		When asked to get into line and cease talking, Philip raised his fist and slapped one fist into his other hand.

What prompts him to shake his fist?

Date	Teacher's Comments	Teaching Assistant's Comments
3-8	He was asked to comply with my request.	
3-9	He was asked to start his work.	He shakes his fist when he is asked to do something.
3-10	He was once again directed to finish his assignment.	
3-11	He was asked to finish his math.	
3-12		I asked him to get in line and quit talking.

What does Philip do after shaking his fist?

Date	Teacher's Comments	Teaching Assistant's Comments
3-8	Gets red in the face, sulks	
3-9		Gets red, turns away, looks angry, and ignores the person making the request
3-10	Gets angry and resists finishing his work	Folds his hands and glares but does not do his work.
3-11	Turns red and refuses to comply	
3-12	Refuses to work	Appears red and looks explosive
Aggregated Data	• Teacher reports that Philip exhibits signs of anger and inappropriate gestures when asked to comply or complete a task. She also reports that Philip shows physical symptoms of anger when asked to follow directions. The teacher also states that Philip resists following directions and often folds his arms and refuses to work. • The teaching assistant also indicates that upon request Philip refuses to comply and presents angry and inappropriate gestures.	

USING THE COMMUNICATION NOTEBOOK OR JOURNAL DATA IN THE INDIVIDUALIZED EDUATION PROGRAM

Any summary of a communication notebook or journal plays a valuable role in the IEP process. The summary offers the committee a synopsis of the most important information gained over time during the ongoing communication among the participants. In addition, the summary sheet creates a written record of the student's progress in multiple settings with several different observers. This style of summary becomes especially valuable when reviewing IEP goals not readily measured by standardized instruments. The summary documents the input of parents, students, teaching assistants, and other related service personnel and the details of the team approach regarding the student's instruction. It records information that genuinely validates the student's achievement on the IEP. This type of assessment also supports the student-centered focus of the IEP process and the need for all parents to have a voice in decision making.

COMMUNICATION NOTEBOOKS, JOURNALS, AND TECHNOLOGY

Using technology can enhance the use of communication notebooks and journals. The following suggestions delineate methods for utilizing technology when employing these data collection techniques:

- Allow students unable to communicate orally to benefit from using written communication in communication notebooks and journals (Male, 2003).
- Encourage students to utilize pictures from clip art or the Internet to express their feelings if they cannot write (Male, 2003).
- Use word **prediction software** to reduce the number of keystrokes a student will have to make in communication notebooks and journals (Male, 2003).

What Do Communication Notebooks and Journals Contribute to IEP Development?

- They create communication channels that can offer information in goal planning.
- They involve the student, parent, and teacher in collaborative planning and assessment of daily activities.
- They provide opportunities for thoughtful input during convenient times for each respondent.
- They increase the amount of communication between home and school on a daily basis.
- They offer ways of quickly achieving understanding about questions that arise during the school day and school year.

- Select adaptive keyboards or talking word processors to record entries (Male, 2003).
- Choose a device such as IntelliKeys or IntelliTalk to enable access to picture libraries that aid the writing process.

SUMMARY

- Communication notebooks and journals provide opportunities for data collection in less structured formats from a variety of perspectives.
- These tools document continuous dialogue among families, teachers, teaching assistants, and related service personnel to obtain assessment data that reflect issues of culture and language.
- Their simple nature allows the teacher to design a communication system to match the student's selected IEP goals and ensure genuine data collection to reflect real life.
- Communication notebooks and journals require the IEP team to collect data regarding common everyday problems or successes.
- Summarizing data gleaned from communication notebook and journal systems can answer specific assessment questions.
- Communication notebooks and journals provide specific evaluation data for the IEP decision-making process.

COMPREHENSION CHECK

1. How useful are communication notebooks and journals in providing assessment data to document student growth?
2. Explain the function of qualitative data in communication notebooks and journals.
3. Compare and contrast information received from standardized testing to information gleaned from communication notebooks and journals.

ACTIVITIES

1. Design a communication notebook or journal system for a student receiving specific services in your field placement setting.
2. Think about the feelings and perceptions of parents of students with special needs. How do you think a communication notebook or journal would encourage such parents to be self-advocates for their student in the assessment process? Write an introductory letter to a parent explaining this important assessment responsibility.
3. Write a journal entry that describes how you performed during this class session to document your progress in understanding communication notebooks and journals.

REFERENCES

Baca, L. M., & Cervantes, H. T. (2004). *The bilingual special education interface*. Upper Saddle River, NJ: Merrill/Prentice Hall.

Bondurant-Utz, J. (2002). *Practical guide to assessing infants and preschoolers with special needs*. Upper Saddle River, NJ: Merrill/Prentice Hall.

Bos, C. S., & Vaughn, S. (2002). *Strategies for teaching students with learning and behavior problems*. Boston: Allyn & Bacon.

Denzin, N. K., & Lincoln, Y. S. (Eds.). (2000). *Handbook of qualitative research*. San Diego, CA: Sage Publications.

English, L. M., & Gillen, M. A. (2001). Journal writing in practice: From vision to reality. *New Directions for Adult and Continuing Education, 90,* 87–94.

Geertz, C. (1973). *The interpretation of cultures: Selected essays*. New York: Basic Books.

Hamill, L., & Everington, C. (2002). *Teaching students with moderate to severe disabilities: An applied approach for inclusive environments*. Upper Saddle River, NJ: Merrill/Prentice Hall.

Hill, B. C., & Ruptick, C. (1994). *Practical aspects of authentic assessment: Putting the pieces together*. Norwood, MA: Christopher-Gordon Publishers, Inc.

Jayanthi, M., Bursuck, W., Epstein, M. H., & Polloway, E. A. (1997). Strategies for successful homework. *Teaching Exceptional Children, 30*(1), 4–7.

Kerr, M. M., & Nelson, C. M. (2002). *Strategies for addressing behavior problems in the classroom* (4th ed.). Upper Saddle River, NJ: Merrill/Prentice Hall.

Kulm, G. (1994). *Mathematics assessment*. San Francisco, CA: Jossey-Bass.

Male, M. (2003). *Technology for inclusion: Meeting the special needs of all students* (4th ed.). Boston: Allyn & Bacon.

Mastropieri, M. A., & Scruggs, T. E. (2000). *The inclusive classroom: Strategies for effective instruction*. Upper Saddle River, NJ: Merrill/Prentice Hall.

Peyton, J. K. (1993). *Dialogue journals: Interactive writing to develop language and literacy*. ERIC Digests, Report: EDO-FL-93–01.

Sattler, J. M. (2001). *Assessment of children: Cognitive applications*. San Diego, CA: Jerome M. Sattler, Publisher, Inc.

Spinelli, C. G. (2002). *Classroom assessment for students with special needs in inclusive settings*. Upper Saddle River, NJ: Merrill/Prentice Hall.

Stiggins, R. J. (2001). *Student-involved classroom assessment* (3rd ed.). Upper Saddle River, NJ: Merrill/Prentice Hall.

Turnbull, A. P., & Turnbull, H. R. (2001). *Families, professionals, and exceptionality: Collaborating for empowerment* (4th ed.). Upper Saddle River, NJ: Merrill/Prentice Hall.

Westling, D. L., & Fox, L. (2000). *Teaching students with severe disabilities* (2nd ed.). Upper Saddle River, NJ: Merrill/Prentice Hall.

Williams, V. I., & Cartledge, G. (1997). Passing notes to parents. *Teaching Exceptional Children, 30*(1), 30–35.

REPORTING THE RESULTS

III

WRITING AUTHENTIC ASSESSMENT REPORTS

10

Chapter Focus

Authentic assessment reports unite data collected using various tools to form real-world depictions of student achievement. Reports help the IEP team to focus on strengths and priority needs for program planning. This chapter informs the reader about the steps involved in creating quality authentic assessment reports. The report incorporates the strengths of the student, competencies achieved, priority needs for further work, and recommendations about future planning.

LEARNER OBJECTIVES

- Explain the reason for using authentic assessment reports.
- Describe the foundations for authentic assessment reports.
- Understand the components of an authentic assessment report.
- Explain how the authentic assessment report accommodates cultural and linguistic diversity.
- Describe how technology aids report development.

QUALITY AUTHENTIC ASSESSMENT REPORTS

The quality of the authentic assessment report significantly impacts the decision-making process of the IEP team. Sattler (2001) identifies three major characteristics of a quality authentic assessment report: (a) organization, (b) clarity of findings, and (c) readability.

In addition, quality assessment reports do the following:

- Highlight the reasons for the assessment
- Compare the current information with previous data
- Determine which questions continue to remain unanswered
- Omit irrelevant information
- Include sources to clarify the student's progress
- Feature clear descriptions of the student's abilities and needs
- Consider all sources of information
- Reflect concise, clear, and error-free information
- Communicate in understandable and unbiased language.

THE RATIONALE FOR AUTHENTIC ASSESSMENT REPORTS

The review of authentic assessment results guides IEP teams to identify current strengths and priority needs while evaluating student progress on program goals. These outcomes describe the "rich array" of the student's knowledge and skills, whereas the results obtained from standardized instruments capture performance on one specific day (Tombari & Borich, 1999). Authentic procedures demand realistic functioning in a genuine context (Taylor, 2003). The process provides a picture of the student developed from multiple procedures across applicable settings. These glimpses, demonstrated over time, supply a description of the student that no other assessment technique imparts.

Authentic assessments closely linked to daily classroom activities emphasize the student's ability to complete specific goals (Nitko, 2004). Recent changes to IDEIA 2004 stress the need for assessments that acknowledge a strong relationship between appraisal results and the development of IEP goals. Using authentic assessment reports helps to cement the bond between assessment and intervention.

For example, Martin, Marshall, and Sale (2004) studied 1,638 secondary IEP meeting participants from 393 meetings across a 3-year time span. They determined that altering the focus of IEP meetings from a deficit-driven perspective to a strength-based, student-and-family interest orientation improved the partnership within the team. Furthermore, they indicated that the value-added benefits of this focus result in increased participation and positive attitudes toward the special education process.

Overall, authentic assessment reports supply the IEP team with an evaluative synopsis that increases understanding and explains student performance through an in-depth investigation (Bassey, 1999). The authentic assessment approach brings multiple perspectives together in a cohesive format verified through several sources. Using this arrangement, the IEP team considers how the information fits together rather than looking at individual assessment pieces in isolation. This method assists the IEP team members in making decisions by providing opportunities to view the student in a holistic, personalized manner.

DIMENSIONS OF THE AUTHENTIC ASSESSMENT REPORT

While every authentic assessment contains a variety of components based on the student's individual strengths and needs, certain dimensions of the process remain constant. Six key dimensions exist to ensure the quality and accuracy of the authentic assessment process. Each of these aspects provides strength and depth to the procedure while creating a real-world appraisal of the student's achievement:

1. Observation of performance over time
2. Use of realistic functioning to pinpoint daily improvement
3. Inclusion of a variety of perspectives from various sources and settings
4. Observation of each student in context while involved in educational activities to obtain active knowledge
5. Application of a variety of methods to measure growth in different types of students
6. Assurance of the reliability and validity of the process

Using these factors results in a problem-solving method that links assessment and intervention that best fit student strengths and needs rather than relying on standard procedures (McNamara & Hollinger, 2003).

Observation of Performance Over Time

Ongoing assessment affords educators the opportunity to evaluate a student daily, over time, and cumulatively to document continuous growth. Evaluating student progress indicates program effectiveness, monitors IEP placement decisions, and creates records regarding the response to unique student needs (Venn, 2004). Continuous assessment supplies accountability documentation required by federal and state laws for students with disabilities enrolled in special education programs. Also, instead of scrutinizing student functioning on one specific day using a standardized instrument, authentic assessment captures the daily fluctuations in development over a period of time.

Use of Realistic Functioning to Isolate Improvement

Standardized assessment uses contrived activities to monitor student learning during a specific administration. Student variables, such as fatigue, hunger, illness, and anxiety, impact the results. The use of standardized instruments that differentiate among developmental levels of individuals with and without disabilities may underestimate the ability of students with a disability (Losardo & Notari-Syverson, 2001). Standardized assessment data leave the IEP team to make decisions based on an observation of student abilities through a single snapshot. Authentic assessment provides opportunities for evaluation to take place in the classroom using activities completed in the learning cycle that provide a critical link between assessment and intervention.

Inclusion of a Variety of Perspectives

Authentic assessment also incorporates the perspectives of many individuals associated with the student to broaden insight into the student's abilities. The law requires that no important area of performance be excluded from a full and individual evaluation. For instance, health, vision, hearing, social and emotional status, general intelligence and academic performance, and communication and motor abilities must all be integrated into the report. Several sources gather this pertinent information (McLoughlin & Lewis, 2001). Special educators and other professionals, parents, and school administrators make important educational decisions regarding the student. Creating strong authentic assessment evaluations includes increasing the participation of these personnel in the process. By using this active participant method, all members become capable of talking about issues and potential programming as they have seen the student firsthand in his environment. This awareness of student strengths, needs, and goals helps in formulating future planning.

Observation of Each Student in Context

Observations elicit knowledge about a student performing in an environment and establish an experiential picture of actual skill levels. A number of observations gathered over time demonstrates the quality and depth of the student's performance. Knowledge collected through authentic assessment indicates the status of learning to establish clear, comprehensive ideas about optimal student learning. Observing for mastery and generalization supplies the impetus for revisiting a goal or the design of new goals built on prior knowledge. This dimension serves to provide the IEP team with precise information about specific daily functioning rather than a global understanding of contrived skills.

Application of a Variety of Methods to Measure Growth

Authentic assessment includes evidence of a variety of methods used to evaluate the student's progress toward the annual goal. The tools and techniques described in this text represent numerous methods for gaining information about a student's performance. Utilizing a range of methods increases the team's confidence in genuine results. This assurance improves decision making and supports the team in making fact-based decisions that reflect the student's strengths and needs.

Using authentic assessment procedures in which the data collection occurs in the classroom and other environments offers the IEP team the opportunity to gather information tailored to the student. Different types of students require various understandings of cultural and linguistic diversity; gender differences (Nitko, 2004); family characteristics and structures; socioeconomic status; poverty and its influences; and religious beliefs (McLean, Wolery, & Bailey, 2004). Authentic assessments reflect each student's capabilities with respect to their IEP goals rather than evaluating progress on an isolated measure.

Ensuring Reliability and Validity

A key component of ensuring that reliability and validity exist in an authentic assessment concerns the ability of the team to obtain information from multiple sources and multiple settings (McLean, Wolery, & Bailey, 2004). Relying on one person to provide all the data presents considerable reliability issues. Compiling information from various sources in multiple settings produces trustworthiness, a form of reliability. Without relying on one source or one tool, the team establishes a realistic picture viewed from several perspectives. These realistic threads comprise the holistic picture that authentic assessment attempts to create.

Gallagher (1998) discusses the establishment of validity in authentic assessment in terms of content, construct, and criterion related. By ensuring a match between assessment tasks and IEP goals, the team verifies the content validity of a student's authentic assessment. The team addresses construct validity by examining the realism scale provided with each synopsis. When looking across assessment tools, criterion-related validity reveals common threads or results gathered across the tools.

Reliability, according to Gallagher (1999), indicates the dependability of a particular assessment process. The IEP team must guarantee that the results of an authentic assessment for a particular student culminate in reliable conclusions. To ensure reliability, consider the following steps:

- Increase the number and variety of activities used to measure the student's mastery (Tombari & Borich, 1999).
- Enhance the number of times assessment activities occur (Tombari & Borich, 1999).
- Ensure that goals are clearly written (Tombari & Borich, 1999) and measurable.
- Improve scoring objectivity by using rubrics when appropriate (Tombari & Borich, 1999).
- Provide training for informants to ensure understanding of the criteria (Nitko, 2004).
- Monitor informant use of tools over time to ensure continued consistency (Nitko, 2004).
- Supply written, detailed descriptors to clarify the level of each criterion on assessment components (Cohen & Spenciner, 2003).

In addition to confirming reliability using the techniques just described, the IEP team verifies reliability by answering these seven questions proposed by Bassey (1999).

1. Have the team members been engaged over a period of time in the evaluation process?
2. Have the observations been persistent and have observers looked for valuable details to round out the information obtained from other sources?

3. Has the data collected been supported by other sources, including traditional measures?
4. Have all members of the IEP team verified the findings?
5. Is the evaluation detailed enough to ensure confidence in the findings?
6. Is sufficient documentation for conclusions available from various assessment tools?
7. Have all the sources, including different tools, raters, and perspectives, been considered in the development of the final written narrative summary?
8. Has the IEP team considered alternative ways of viewing the data to verify the relevance of their conclusions?

CREATING AN AUTHENTIC ASSESSMENT REPORT

Authentic assessment reports consist of strength-based descriptions of student progress for the IEP team. The IEP team regards all perspectives and information as valuable. Either a notebook or an electronic file, including all data collected, forms the authentic assessment report. The reports contain (a) identifying and historical record information, (b) the IEP current goals, (c) a listing of the assessment tools and methods used to record the data in order to evaluate these goals, including a description of the multiple settings and perspectives used in the process, (d) a synopsis of the data, listing student strengths, priority needs, and competencies achieved, along with a rating of realism for the authentic assessment, and (e) the actual documents collected from each tool (Losardo & Notari-Syverson, 2001). The results inform all team members of the student's authentic assessment results prior to or during the IEP team meeting.

Identifying Information

The first section of the report includes items such as name, address, phone number, parent names, age, birth date, ethnicity, school picture, student identification number, current eligibility category, school, homeroom, teachers' names, and current education placements. Figure 10.1 presents the section of a sample assessment report displaying the identifying information for a student.

Historical Records

This component reveals information about the student's historical records, including absences, health history, classroom situations, other mitigating facts having an impact on the student's ability to master the IEP goals successfully. The information appears in a concise narrative format and does not replace other records from the student's folder. It simply summarizes historical data to alert the IEP team to significant factors. Figure 10.2 provides the section of a sample assessment report displaying the historical information for a student.

Figure 10.1   Identifying Information for Marla, a Student

Phone number: 214-383-5500

Parent names: Martha and Michael Frasier

Age: 6

Birthdate: March 1, 1998

Ethnicity: African American

School picture:

Student identification number: 464-935-8578

Current eligibility category: Autism

School/homeroom: Merkett Elementary

Teachers' names: Ms. Peabody—Classroom Teacher; Ms. Carlson—Special Education Teacher; Ms. Applewhite—Classroom Teaching Assistant; Mrs. Wilson—Special Education Teacher; Mrs. Blair—Speech Language Pathologist

Current education placement: Inclusionary kindergarten

Figure 10.2   Historical Information for Marla

Absences: Regular attendance

Health history: Delayed speech; early intervention at age two

Classroom situations or other mitigating facts having an impact on the student's ability to successfully master the IEP goals: Marla receives consistent support from her family. Her mother is a school volunteer and works with the school to meet Marla's needs. She is an only child. She experiences significant delays in language. Her mother sought intervention and help when Marla was 2 years old. Marla has experienced difficulty in play groups with others. She is unable to communicate and physically acts out when others do not understand her messages.

Current Individualized Education Program Goals

A copy of the student's current IEP or a listing of the goals informs the IEP team of current and past goals. While the IEP goals focus on the fundamental purpose of the meeting, the team considers all data collected regarding mastery prior to planning new or dismissing old goals.

Tools Used for Assessment

The IEP team selects appropriate authentic assessment tools to monitor selected IEP goals. In some cases, data collection occurs using only a few tools. At other times, the array of authentic assessment tools completes the process.

Synopsis of the Data Collected

The Annual Goal Synopsis   Taking the time to review the report, including student work and a synopsis of other data collected in the authentic assessment, provides the IEP team with powerful information for decision making (Cobb, 2004). The next section

Figure 10.3   Synopsis of Marla's First Area for Assessment

Student name: Marla

Area for assessment: Expressive language

Tool	Setting	Sources
CBM	Inclusionary first-grade general education classroom	General and special education teachers, teaching assistant, speech therapist
Portfolio-self-reflections	Inclusionary first-grade general education classroom	Student, general and special education teachers, teaching assistant
Rating scales	Inclusionary first-grade general education classroom, Challenger baseball, hippotherapy	General and special education teachers, teaching assistant, parents, coaches, speech therapist
Ecological inventory	Inclusionary first-grade general education classroom	General and special education teachers, teaching assistant, parents, speech therapist
Sociogram	Inclusionary first-grade general education classroom	Peers

96% accuracy in use of visual cue cards to increase expressive language

100% compliance when asked to describe illustrations using simple sentences

100% accuracy in selecting visual cue cards that indicate preferences in literacy skills center

Realism Rating

				X	
Hand over hand	In isolation with prompts	In isolation without prompts	Generalized with prompts	Independent	

of the authentic assessment report presents each area for assessment based on the IEP annual goals. The team compiles the data to emphasize strengths and priority needs, note competencies achieved, and rate the authenticity or realism of the results. This rating reflects the confidence the team places in the assessment results. By considering the realism rating, the IEP team ensures that the data provide information about real-world conditions (Gronlund, 2003). Behind each synopsis, all documentation produced for the annual goal appears. Figures 10.3 through 10.6 present the sections of a sample assessment report for four areas of assessment.

Identifying Strengths and Priority Needs   Presenting the information gathered in the authentic assessment report allows the IEP team to consider specific progress rather than examining the results as a whole. The report lists the specific strengths identified during the evaluation. Conversely, priority needs also appear in this section. The IEP team decisions reflect the link between assessment and intervention based on these strengths and priority needs. The use of an individual synopsis for each area makes linking assessment and intervention easier. By including the tools and results, the team promotes reliance on strengths and addresses priority needs from a strength-based perspective. The process allows the team to thoroughly evaluate present areas of mastery impacting the team's selection of new priorities. In addition, the process points the

Figure 10.4   Synopsis of the Data Collected for Second Area for Marla's Assessment

Student name: Marla		
Area for assessment: Receptive language		
Tool	**Setting**	**Sources**
CBA	Inclusionary first-grade general education classroom	General and special education teachers, teaching assistant, speech therapist
Rating scales	Inclusionary first-grade general education classroom	General and special education teachers, teaching assistant, speech therapist
100% accuracy with a rate of learning new visual cue cards for receptive language at 2 cards per week		
Accuracy rate for learning new visual cue cards for receptive language at 5 cards per week drops to 40%		
Understands receptive language paired with visual cue cards best on a one-to-one basis		

Realism Rating				
			X	
Hand over hand	In isolation with prompts	In isolation without prompts	Generalized with prompts	Independent

Figure 10.5 Synopsis of the Data Collected for Third Area for Marla's Assessment

Student name: Marla		
Area for assessment: Behavior		
Tool	**Setting**	**Sources**
Interviews	Inclusionary first-grade general education classroom	General and special education teachers, teaching assistant, speech therapist, student
ABC analysis	Inclusionary first-grade general education classroom	General and special education teachers, teaching assistant, speech therapist
Anecdotal records	Inclusionary first-grade general education classroom	General and special education teachers, teaching assistant, speech therapist
Checklists	Inclusionary first-grade general education classroom, home	General and special education teachers, teaching assistant, speech therapist, parent
Rating scales	Inclusionary first-grade general education classroom, Challenger baseball, hippotherapy	General and special education teachers, teaching assistant, speech therapist, parent, coaches

100% accuracy using visual cue cards to express feelings after aggressive outbursts

Aggressive behavior continues despite intervention

Responds with pushing to any type of attention

Distraction prior to student's response appears to decrease aggressive behaviors

Realism Rating				
X				
Aggression	In isolation with prompts	In isolation without prompts	Generalized with prompts	Independent

team toward conclusions about the need for generalization of skills mastered in isolated settings. Figure 10.7 presents a sample assessment cumulative assessment report.

An IEP Goal Unmastered   Even when a particular skill remains unmastered, the IEP team uses the results of the authentic assessment to verify the steps taken during instruction. The team then evaluates why the student did not master the skill and determines whether to continue with the current area to implement modifications to progress toward mastery.

The Final Product   A final step taken by the IEP team involves the delineation of strengths and priority needs as identified during the authentic assessment. The report allows the team to see the whole student from a variety of perspectives and settings.

Figure 10.6   Synopsis of the Data Collected for Fourth Area for Marla's Assessment

Student name: Marla		
Area for assessment: Reading skills		
Tool	**Setting**	**Sources**
Rating scales	Inclusionary first-grade general education classroom, home	Special education and general education teachers, teaching assistant, speech therapist, parents
Communication notebook	Inclusionary first-grade general education classroom, home	Special education and general education teachers, teaching assistant, speech therapist, parents
Behavioral observations	Inclusionary first-grade general education classroom, home	General and special education teachers, teaching assistant, speech therapist, parents

40% participation in paired reading at school, 25% participation at home

Parent describes less cooperation in reading at home

60% increase in number of reading minutes at school versus home

Realism Rating

No reading	Follows pictures with finger	Follows text with finger	X Paired reading	Independent

Figure 10.7   Marla's IEP Team Performance-Based Authentic Assessment Report

Student name: Marla   April 12

Merkett Elementary School   Ms. Peabody—first grade

Strengths

- Increased expressive and receptive language skills with visual cue card system
- Transferred skills between cue cards and classroom work
- Used visual cue cards to indicate academic choices
- Continued to learn new visual cue cards at a modest rate
- Identified feelings through the visual cue cards after outbursts
- Increased number of reading minutes at pre-primer level

Priority Needs

- Improve learning rate for visual cue cards
- Increase language understanding in group settings
- Reduce aggressive behavior, particularly pushing
- Enhance pre-primer reading minutes at home and in school

Figure 10.8   Description of Assurances for Reliability and Validity for Marla

	Expressive Language	Receptive Language	Lowering Aggressive Behaviors
Settings	Inclusionary first-grade general education classroom, Challenger baseball, hippotherapy	Inclusionary first-grade general education classroom, home	Inclusionary first-grade general education classroom, home
Perspectives	General and special education teachers, teaching assistant, speech therapist, parents, coaches	General and special education teachers, teaching assistant, speech therapist, parents, coaches	General and special education teachers, teaching assistant, speech therapist, parents

Linking home and school progress for many students with disabilities remains a significant target. Unless data collection occurs across several environments, critical information evades the IEP team.

Ensuring Reliability and Validity

This section contains a short description of the methods used to ensure that the results of the authentic assessment represent reliable and valid performances by the student. A description of the team's inclusion of multiple perspectives and numerous settings substantiates the authentic assessment results and recommendations. These multiple perspectives include all of the individuals who work or interact with the student. Additional settings might include different classroom and school surroundings, community activities, and the home environment. If the perspectives result in conflicting data, the IEP team must go back to the assessment process and determine how to reconcile the contradiction. Figure 10.8 provides a description of assurances of the authentic assessment's reliability and validity for a sample student.

MEETING CULTURAL AND LINGUISTIC NEEDS

The IEP team also ensures the reliability and validity of an authentic assessment by paying careful attention to issues of cultural and linguistic diversity and their impact on the assessment process and results. Cohen and Spenciner (2003) identify six areas that the IEP team must address to acknowledge the importance of sensitivity and fairness in assessing students from a variety of cultures:

- Use appropriate tools and methods to consider the impact of the student's culture.
- Employ methods and tools familiar to the student and congruent with the student's cultural values and experiences.

- Select tools and methods that reflect the student's preferred or more skilled language.
- Utilize accommodations and modifications to meet student needs.
- Engage in a variety of techniques to allow the student to demonstrate abilities, including those reflecting cultural experiences.
- Choose tools and methods sensitive to diverse cultures and unique learning styles.

Behaviors viewed within the context of everyday life supply a complete perspective on the student's learning style (Losardo & Notari-Syverson, 2001). Authentic assessment addresses two culturally sensitive areas that impact the validity of test results. First, the influences of the family and the sociocultural background create a profound effect on the student's daily functioning. Second, the student's functioning within her environment provides a clearer framework to consider the evaluation results.

In addition to assessment issues, the IEP team must also be aware of the cultural context through which members create their personal value systems (Dabkowski, 2004). This context impacts team members' ability to work together in joint decision making and, therefore, must be considered as a factor during the team meetings. Issues such as educational outcomes, the nature of the parent–professional partnership, and methods for decision making all reflect cultural beliefs. Authentic assessment reports provide a structure to encourage all members to interact in a partnership role.

DEVELOPMENT OF AUTHENTIC ASSESSMENT REPORT AND TECHNOLOGY

Using technology to gather and organize data collected in an authentic assessment report eases the production of lengthy reports and reduces the amount of time required to manage the evaluation procedures (Sorrells, Reith, & Sindelar, 2004). In addition, long-term storage of the data improves opportunities for IEP teams to consider trends over time. Software packages such as Microsoft Office, which includes Microsoft Word, Excel, Publisher, and Front Page, provide useful tools for the development of the authentic assessment results.

The IEP team collects information on the computer for a variety of students and files individual information in separate folders as the data become available. The cut-and-paste feature allows for the inclusion of records taken directly from the original authentic assessment tool. Scanners permit the inclusion of historical information needed by the team. Video and audio clips incorporated in the electronic file also add realistic information to the report, including audio recordings and video clips of learning situations, footage of class activities, and student presentations (Spinelli, 2002).

Individual organizational tools, such as the Palm Pilot, aid in the collection of data during lessons and then provide an electronic means for moving that data directly into the learning profile notebook (Male, 2003). CD-ROMs, DVDs, and sound cards provide excellent storage methods for electronic learning profiles. The IEP team also utilizes software programs, such as Microsoft PowerPoint, to develop the authentic assessment results for the IEP meeting, thus allowing members of the team to view the information simultaneously.

SUMMARY

- Authentic assessment reports provide vital closure to the evaluation process. Ensuring access to all the data and to the data in summary form informs the IEP team members and creates an opportunity for effective collaboration.
- Providing quality, in-depth, but understandable authentic assessment reports ensures that the IEP team has the opportunity to generate a truly student-centered, multidisciplinary evaluation.
- Authentic assessment reports incorporate identifying and historical information, the IEP goals, the tools used during the assessment, the synopsis of strengths, priority needs, and competencies achieved, as well as a rating of the realism of the assessment to formulate recommendations for future planning.
- Authentic assessment reports accommodate cultural and linguistic diversity by looking across and considering all data, including information from the family.
- The use of technology supports timely report development.

COMPREHENSION CHECK

1. Compare and contrast ways that parents can be involved in the assessment process when using authentic measures, as opposed to standardized measures.
2. What would be the advantages of combining standardized and authentic assessments?
3. Why would authentic assessment be considered a "child-centered process"?

ACTIVITIES

1. Evaluate the use of authentic assessment reports versus standardized results obtained without authentic assessment tools. Role-play a parent's perspective and describe the advantages to discussing authentic results as opposed to standardized assessment results.
2. Create a listing of authentic tools that would aid in decision making in IEP development.
3. Explain how authentic assessment reports improve the IEP team's understanding of student progress through an academic year.

REFERENCES

Bassey, M. (1999). *Report research in educational findings.* Buckingham, England: Open University Press.

Cobb, C. (2004). Effective instruction begins with purposeful assessments. *The Reading Teacher, 57*(4), 386–388.

Cohen, L. G., & Spenciner, L. J. (2003). *Assessment of children and youth with special needs.* Boston: Pearson.

Dabkowski, D. M. (2004). Encouraging active parent participation in IEP team meetings. *Teaching Exceptional Children, 36*(3), 34–39.

Gallagher, J. D. (1998). *Classroom assessment for teachers.* Upper Saddle River, NJ: Merrill/Prentice Hall.

Gronlund, N. E. (2003). *Assessment of student achievement* (7th ed.). Boston: Allyn & Bacon.

Losardo, A., & Notari-Syverson, A. (2001). *Alternative approaches to assessing young children.* Baltimore, MD: Brookes.

Male, M. (2003). *Technology for inclusion: Meeting the special need of all students* (4th ed.). Boston: Allyn & Bacon.

Martin, J. E., Marshall, L. H., & Sale, P. (2004). A three-year study of middle, junior high and high school IEP meetings. *Exceptional Children, 70*(3), 285–297.

McLean, M., Wolery, M., & Bailey, D. B. Jr. (2004). *Assessing infants and preschoolers with special needs* (3rd ed.). Upper Saddle River, NJ: Merrill/Prentice Hall.

McLoughlin, J. A., & Lewis, R. B. (2001). *Assessing students with special needs* (5th ed.). Upper Saddle River, NJ: Merrill/Prentice Hall.

McNamara, K., & Hollinger, C. (2003). Intervention-based assessment: Evaluation rates and eligibility findings. *Exceptional Children, 69*(2), 181–193.

Nitko, A. J. (2004). *Educational assessment of students* (4th ed.). Upper Saddle River, NJ: Prentice Hall.

Sattler, J. M. (2001). *Assessment of children: Cognitive applications* (4th ed.). San Diego: Jerome M. Sattler, Publisher, Inc.

Sorrells, A. M., Reith, H. J., & Sindelar, P. T. (2004). *Critical issues in special education: Access, diversity and accountability.* Boston: Pearson/Allyn & Bacon.

Spinelli, C. G. (2002). *Classroom assessment for students with special needs in inclusive settings.* Upper Saddle River, NJ: Merrill/Prentice Hall.

Taylor, R. L. (2003). *Assessment of exceptional students: Educational and psychological procedures* (6th ed.). Boston: Pearson.

Tombari, M., & Borich, G. (1999). *Authentic assessment in the classroom: Applications and practice.* Upper Saddle River, NJ: Merrill/Prentice Hall.

Venn, J. J. (2004). *Assessing students with special needs* (3rd ed.). Upper Saddle River, NJ: Merrill/Prentice Hall.

Weber, E. (1998). Marks of brain-based assessment: A practical checklist. *NASSP Bulletin, 82*(598), 63–72.

INDEX

Academic Competence Evaluation Scales (ACES), 57
Accelerated Reader with Advantage Learning System, 40
Achenbach, T. M., 69
Active listening skills, 127
Adaptation, ecological inventories and, 161
Adaptive keyboards, 205
Aggregated table summaries, 202–203
Aim lines, curriculum-based measurement and, 54–55
AIMSweb, 60
Albert, L. R., 66
Albin, R. W., 83
Allinder, R., 43, 44, 45, 50
Alper, S., 5, 10, 11, 27, 28, 31, 33, 160, 162, 170, 177
Alt, M. J., 167
Alta Vista's Babel Fish, 154–155, 190
Amplitude, behavioral observation and, 70
Analytic scoring, rubrics and, 106
Anecdotal observations, 198
Anecdotal recording, 72–73, 79
Annual goals, authentic assessment reports and, 216–217
Antecedent-behavior-consequence (A-B-C) analysis, 77–78, 81, 200
Archiving interviews and questionnaires, 130
Art-based portfolios, 100
Artesani, T. M., 76, 77, 81, 82, 83, 85
Assessment of Practices in Early Elementary Classrooms (APEEC), 167
Assessment reports. See Authentic assessment reports
Assistive technology
  commercially available tools, 180
  environmental assessments and, 180–183
  Functional Evaluation for Assistive Technology (FEAT) tools, 180–181

issues regarding, 181–182
notebooks and, 192
Audio recordings
  authentic assessment and, 221
  communication journals and, 191
  participant-observer observations and, 79
Auditory modality deficits, 8
Auditory processing problems, questionnaires and, 121
Augmentative or Alternative Communication Feature Match Software, 180
Augmentative/Alternative Technology Assessment Tool, 180
Authentic assessment. See also Authentic assessment reports
  advantages of, 18–19
  annual goals and, 17
  contextual measures and, 15–16
  cultural diversity and, 17–18
  cumulative measures and, 14–15
  depth of development and, 12
  disadvantages of, 19
  distinguishing from informal assessment, 4–5
  dual role of technology and, 19–20
  evaluating inclusionary programs and, 13
  evaluating potential for transitions and, 13–14
  evaluating service delivery and, 13
  examining goals and objectives, 11
  future planning and, 12
  individualized education program development and, 12–13, 19
  information obtained from, 14–16
  multiple intelligences and, 7–8
  naturalistic data and, 6–7
  nature of, 4
  No Child Left Behind and, 10
  plan guides and, 11
  preferred modalities and, 8
  reliability and validity and, 9–10
  results of, 11–14
  special education and, 10–11

standards-based individual education programs, 11–12
strength-based evaluations and, 5–6
strengths from outside sources and, 8–9
technique verification questions, 4
Authentic assessment reports
  annual goals synopsis and, 216–217
  creation of, 214–221
  cultural diversity and, 220–221
  dimensions of, 211–214
  final product, 218–220
  historical records and, 214
  identifying information and, 214
  individualized education program goals and, 215
  linguistic diversity and, 220–221
  measuring growth and, 212–213
  nature of, 210
  observation of students in context and, 212
  performance observation over time and, 211
  rationale for, 210–211
  realistic functioning to isolate improvement and, 211–212
  reliability and validity assurance and, 213–214, 220
  strengths and priority needs identification and, 217–218
  synopsis of data gathered and, 216–220
  technology use and, 221
  tools used and, 216
  unmastered IEP goals and, 218
  variety of perspectives and, 212
Averages, checklists and rating scales and, 149–150

Baca, L. M., 17, 25, 68, 117, 118, 163, 189
Bailey, D. B., Jr., 134, 137, 139, 153, 162, 177, 213
Baldwin, L., 145
Barnett, D. W., 159
Bartels, M., 135
Bassey, M., 210, 213